ULTIMATE FANTASTIC FOUR

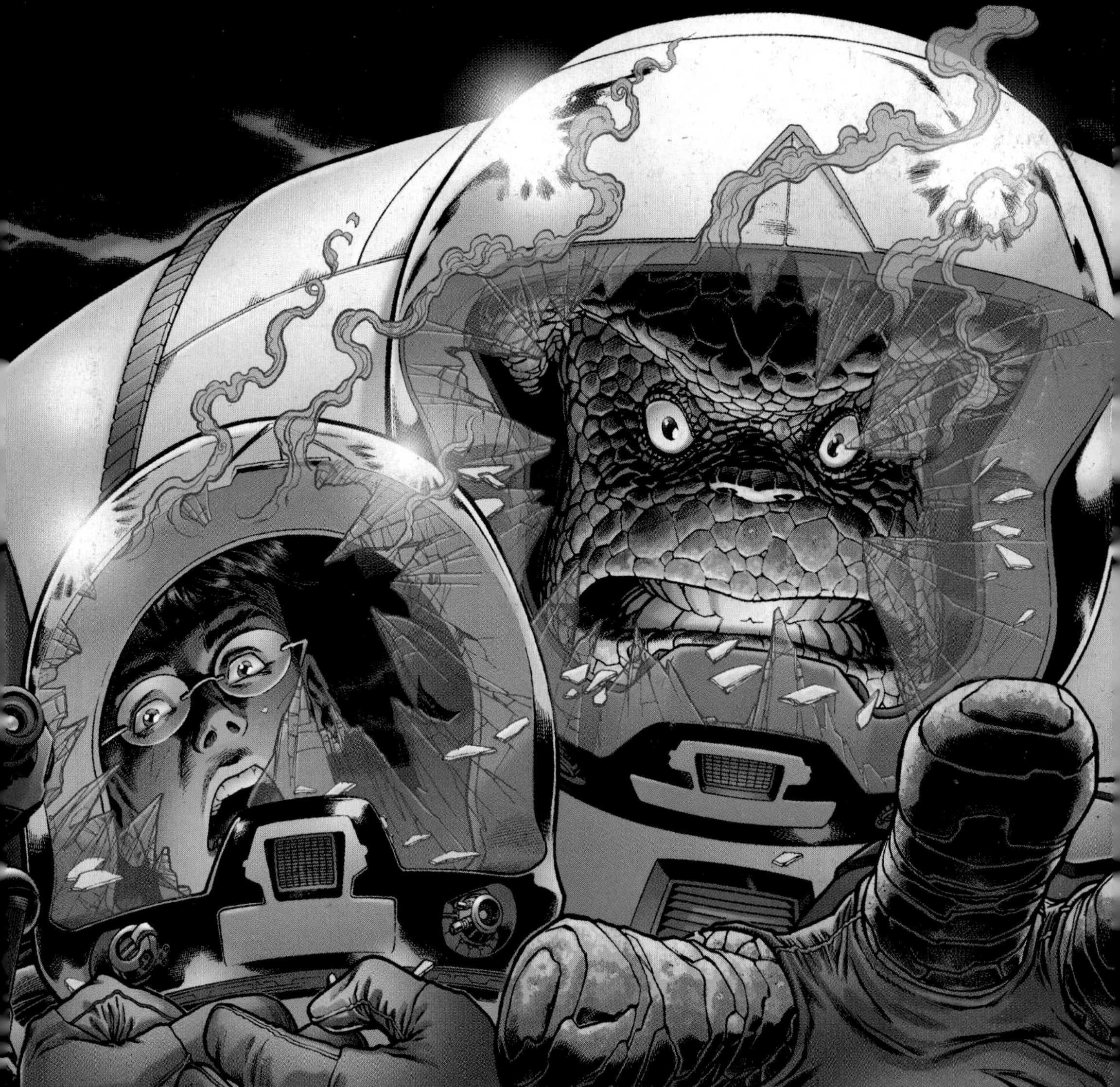

N-ZONE

ULTIMATE FANTASTIC FOUR

N-ZONE

writer
WARREN ELLIS

pencils
ADAM KUBERT

inks
JOHN DELL & SCOTT HANNA
WITH MARK MORALES & LARY STUCKER

colors
DAVE STEWART

letters
CHRIS ELIOPOULOS

assistant editor
JOHN BARBER

associate editor
NICK LOWE

editor
RALPH MACCHIO

collection editor
JENNIFER GRÜNWALD

senior editor, special projects
JEFF YOUNGQUIST

director of sales
DAVID GABRIEL

production
TERNARD SOLOMON

book designer
MEGHAN KERNS

creative director
TOM MARVELLI

editor in chief
JOE QUESADA

publisher
DAN BUCKLEY

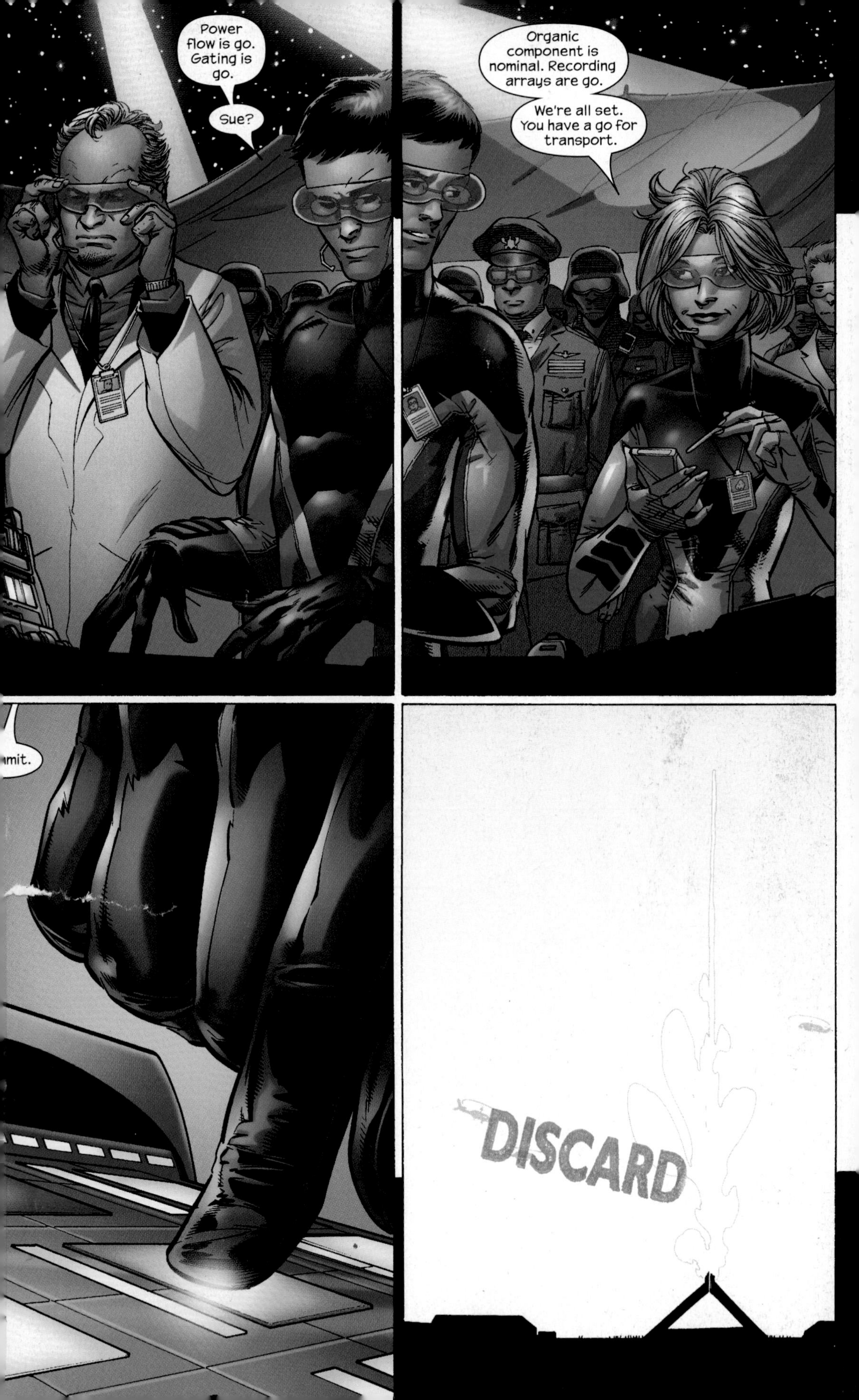
Power flow is go. Gating is go.
Sue?
Organic component is nominal. Recording arrays are go.
We're all set. You have a go for transport.

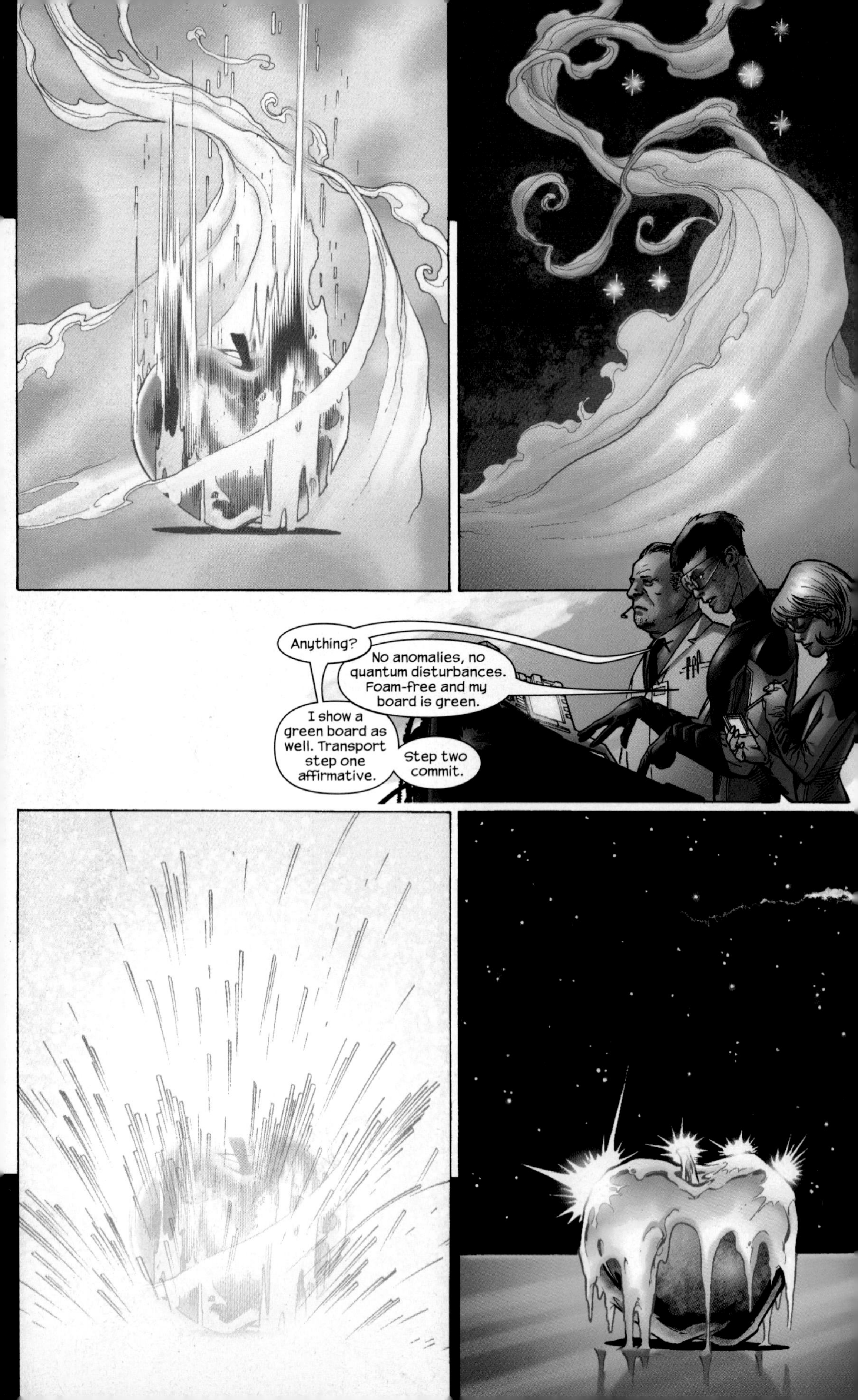
Anything?
No anomalies, no quantum disturbances. Foam-free and my board is green.
I show a green board as well. Transport step one affirmative.
Step two commit.

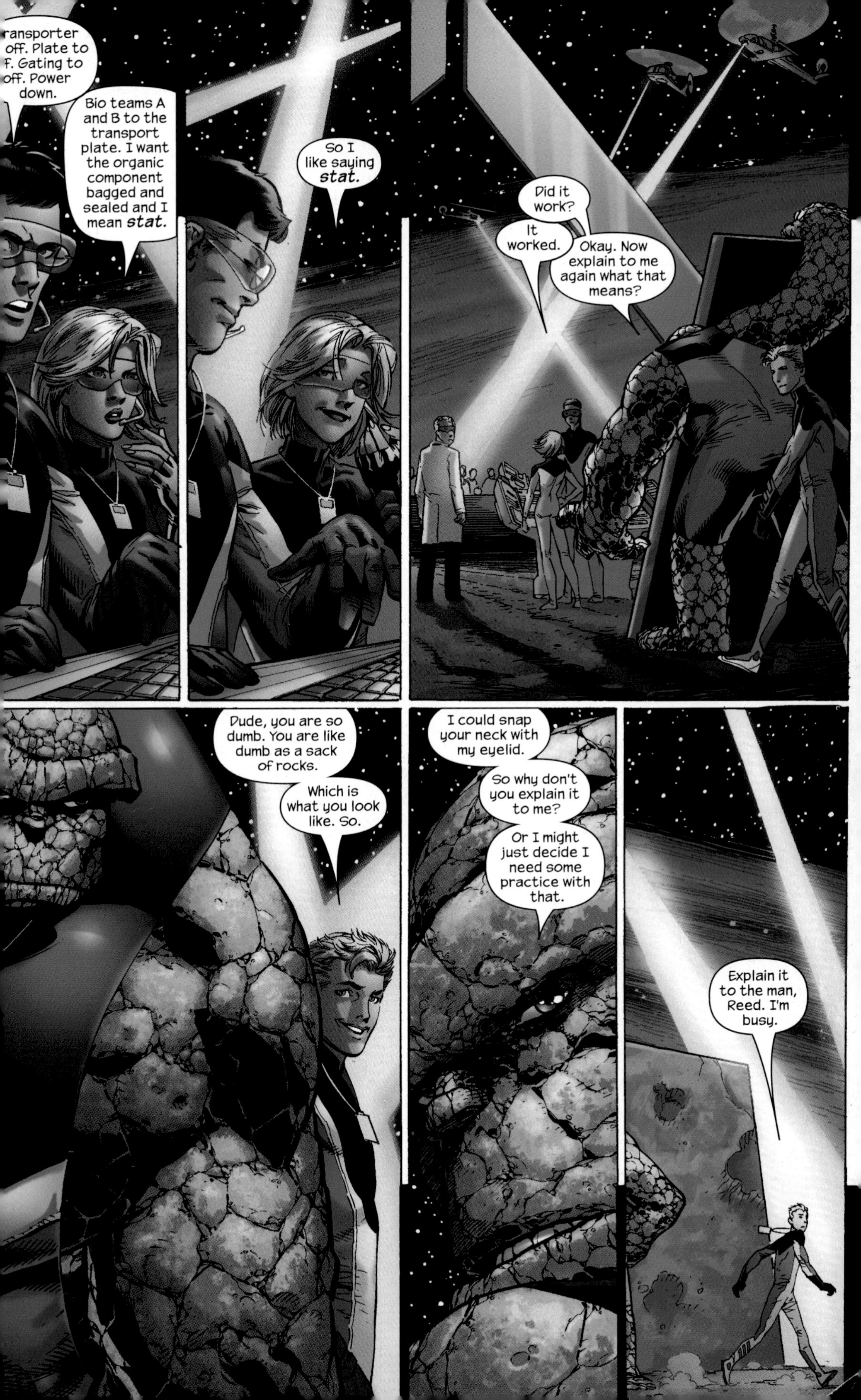
ransporter off. Plate to F. Gating to off. Power down.
Bio teams A and B to the transport plate. I want the organic component bagged and sealed and I mean *stat.*
So I like saying *stat.*
Did it work?
It worked.
Okay. Now explain to me again what that means?
Dude, you are so dumb. You are like dumb as a sack of rocks.
Which is what you look like. So.
I could snap your neck with my eyelid.
So why don't you explain it to me?
Or I might just decide I need some practice with that.
Explain it to the man, Reed. I'm busy.

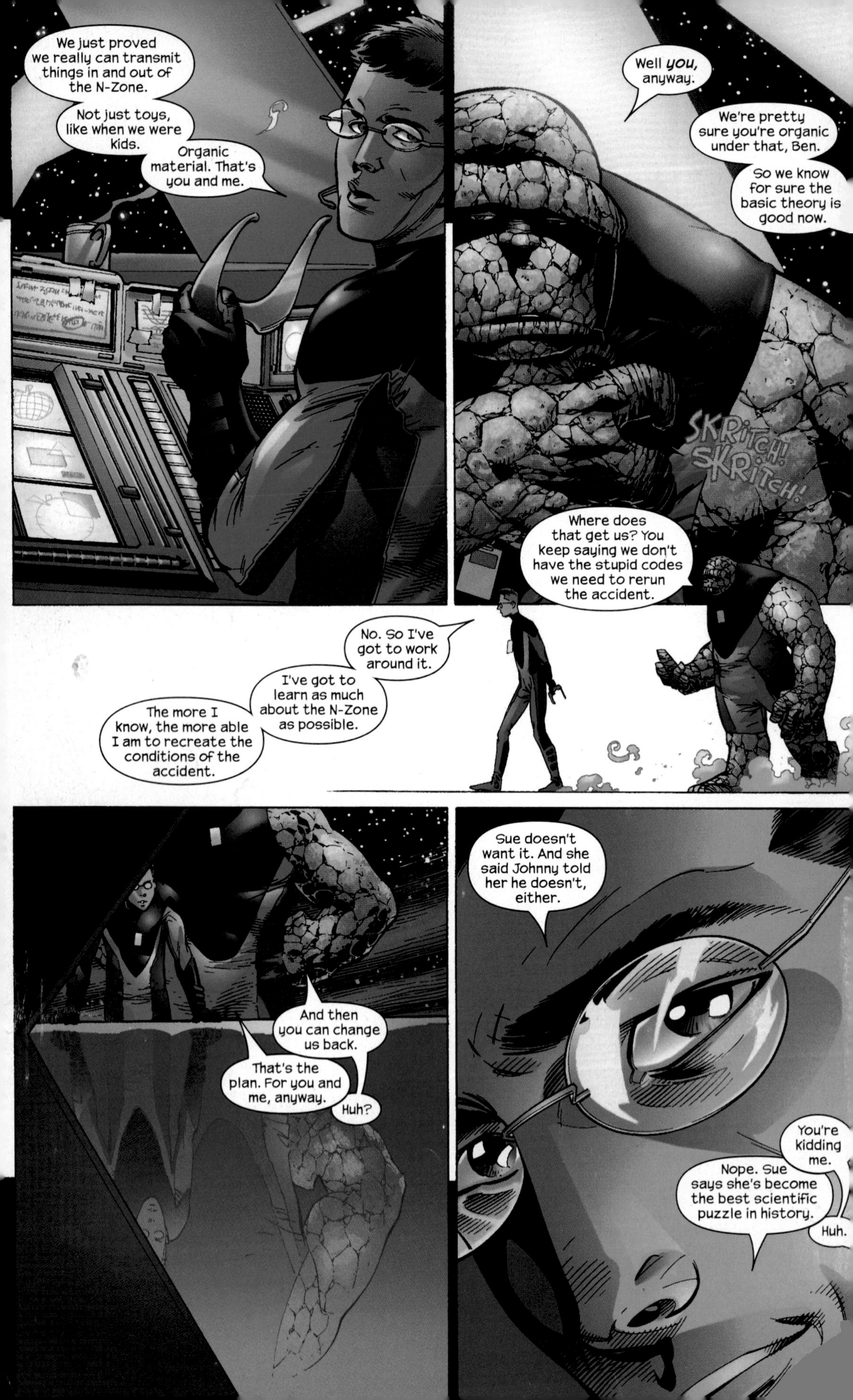
We just proved we really can transmit things in and out of the N-Zone.
Not just toys, like when we were kids.
Organic material. That's you and me.
Well *you*, anyway.
We're pretty sure you're organic under that, Ben.
So we know for sure the basic theory is good now.
SKRITCH! SKRITCH!
Where does that get us? You keep saying we don't have the stupid codes we need to rerun the accident.
No. So I've got to work around it.
I've got to learn as much about the N-Zone as possible.
The more I know, the more able I am to recreate the conditions of the accident.
And then you can change us back.
That's the plan. For you and me, anyway.
Huh?
Sue doesn't want it. And she said Johnny told her he doesn't, either.
You're kidding me.
Nope. Sue says she's become the best scientific puzzle in history.
Huh.

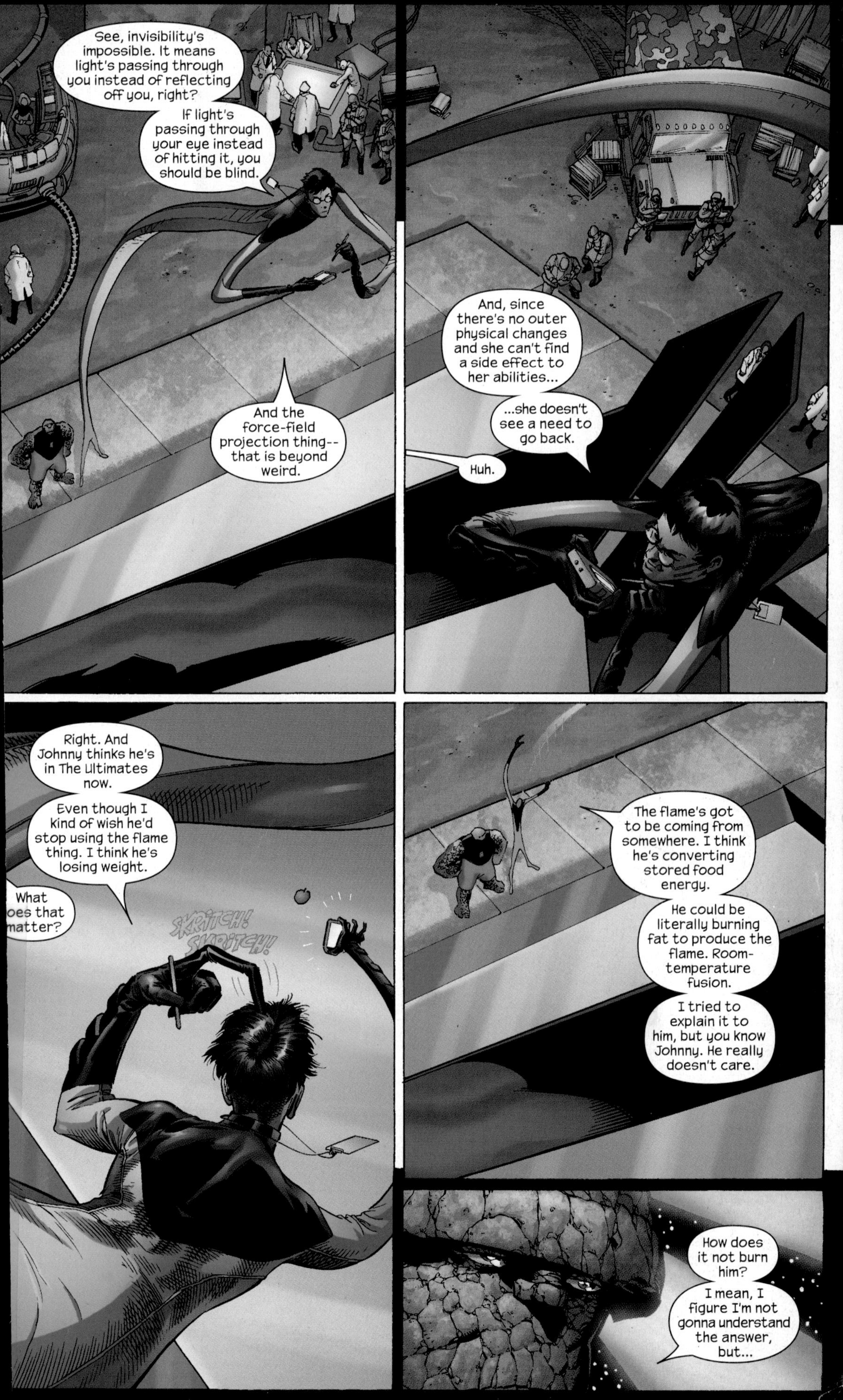
See, invisibility's impossible. It means light's passing through you instead of reflecting off you, right?
If light's passing through your eye instead of hitting it, you should be blind.
And the force-field projection thing--that is beyond weird.
And, since there's no outer physical changes and she can't find a side effect to her abilities...
...she doesn't see a need to go back.
Huh.
Right. And Johnny thinks he's in The Ultimates now.
Even though I kind of wish he'd stop using the flame thing. I think he's losing weight.
What oes that matter?
SKRITCH! SKRITCH!
The flame's got to be coming from somewhere. I think he's converting stored food energy.
He could be literally burning fat to produce the flame. Room-temperature fusion.
I tried to explain it to him, but you know Johnny. He really doesn't care.
How does it not burn him?
I mean, I figure I'm not gonna understand the answer, but...

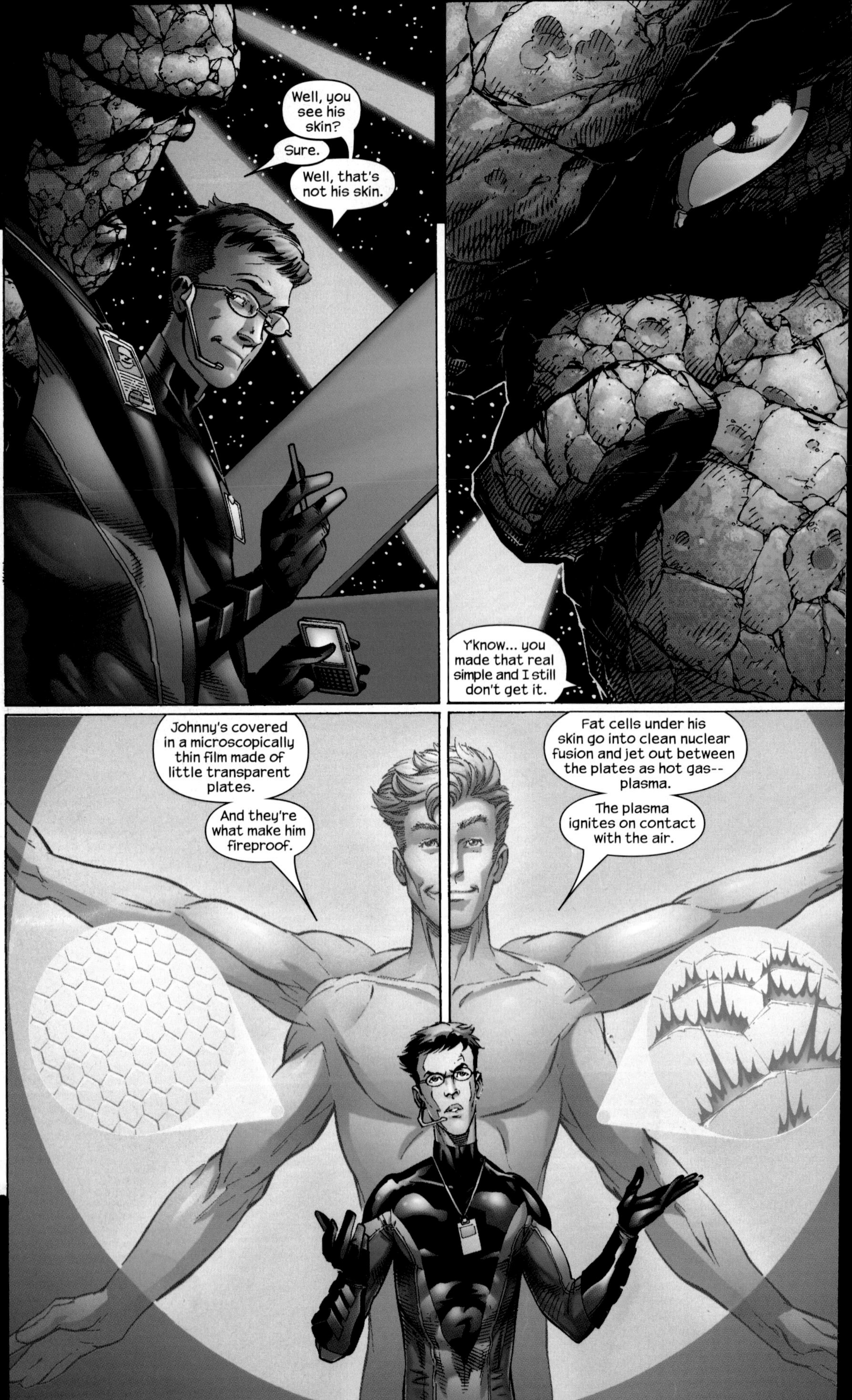

Well, you see his skin?
Sure.
Well, that's not his skin.
Y'know... you made that real simple and I still don't get it.
Johnny's covered in a microscopically thin film made of little transparent plates.
And they're what make him fireproof.
Fat cells under his skin go into clean nuclear fusion and jet out between the plates as hot gas-- plasma.
The plasma ignites on contact with the air.

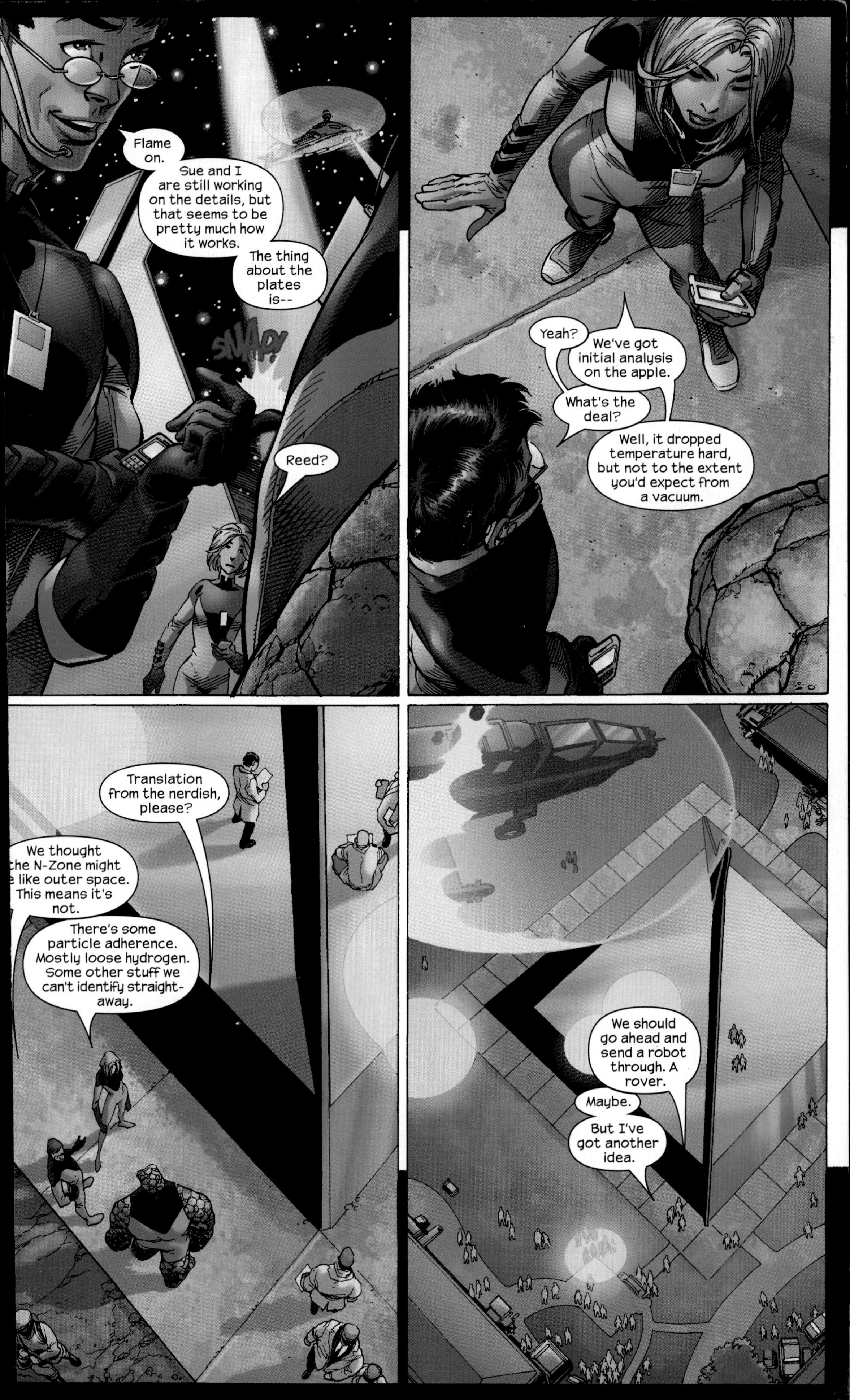

Flame on.
Sue and I are still working on the details, but that seems to be pretty much how it works.
The thing about the plates is--
SNAP!
Reed?
Yeah?
We've got initial analysis on the apple.
What's the deal?
Well, it dropped temperature hard, but not to the extent you'd expect from a vacuum.
Translation from the nerdish, please?
We thought the N-Zone might be like outer space. This means it's not.
There's some particle adherence. Mostly loose hydrogen. Some other stuff we can't identify straight-away.
We should go ahead and send a robot through. A rover.
Maybe.
But I've got another idea.

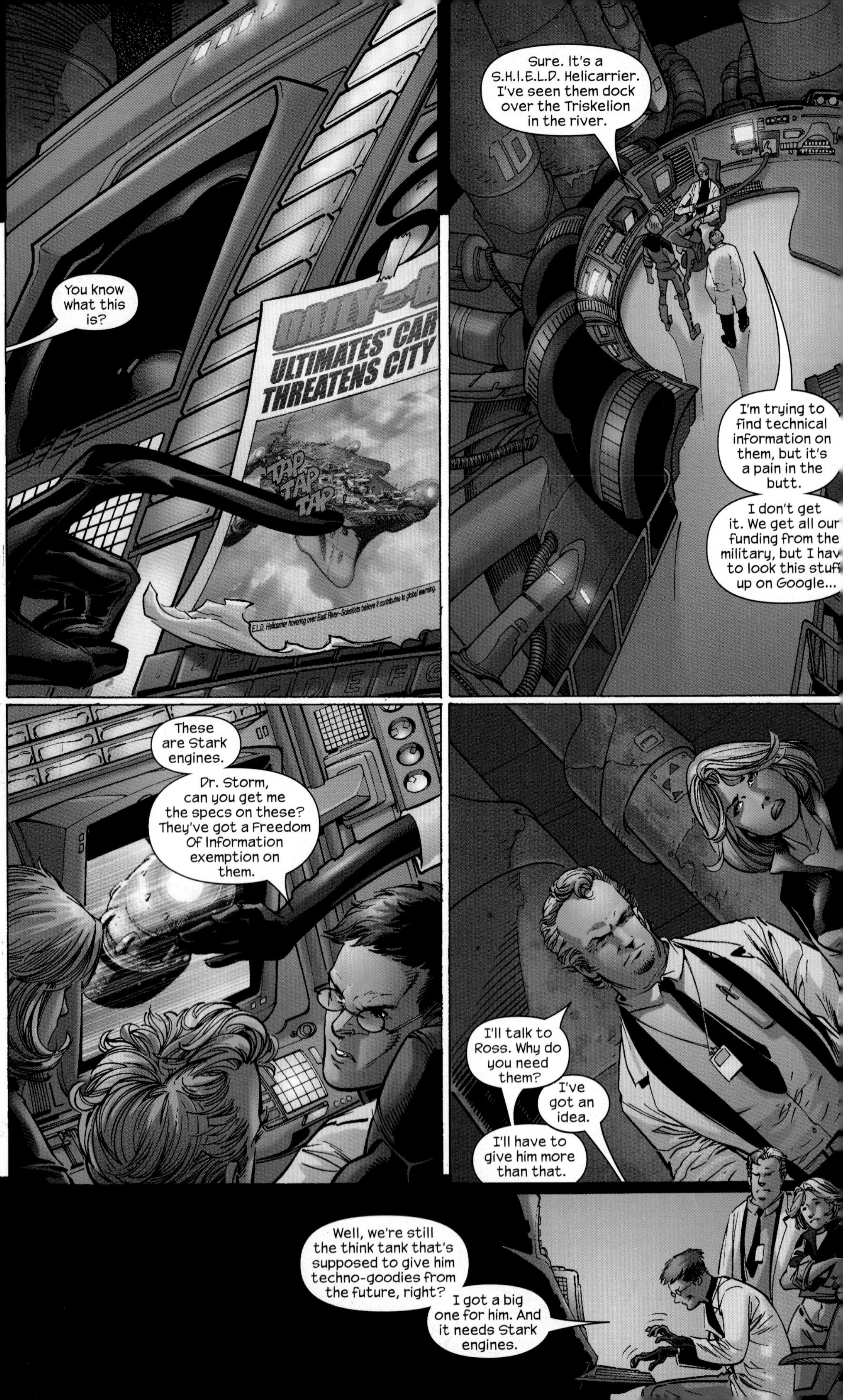
You know what this is?
DAILY
ULTIMATES' CAR
THREATENS CITY
TAP TAP TAP
E.L.D. Helicarrier hovering over East River--Scientists believe it contributes to global warming.
Sure. It's a S.H.I.E.L.D. Helicarrier. I've seen them dock over the Triskelion in the river.
I'm trying to find technical information on them, but it's a pain in the butt.
I don't get it. We get all our funding from the military, but I hav to look this stuff up on Google...
These are Stark engines.
Dr. Storm, can you get me the specs on these? They've got a Freedom Of Information exemption on them.
I'll talk to Ross. Why do you need them?
I've got an idea.
I'll have to give him more than that.
Well, we're still the think tank that's supposed to give him techno-goodies from the future, right?
I got a big one for him. And it needs Stark engines.

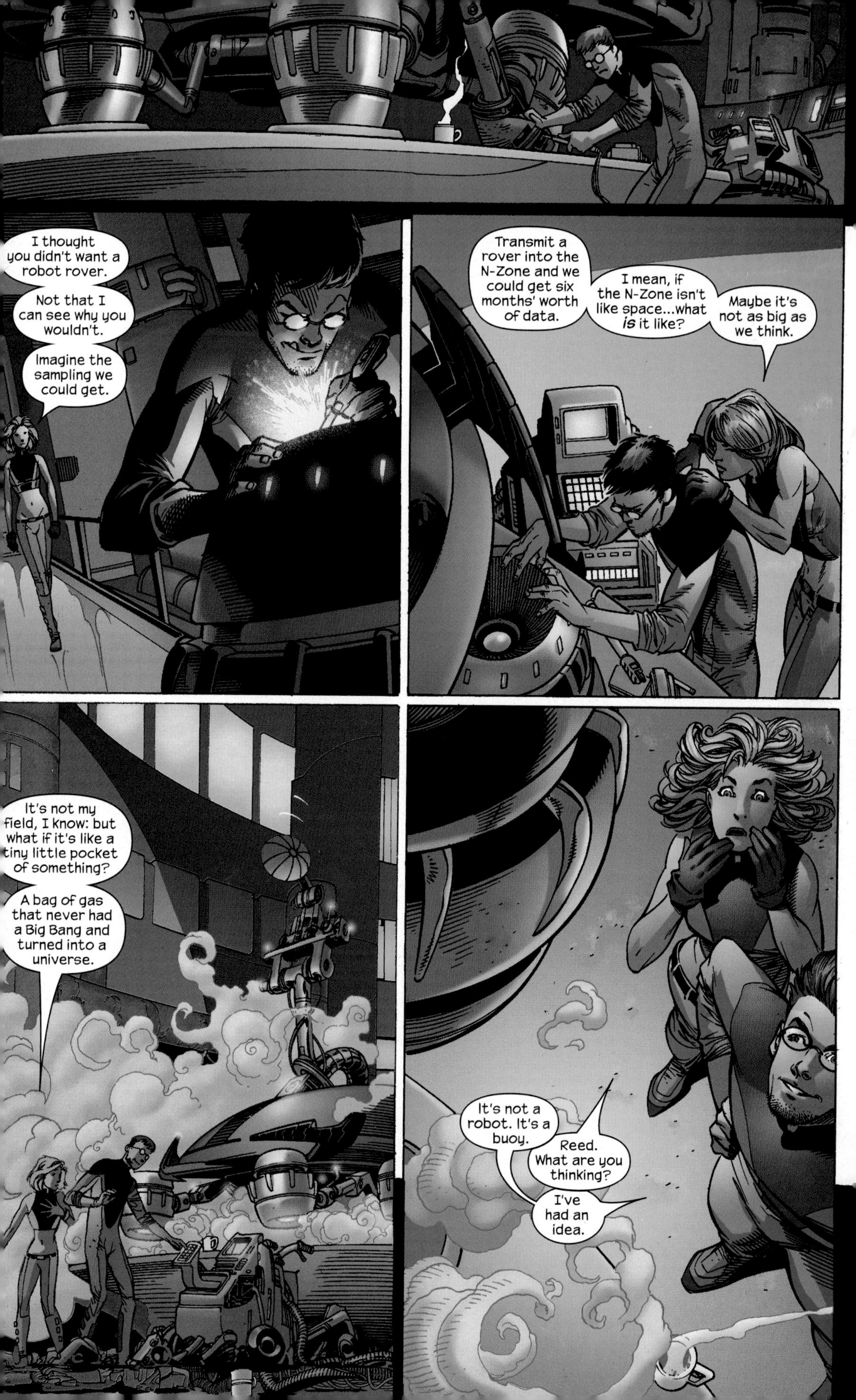
I thought you didn't want a robot rover.
Not that I can see why you wouldn't.
Imagine the sampling we could get.
Transmit a rover into the N-Zone and we could get six months' worth of data.
I mean, if the N-Zone isn't like space...what *is* it like?
Maybe it's not as big as we think.
It's not my field, I know: but what if it's like a tiny little pocket of something?
A bag of gas that never had a Big Bang and turned into a universe.
It's not a robot. It's a buoy.
Reed. What are you thinking?
I've had an idea.

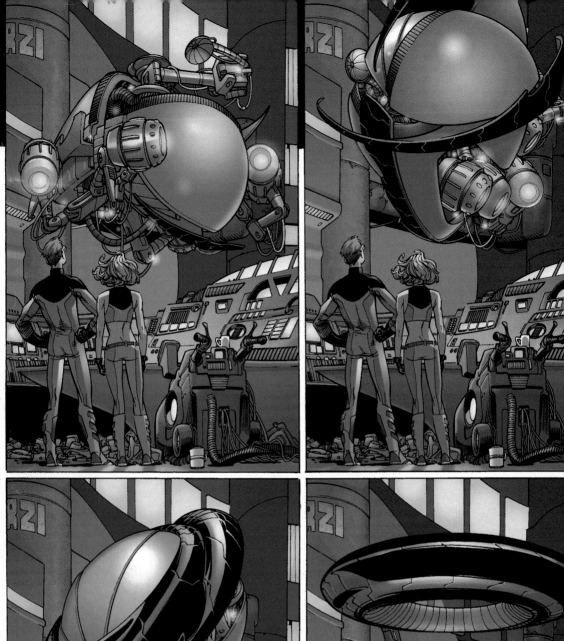

You made a robot hula hoop.

No, no--a hovering robot hula hoop.

You want I should call the TV news now, or should I practice a few tricks with it first?

Leave me alone.

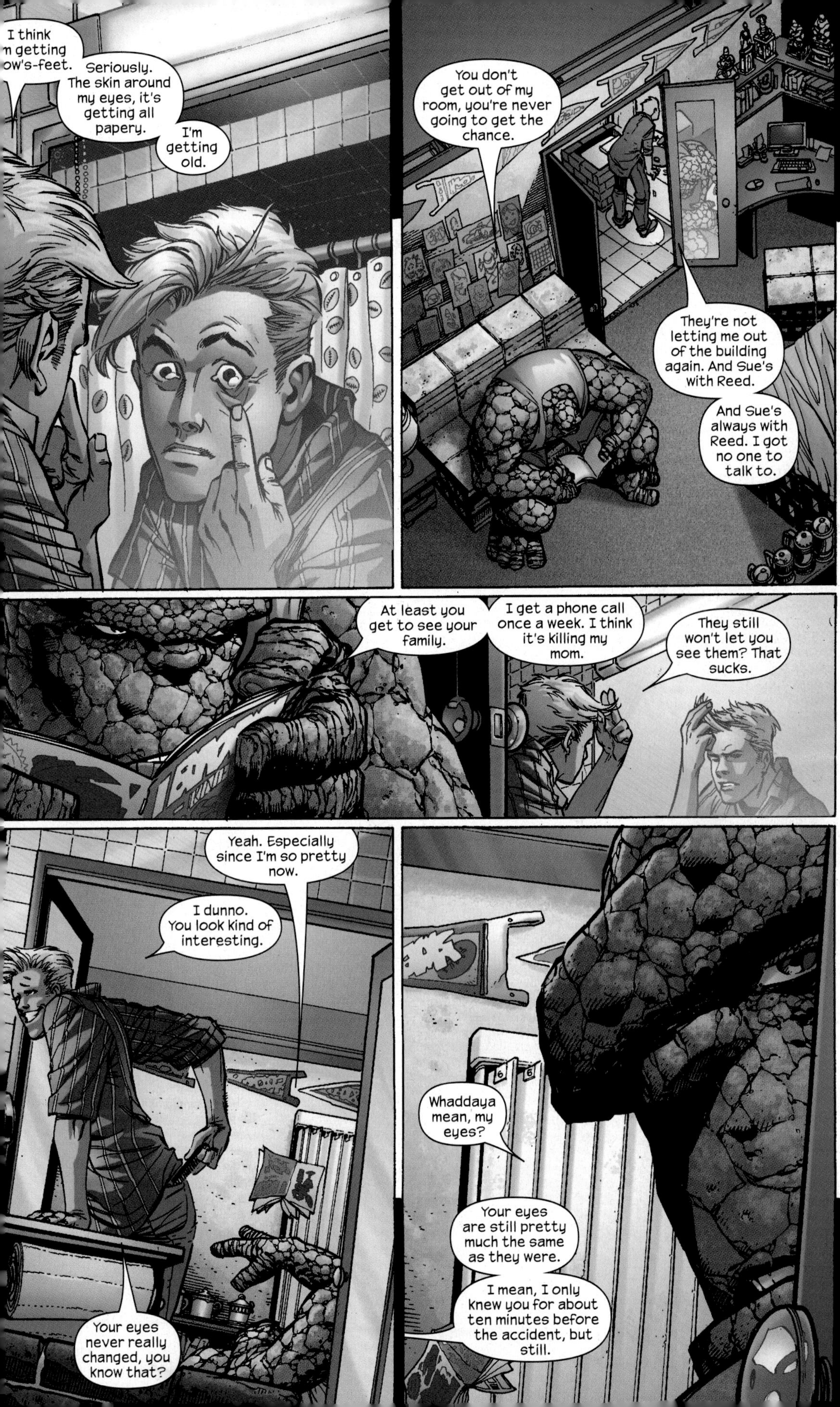

I think m getting ow's-feet.
Seriously. The skin around my eyes, it's getting all papery.
I'm getting old.
You don't get out of my room, you're never going to get the chance.
They're not letting me out of the building again. And Sue's with Reed.
And Sue's always with Reed. I got no one to talk to.
At least you get to see your family.
I get a phone call once a week. I think it's killing my mom.
They still won't let you see them? That sucks.
Yeah. Especially since I'm so pretty now.
I dunno. You look kind of interesting.
Your eyes never really changed, you know that?
Whaddaya mean, my eyes?
Your eyes are still pretty much the same as they were.
I mean, I only knew you for about ten minutes before the accident, but still.

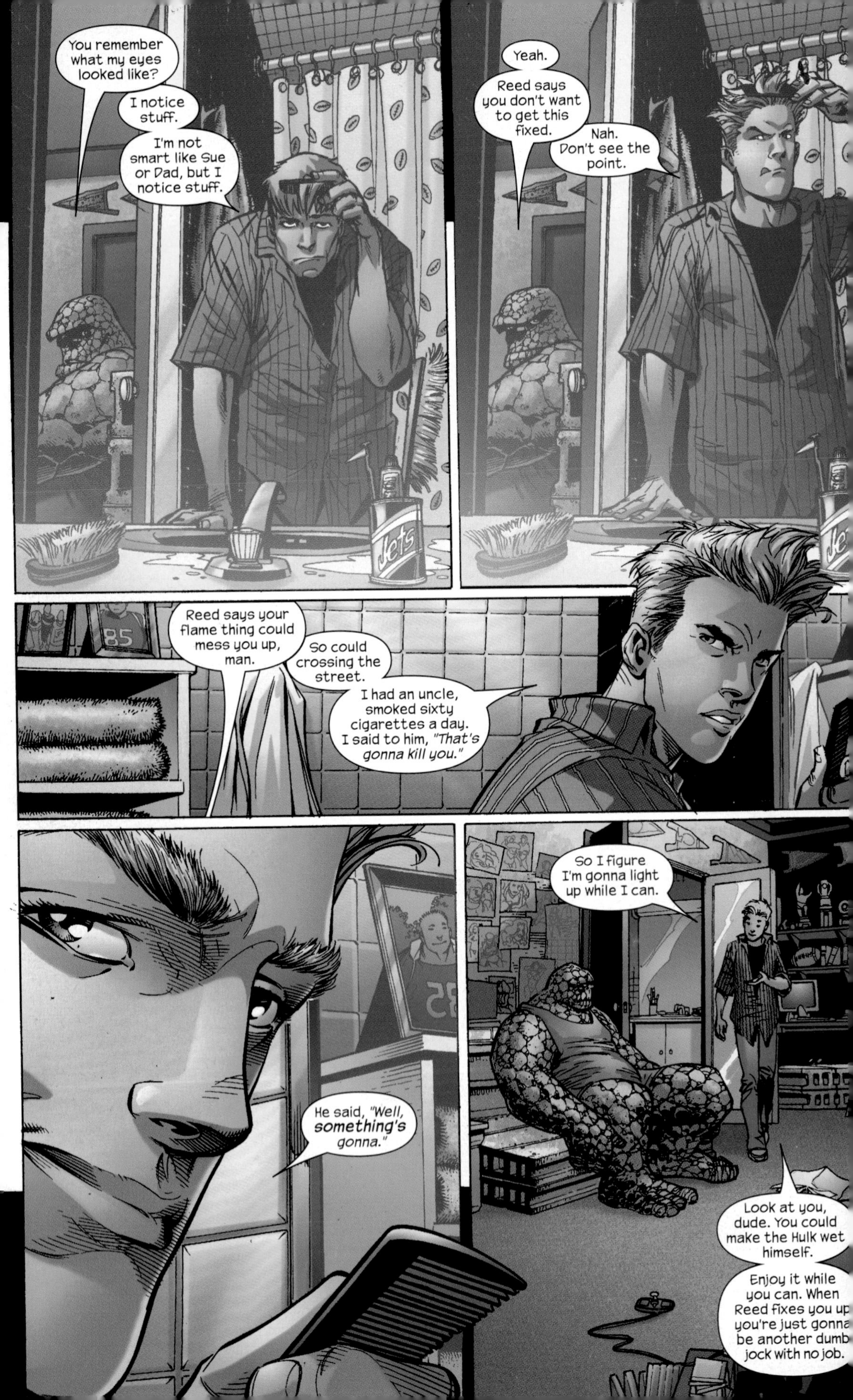
You remember what my eyes looked like?
I notice stuff.
I'm not smart like Sue or Dad, but I notice stuff.
Yeah.
Reed says you don't want to get this fixed.
Nah. Don't see the point.
Jets
85
Reed says your flame thing could mess you up, man.
So could crossing the street.
I had an uncle, smoked sixty cigarettes a day. I said to him, *"That's gonna kill you."*
He said, "Well, ***something's*** *gonna."*
So I figure I'm gonna light up while I can.
Look at you, dude. You could make the Hulk wet himself.
Enjoy it while you can. When Reed fixes you up you're just gonna be another dumb jock with no job.

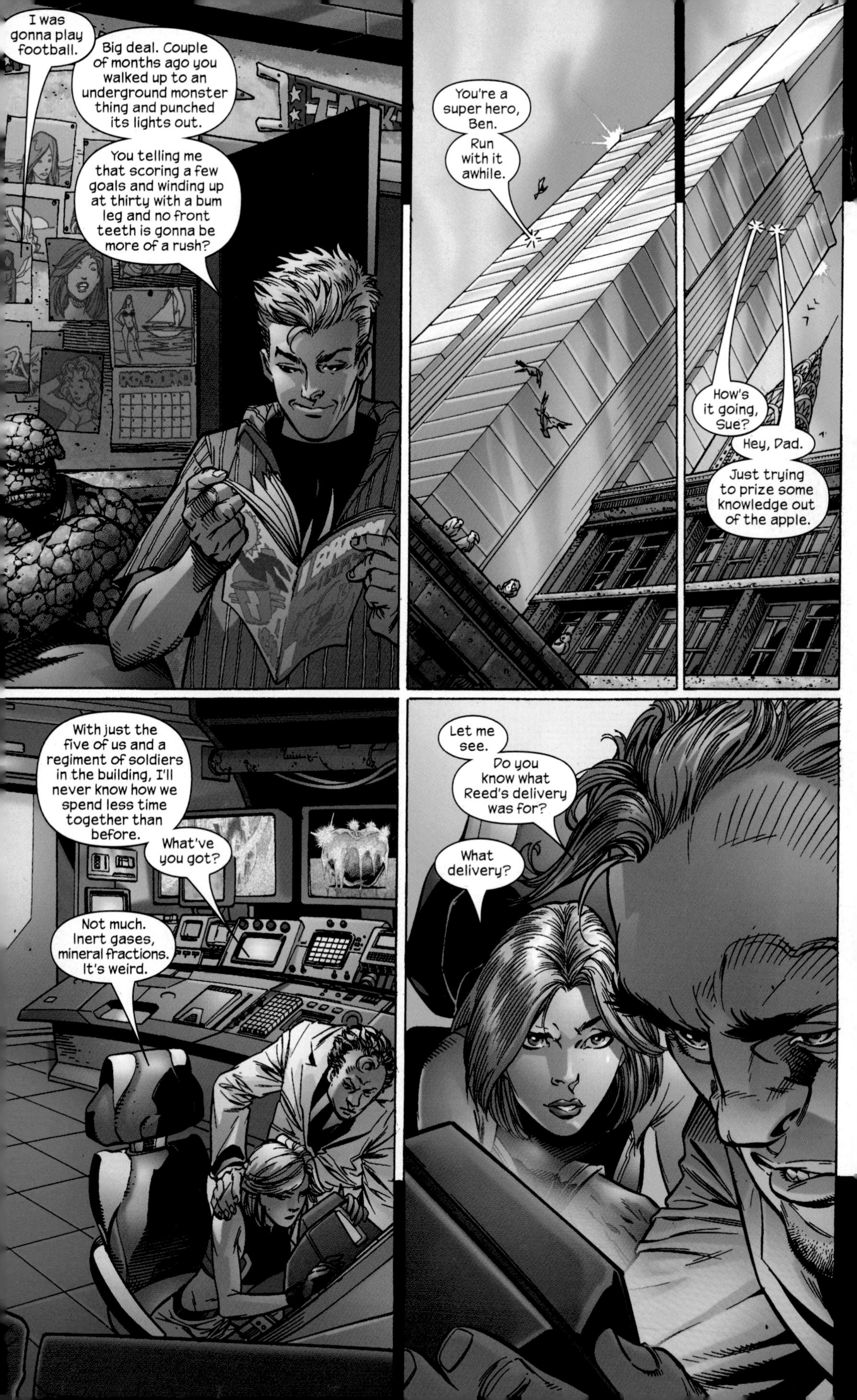
I was gonna play football.
Big deal. Couple of months ago you walked up to an underground monster thing and punched its lights out.
You telling me that scoring a few goals and winding up at thirty with a bum leg and no front teeth is gonna be more of a rush?
You're a super hero, Ben.
Run with it awhile.
How's it going, Sue?
Hey, Dad.
Just trying to prize some knowledge out of the apple.
With just the five of us and a regiment of soldiers in the building, I'll never know how we spend less time together than before.
What've you got?
Not much. Inert gases, mineral fractions. It's weird.
Let me see.
Do you know what Reed's delivery was for?
What delivery?

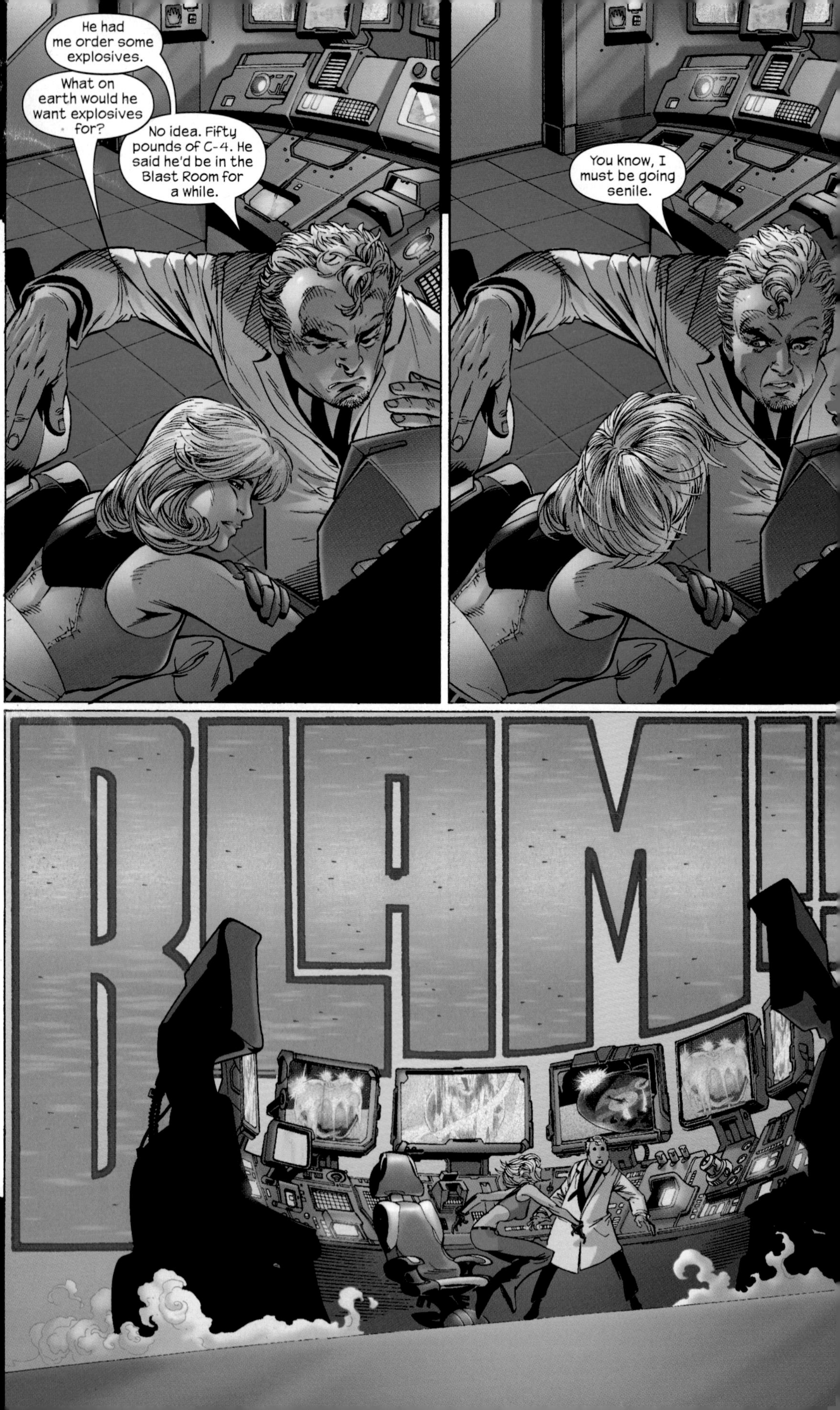
He had me order some explosives.
What on earth would he want explosives for?
No idea. Fifty pounds of C-4. He said he'd be in the Blast Room for a while.
You know, I must be going senile.
BLAM

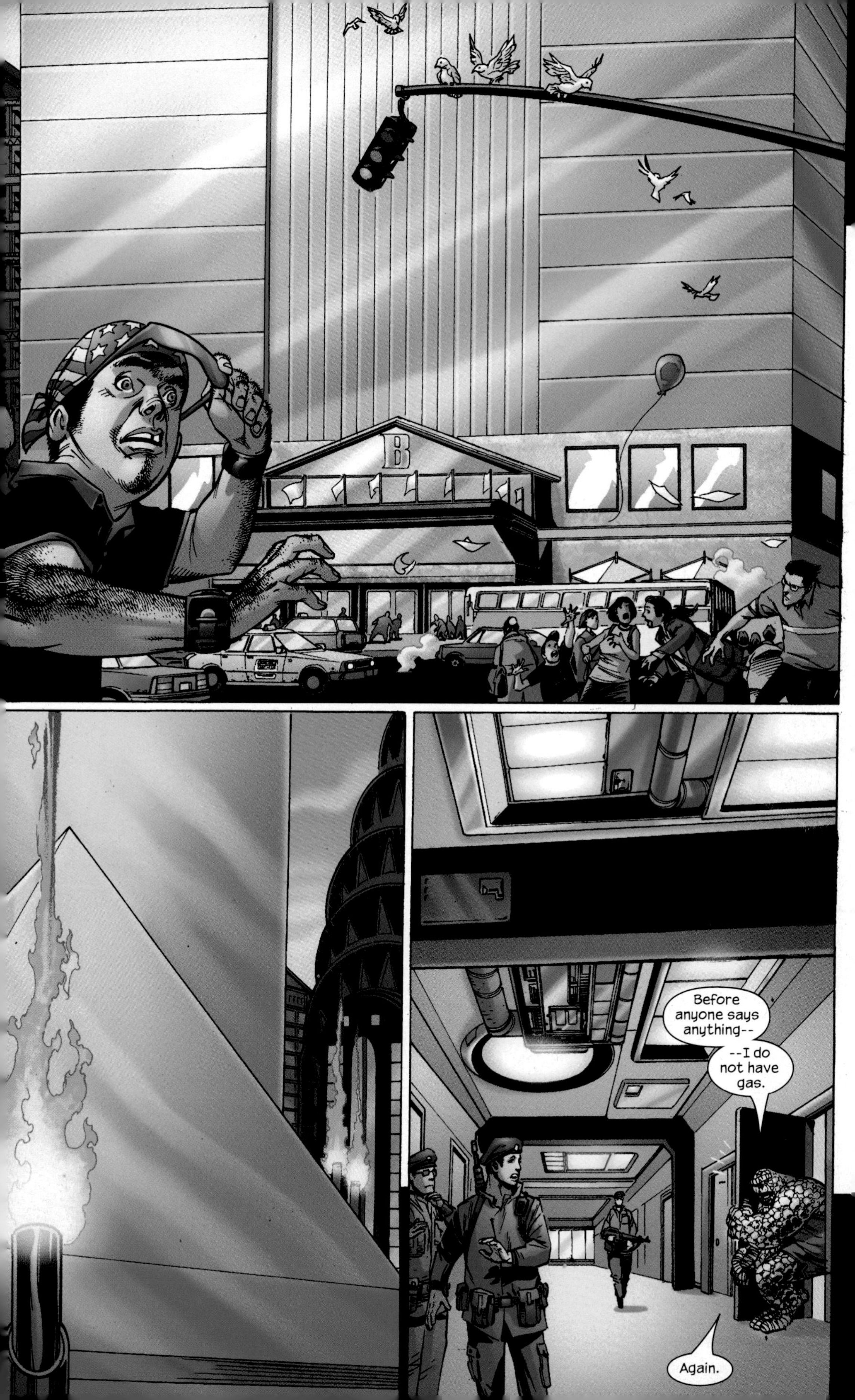
Before anyone says anything--
--I do not have gas.
Again.

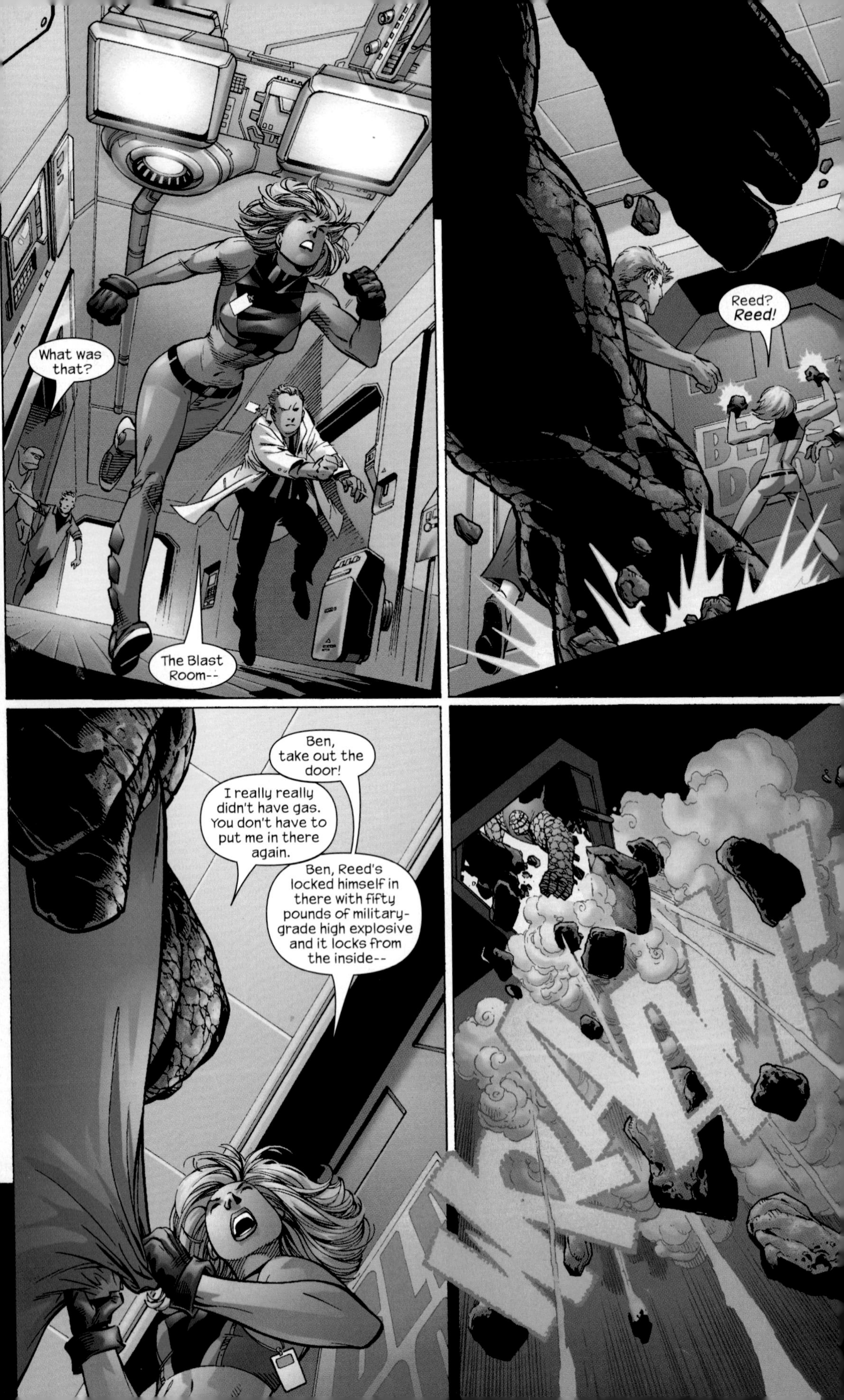
What was that?
The Blast Room--
Reed? Reed!
Ben, take out the door!
I really really didn't have gas. You don't have to put me in there again.
Ben, Reed's locked himself in there with fifty pounds of military-grade high explosive and it locks from the inside--

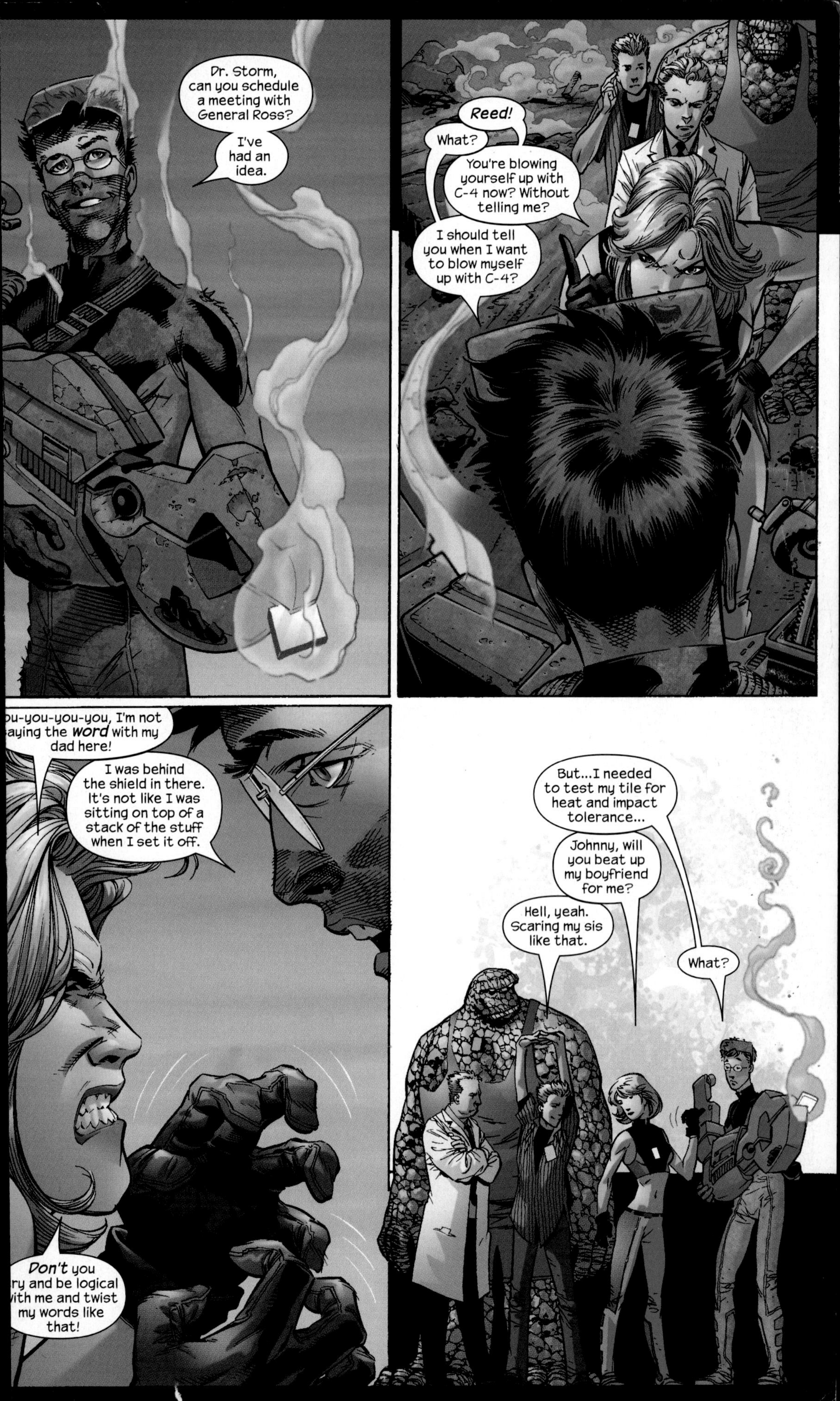
Dr. Storm, can you schedule a meeting with General Ross?
I've had an idea.
Reed!
What?
You're blowing yourself up with C-4 now? Without telling me?
I should tell you when I want to blow myself up with C-4?
ou-you-you-you, I'm not aying the *word* with my dad here!
I was behind the shield in there. It's not like I was sitting on top of a stack of the stuff when I set it off.
Don't you ry and be logical ith me and twist my words like that!
But...I needed to test my tile for heat and impact tolerance...
Johnny, will you beat up my boyfriend for me?
Hell, yeah. Scaring my sis like that.
What?

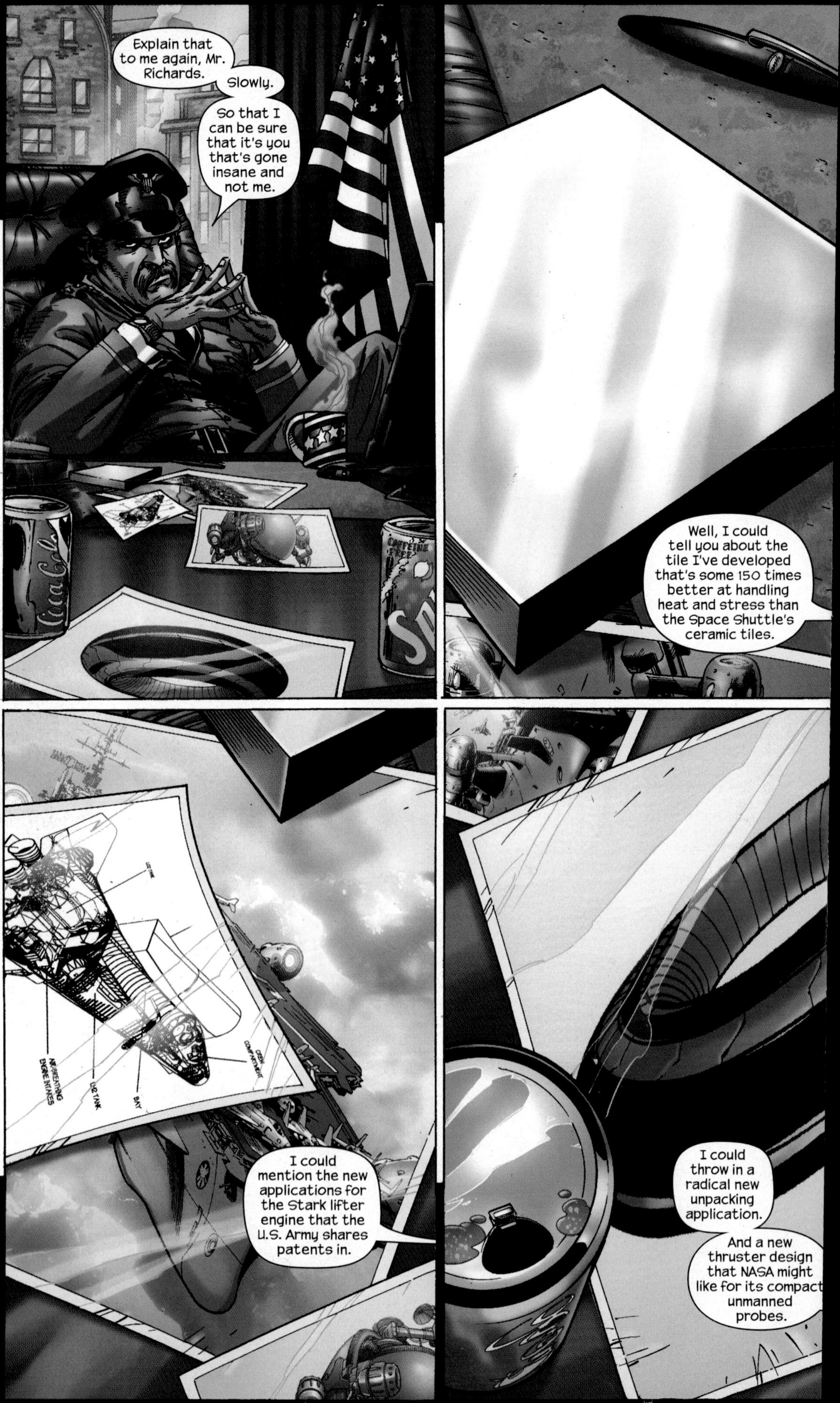
Explain that to me again, Mr. Richards.
Slowly.
So that I can be sure that it's you that's gone insane and not me.
Well, I could tell you about the tile I've developed that's some 150 times better at handling heat and stress than the Space Shuttle's ceramic tiles.
I could mention the new applications for the Stark lifter engine that the U.S. Army shares patents in.
I could throw in a radical new unpacking application.
And a new thruster design that NASA might like for its compact unmanned probes.

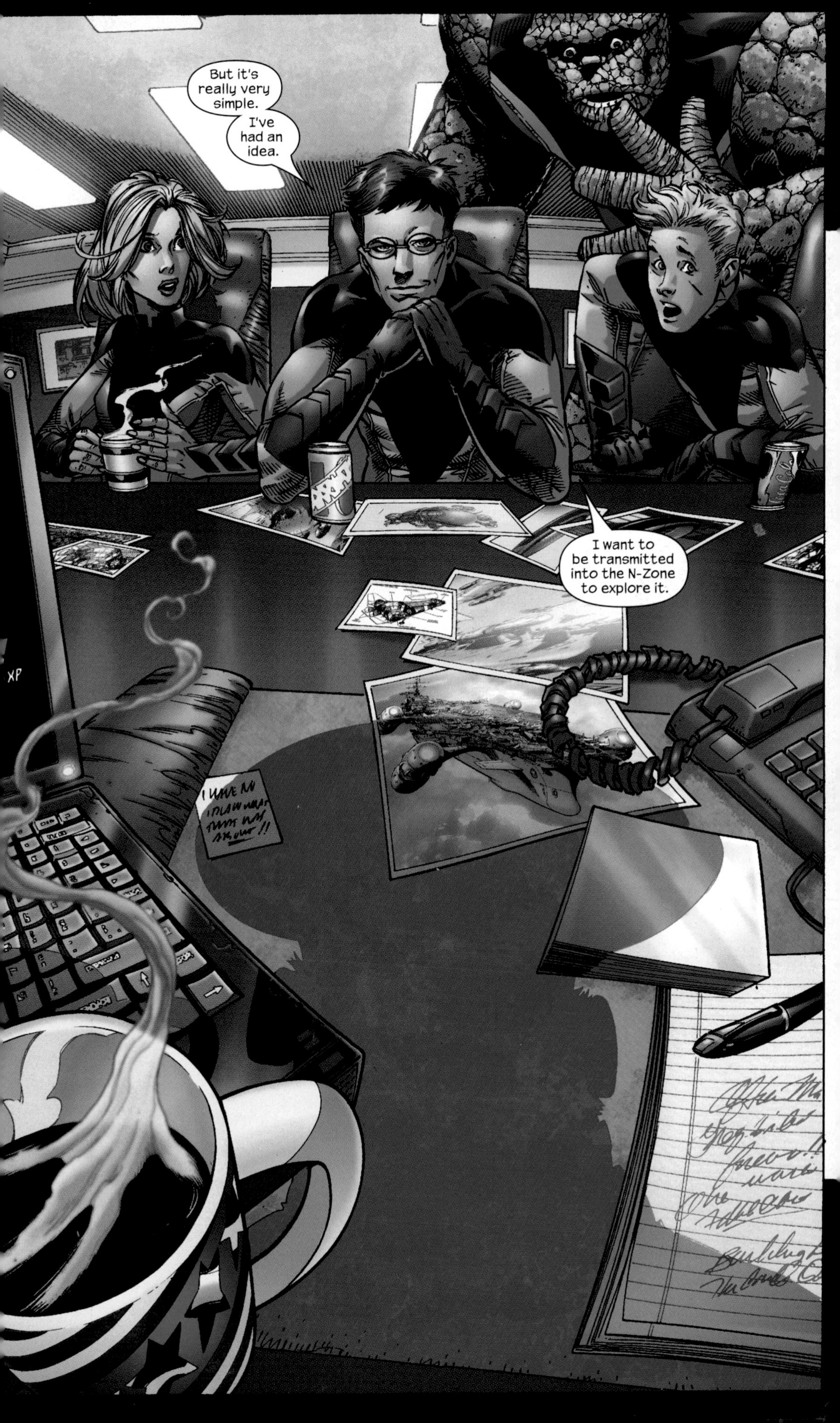
But it's really very simple.
I've had an idea.
I want to be transmitted into the N-Zone to explore it.

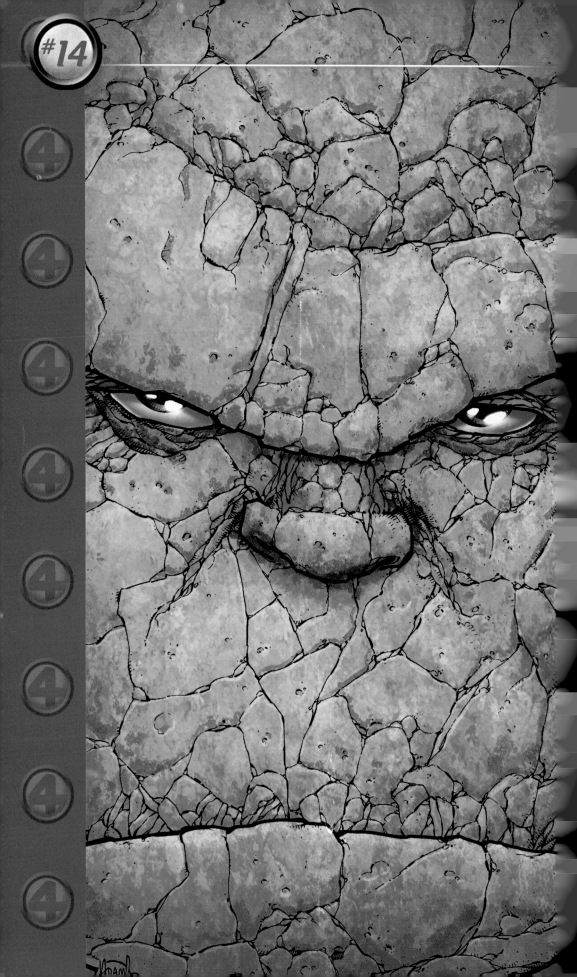

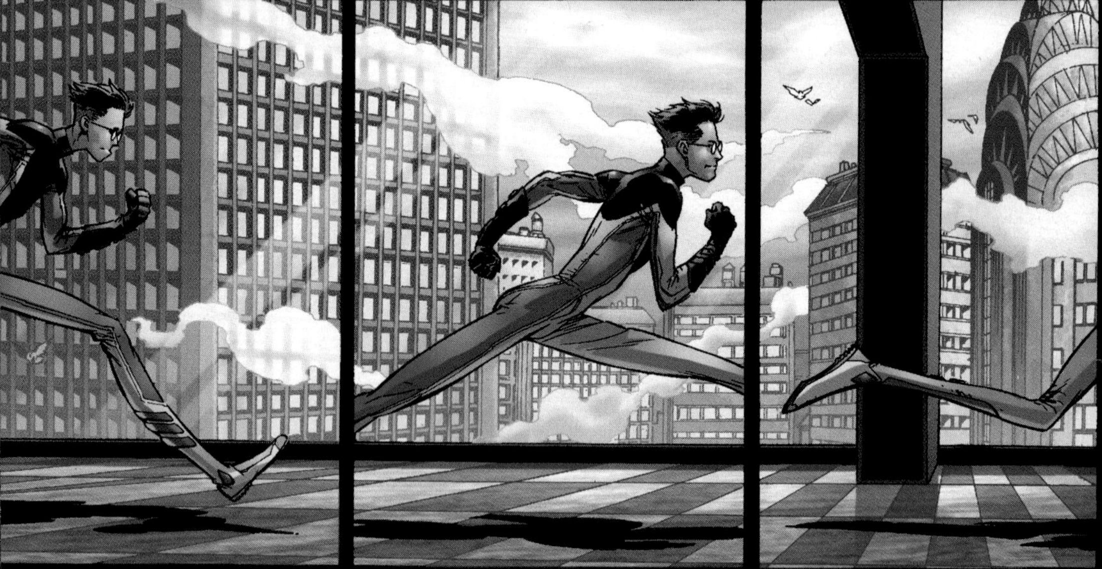

N-ZONE

TWO of SIX

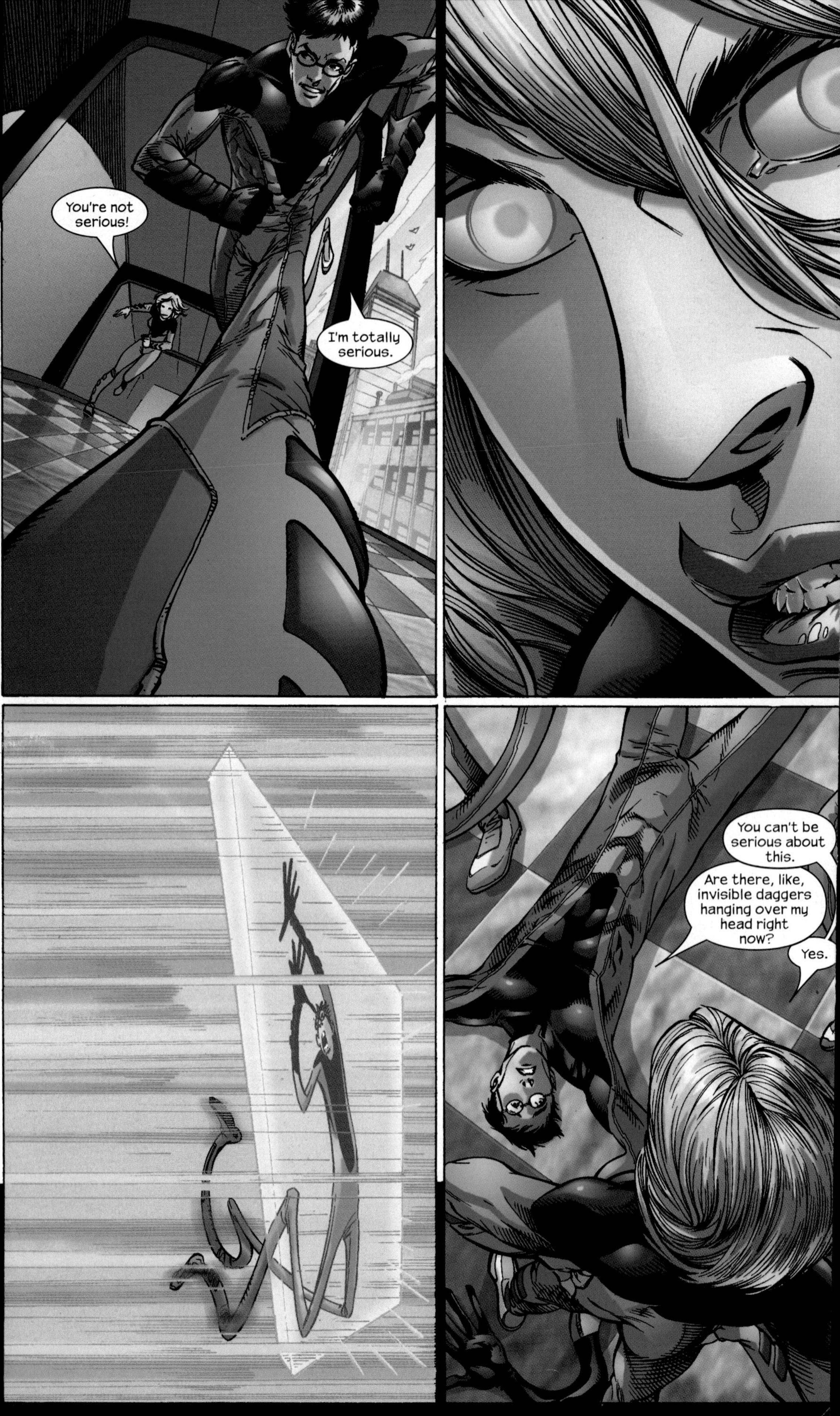
You're not serious!
I'm totally serious.
You can't be serious about this.
Are there, like, invisible daggers hanging over my head right now?
Yes.

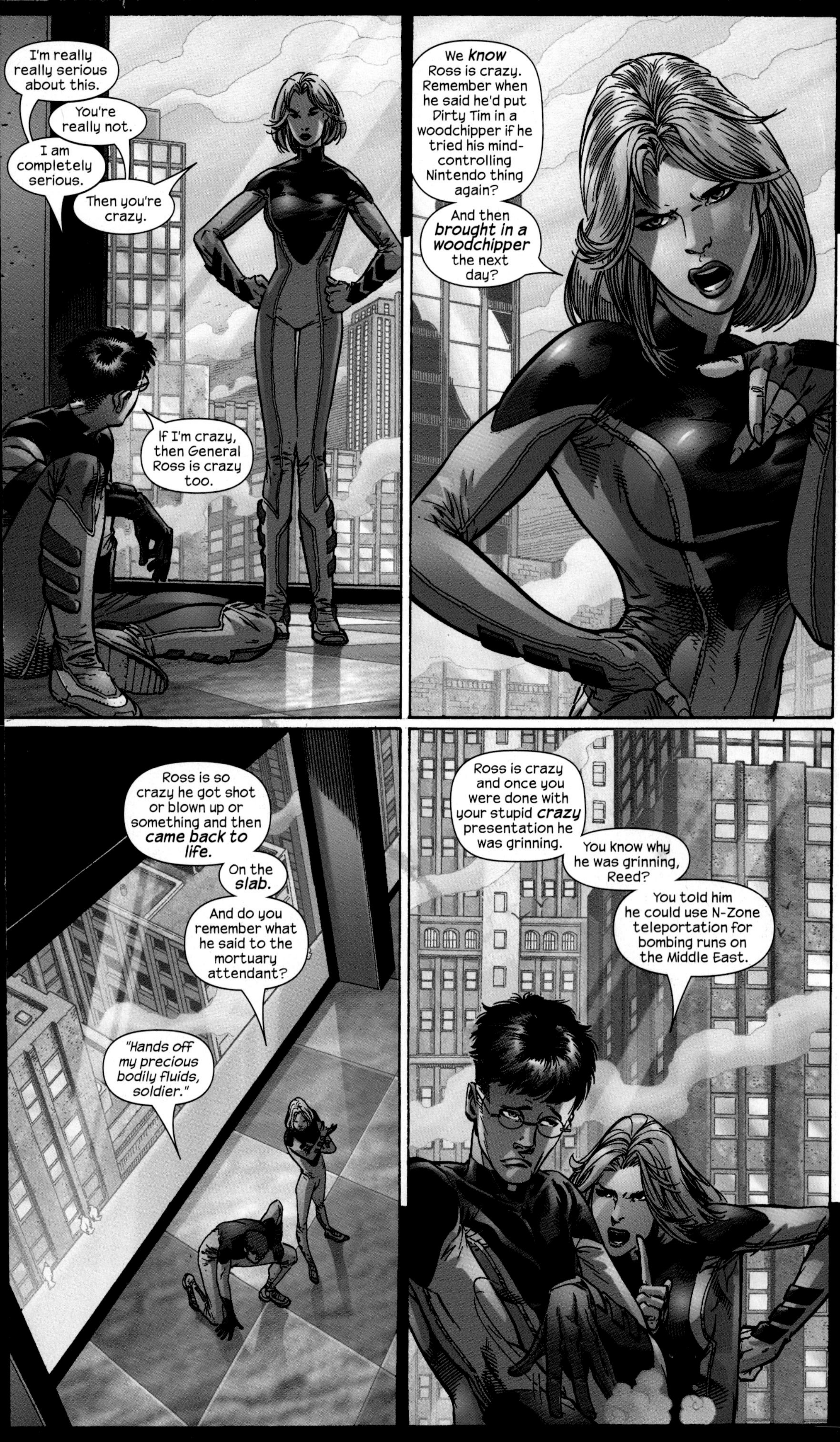
I'm really really serious about this.
You're really not.
I am completely serious.
Then you're crazy.
If I'm crazy, then General Ross is crazy too.
We know Ross is crazy. Remember when he said he'd put Dirty Tim in a woodchipper if he tried his mind-controlling Nintendo thing again?
And then brought in a woodchipper the next day?
Ross is so crazy he got shot or blown up or something and then came back to life.
On the slab.
And do you remember what he said to the mortuary attendant?
"Hands off my precious bodily fluids, soldier."
Ross is crazy and once you were done with your stupid crazy presentation he was grinning.
You know why he was grinning, Reed?
You told him he could use N-Zone teleportation for bombing runs on the Middle East.

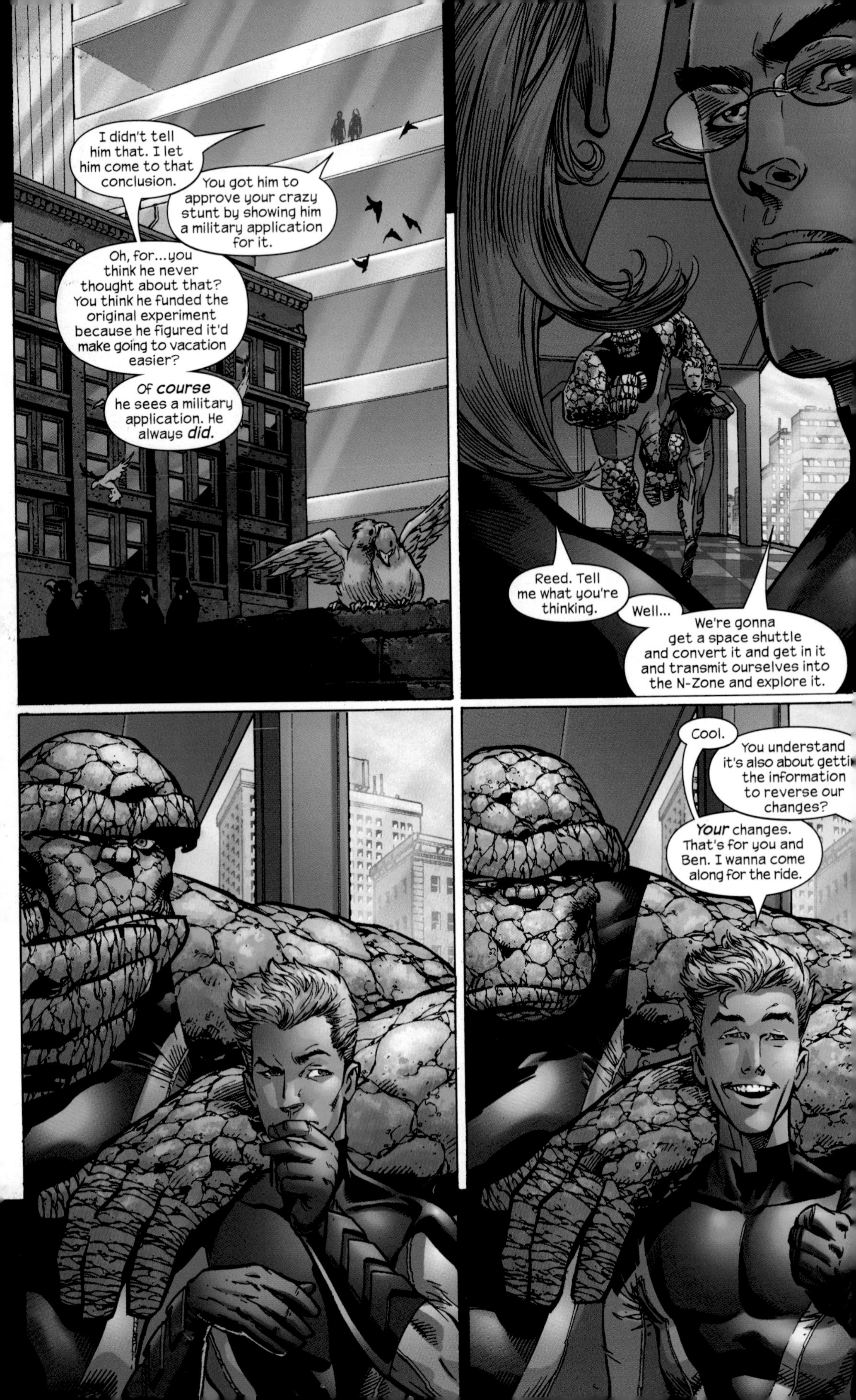
I didn't tell him that. I let him come to that conclusion.
You got him to approve your crazy stunt by showing him a military application for it.
Oh, for...you think he never thought about that? You think he funded the original experiment because he figured it'd make going to vacation easier?
Of *course* he sees a military application. He always *did.*
Reed. Tell me what you're thinking.
Well...
We're gonna get a space shuttle and convert it and get in it and transmit ourselves into the N-Zone and explore it.
Cool.
Your changes. That's for you and Ben. I wanna come along for the ride.

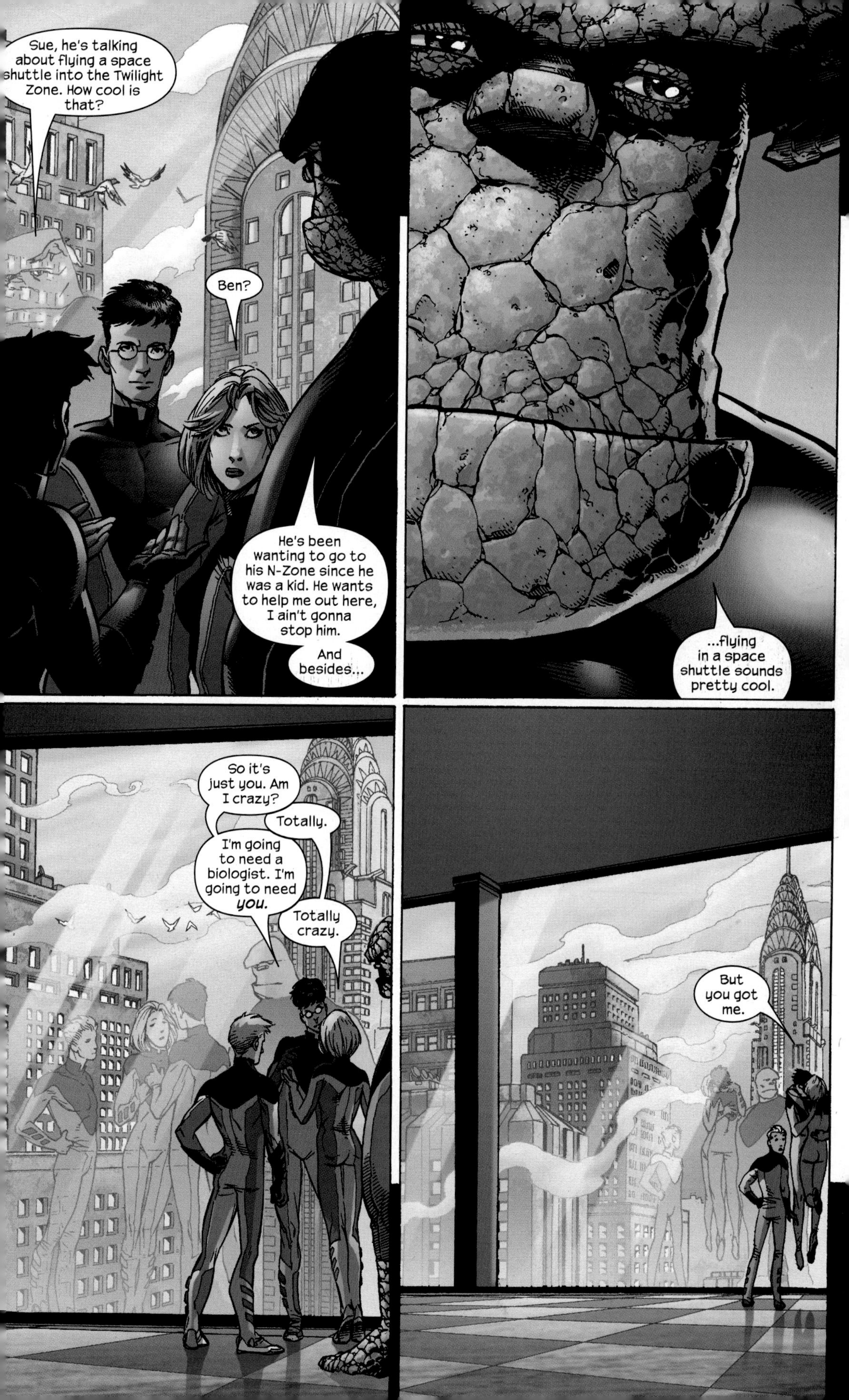
Sue, he's talking about flying a space shuttle into the Twilight Zone. How cool is that?
Ben?
He's been wanting to go to his N-Zone since he was a kid. He wants to help me out here, I ain't gonna stop him.
And besides...
...flying in a space shuttle sounds pretty cool.
So it's just you. Am I crazy?
Totally.
I'm going to need a biologist. I'm going to need *you.*
Totally crazy.
But you got me.

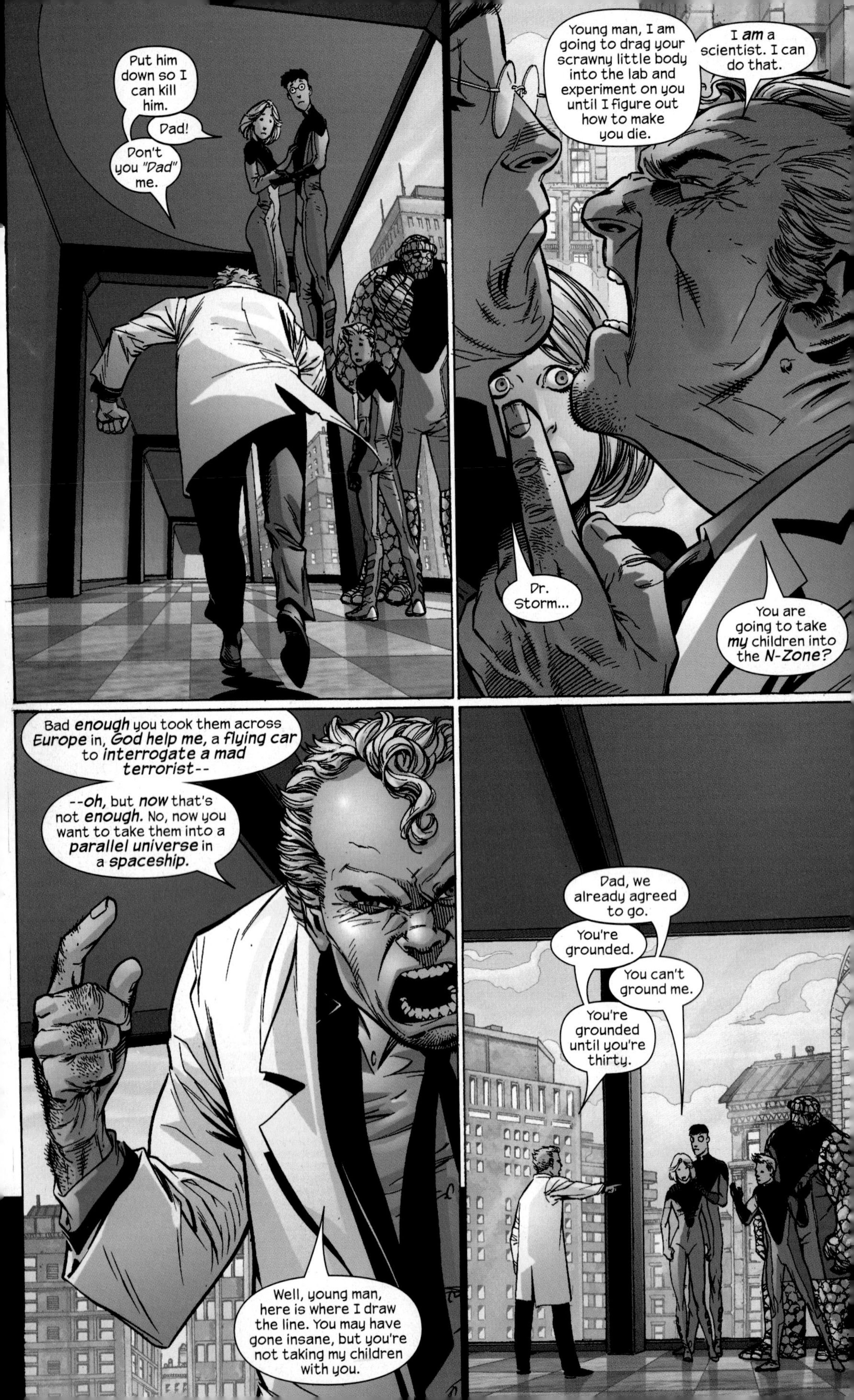
Put him down so I can kill him.
Dad!
Don't you "Dad" me.
Young man, I am going to drag your scrawny little body into the lab and experiment on you until I figure out how to make you die.
I am a scientist. I can do that.
Dr. Storm...
You are going to take my children into the N-Zone?
Bad enough you took them across Europe in, God help me, a flying car to interrogate a mad terrorist--
--oh, but now that's not enough. No, now you want to take them into a parallel universe in a spaceship.
Well, young man, here is where I draw the line. You may have gone insane, but you're not taking my children with you.
Dad, we already agreed to go.
You're grounded.
You can't ground me.
You're grounded until you're thirty.

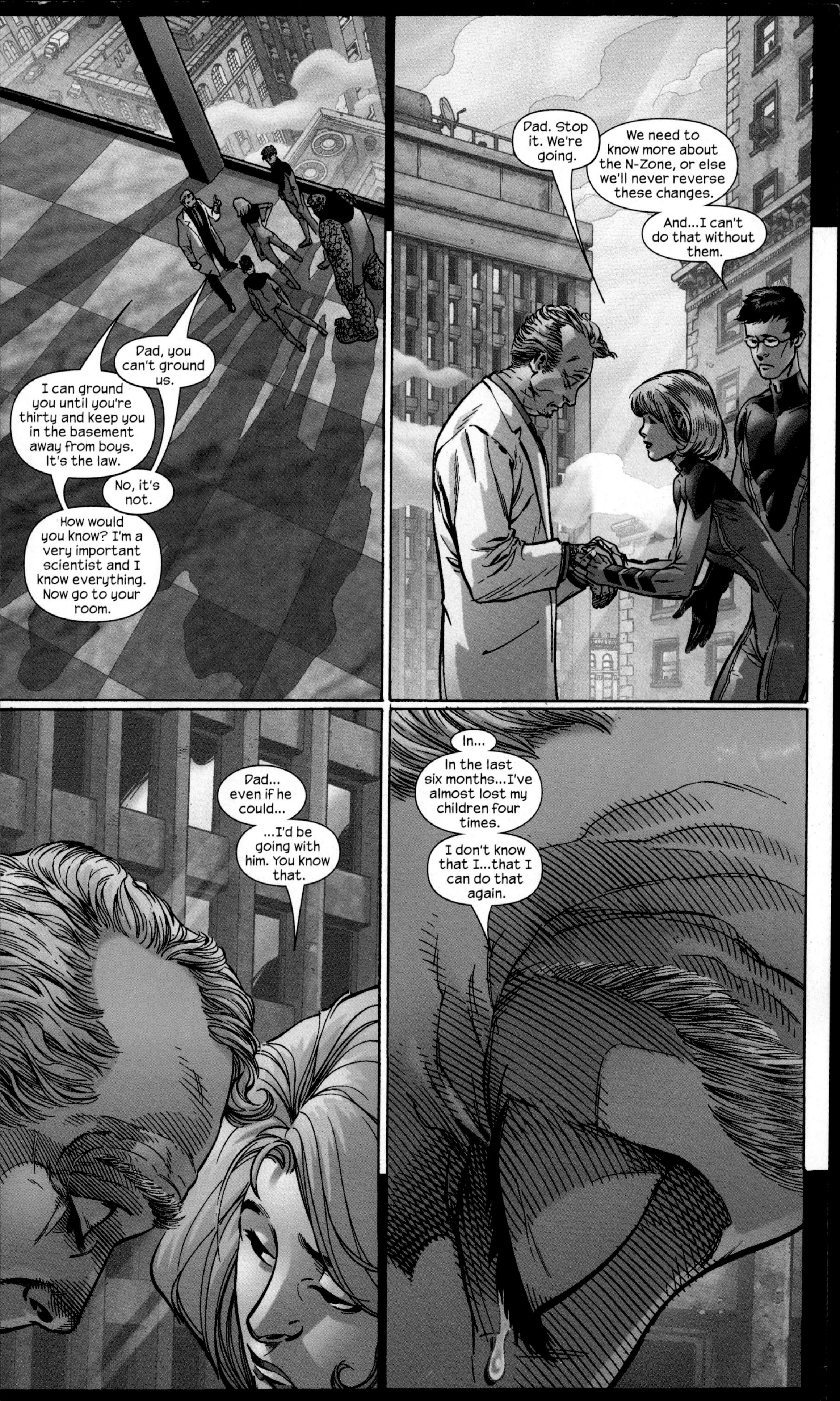
Dad, you can't ground us.
I can ground you until you're thirty and keep you in the basement away from boys. It's the law.
No, it's not.
How would you know? I'm a very important scientist and I know everything. Now go to your room.
Dad. Stop it. We're going.
We need to know more about the N-Zone, or else we'll never reverse these changes.
And...I can't do that without them.
Dad... even if he could...
...I'd be going with him. You know that.
In...
In the last six months...I've almost lost my children four times.
I don't know that I...that I can do that again.

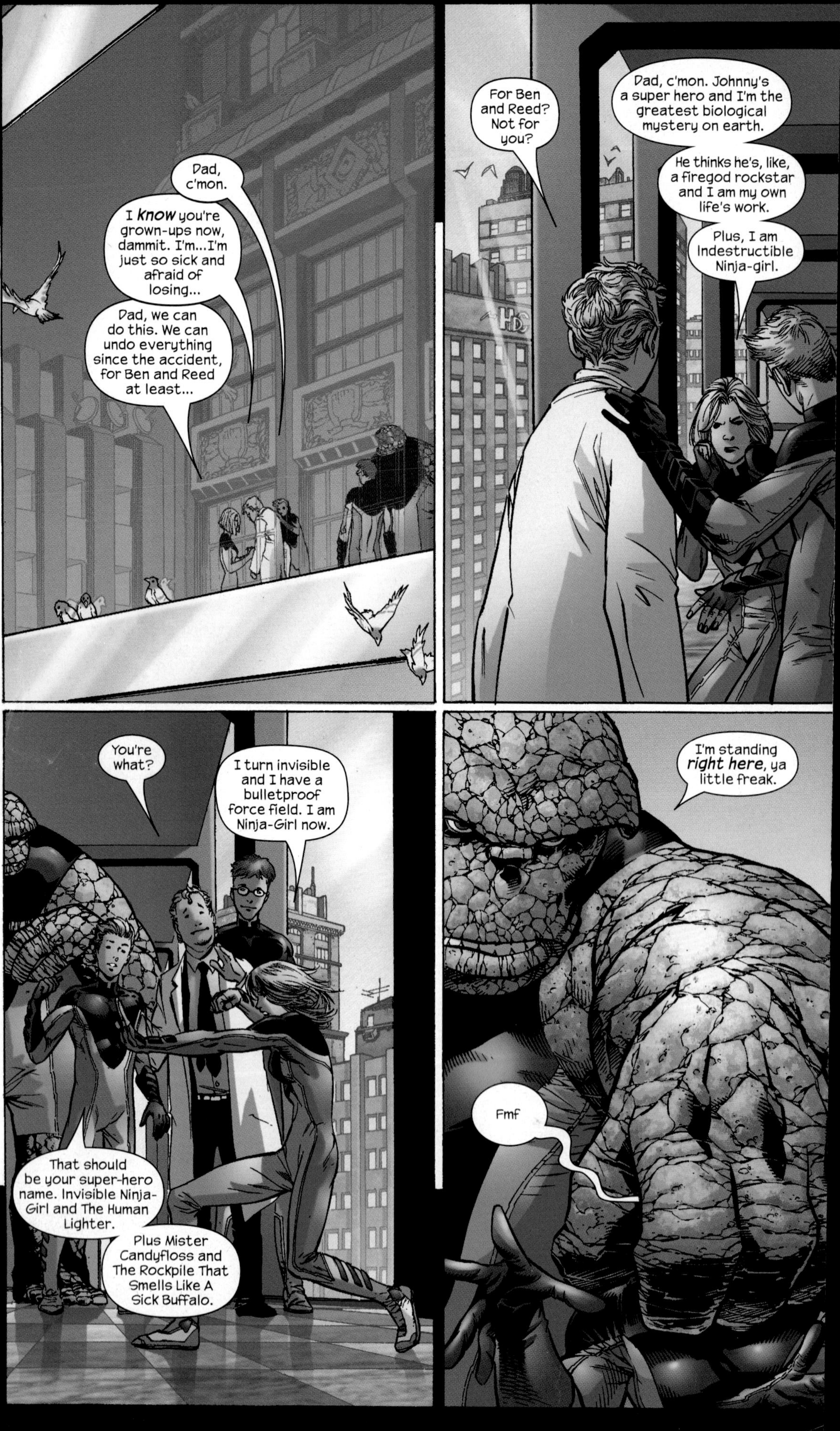
Dad, c'mon.
I KNOW you're grown-ups now, dammit. I'm...I'm just so sick and afraid of losing...
Dad, we can do this. We can undo everything since the accident, for Ben and Reed at least...
For Ben and Reed? Not for you?
Dad, c'mon. Johnny's a super hero and I'm the greatest biological mystery on earth.
He thinks he's, like, a firegod rockstar and I am my own life's work.
Plus, I am Indestructible Ninja-girl.
You're what?
I turn invisible and I have a bulletproof force field. I am Ninja-Girl now.
That should be your super-hero name. Invisible Ninja-Girl and The Human Lighter.
Plus Mister Candyfloss and The Rockpile That Smells Like A Sick Buffalo.
I'm standing right here, ya little freak.
Fmf

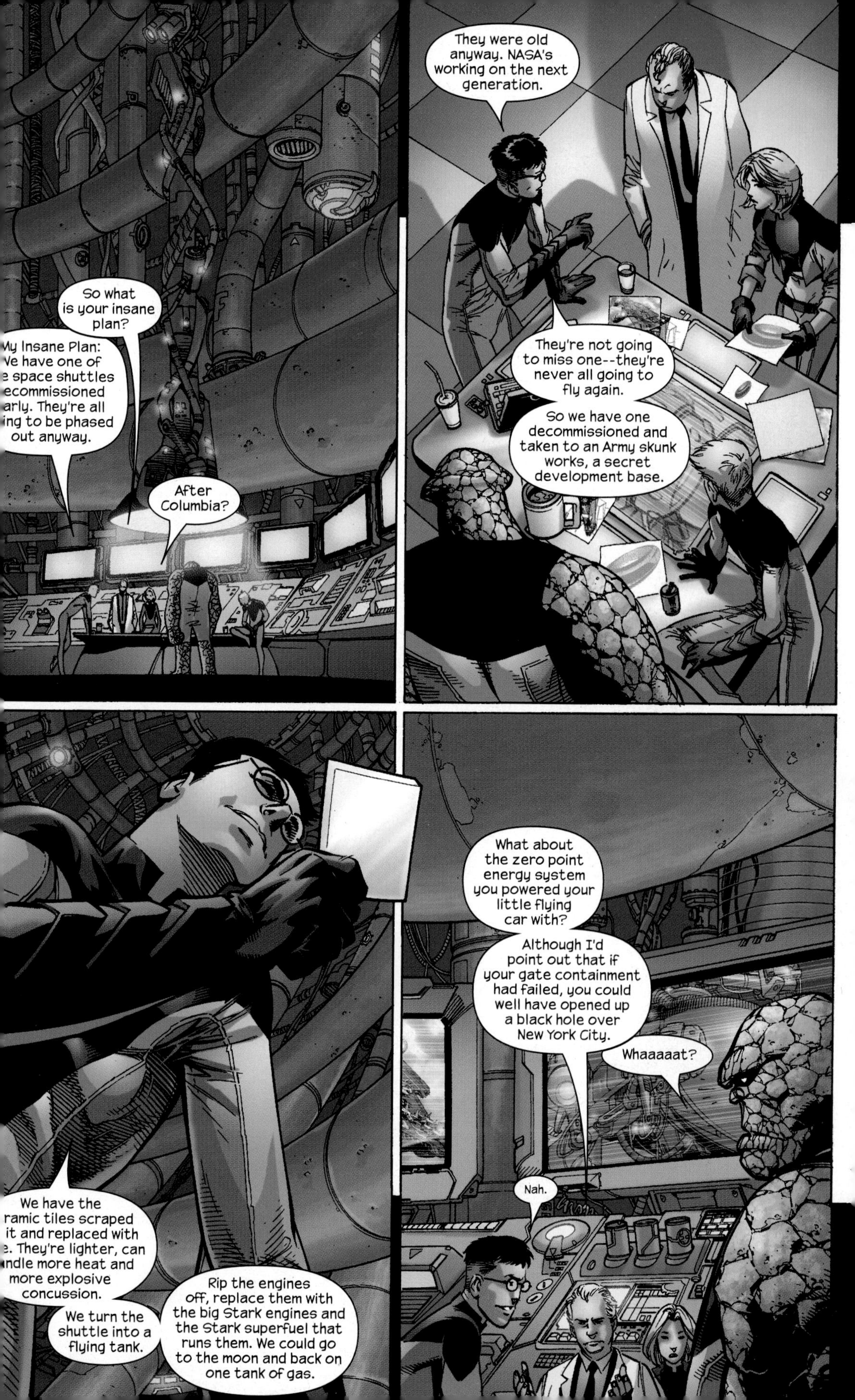
So what is your insane plan?
ly Insane Plan: Ve have one of e space shuttles ecommissioned arly. They're all ing to be phased out anyway.
After Columbia?
They were old anyway. NASA's working on the next generation.
They're not going to miss one--they're never all going to fly again.
So we have one decommissioned and taken to an Army skunk works, a secret development base.
We have the ramic tiles scraped it and replaced with e. They're lighter, can ndle more heat and more explosive concussion.
We turn the shuttle into a flying tank.
Rip the engines off, replace them with the big Stark engines and the Stark superfuel that runs them. We could go to the moon and back on one tank of gas.
What about the zero point energy system you powered your little flying car with?
Although I'd point out that if your gate containment had failed, you could well have opened up a black hole over New York City.
Whaaaaat?
Nah.

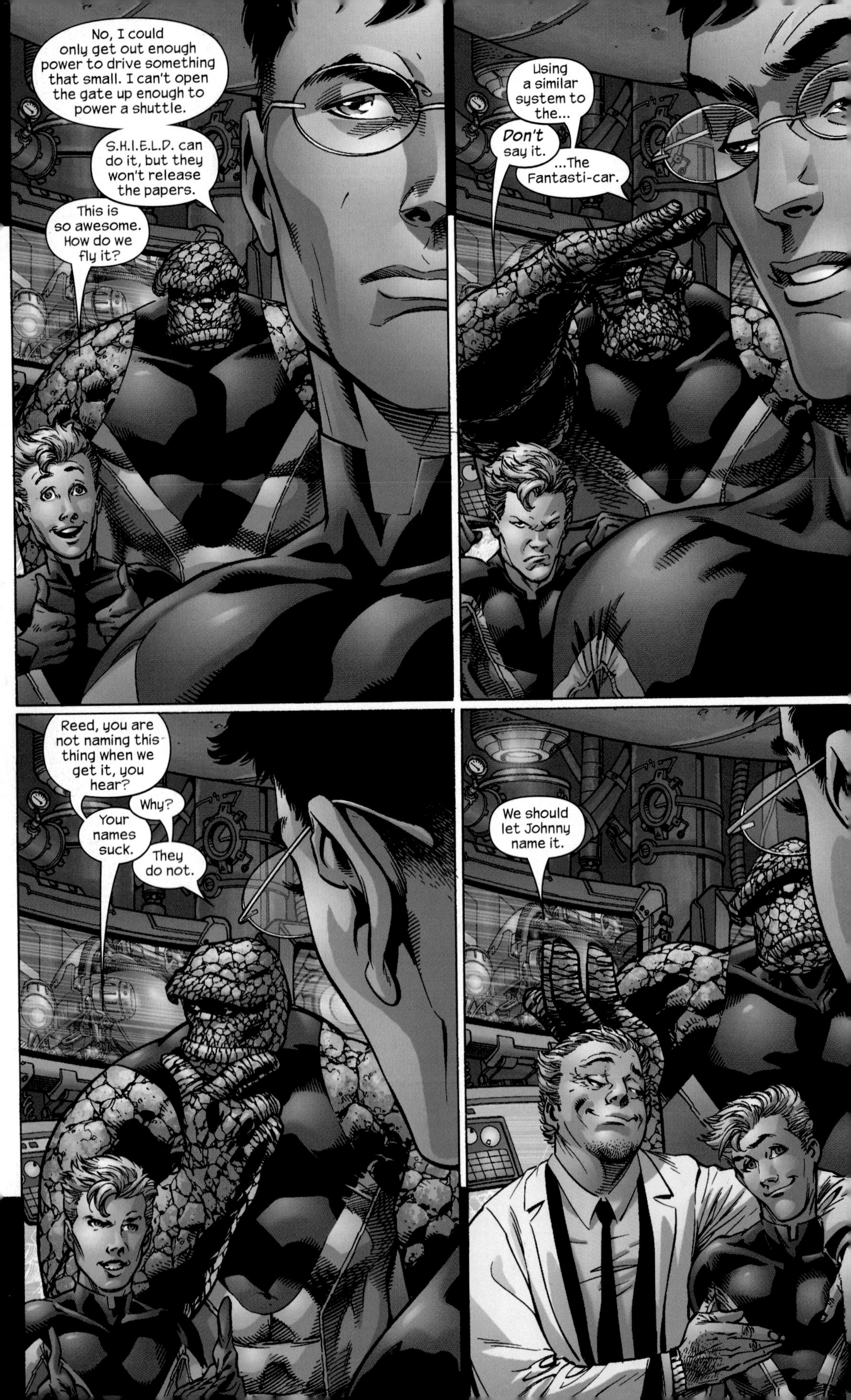
No, I could only get out enough power to drive something that small. I can't open the gate up enough to power a shuttle.
S.H.I.E.L.D. can do it, but they won't release the papers.
This is so awesome. How do we fly it?
Using a similar system to the...
Don't say it.
...The Fantasti-car.
Reed, you are not naming this thing when we get it, you hear?
Why?
Your names suck.
They do not.
We should let Johnny name it.

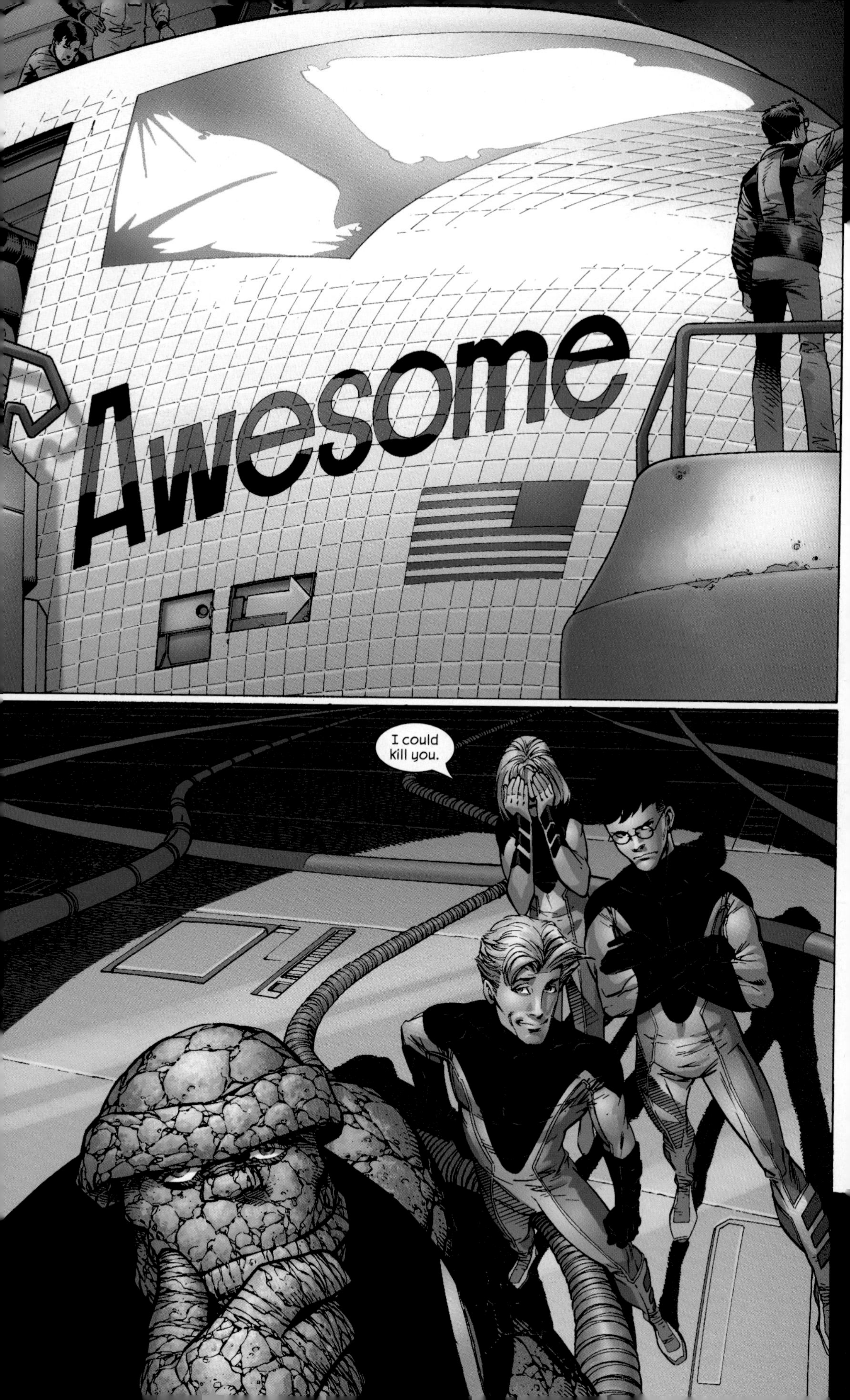
Awesome
I could kill you.

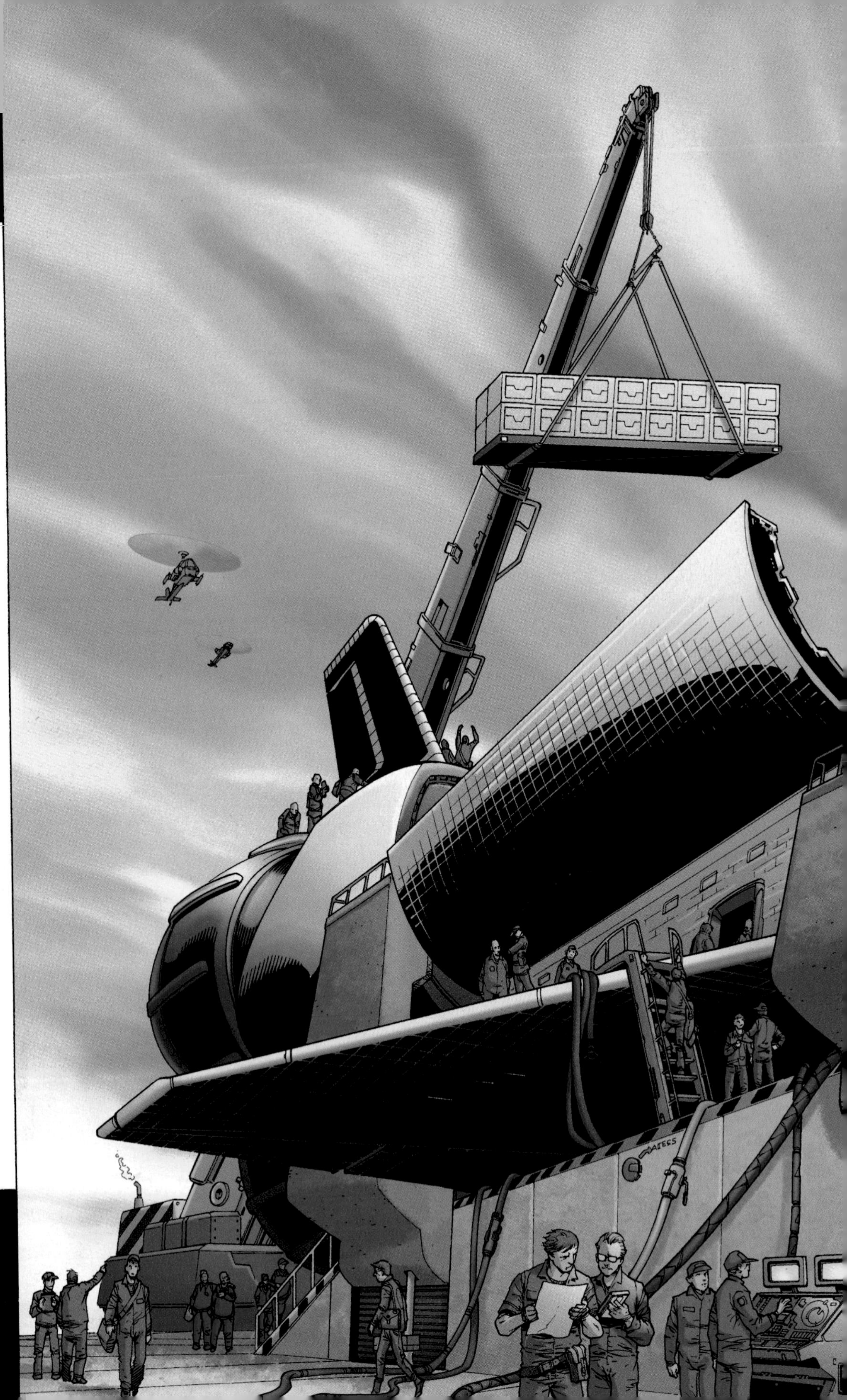

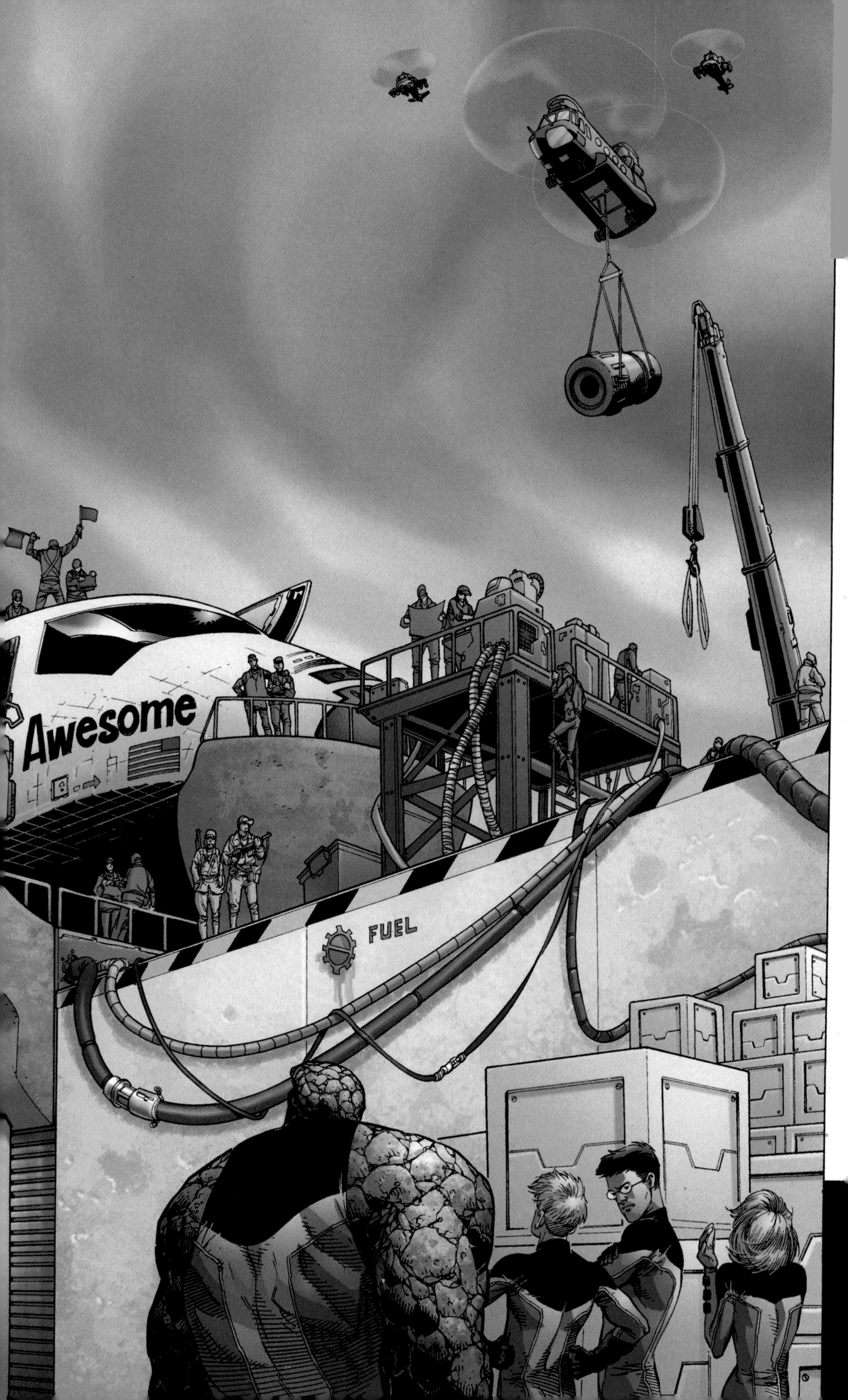
Awesome
FUEL

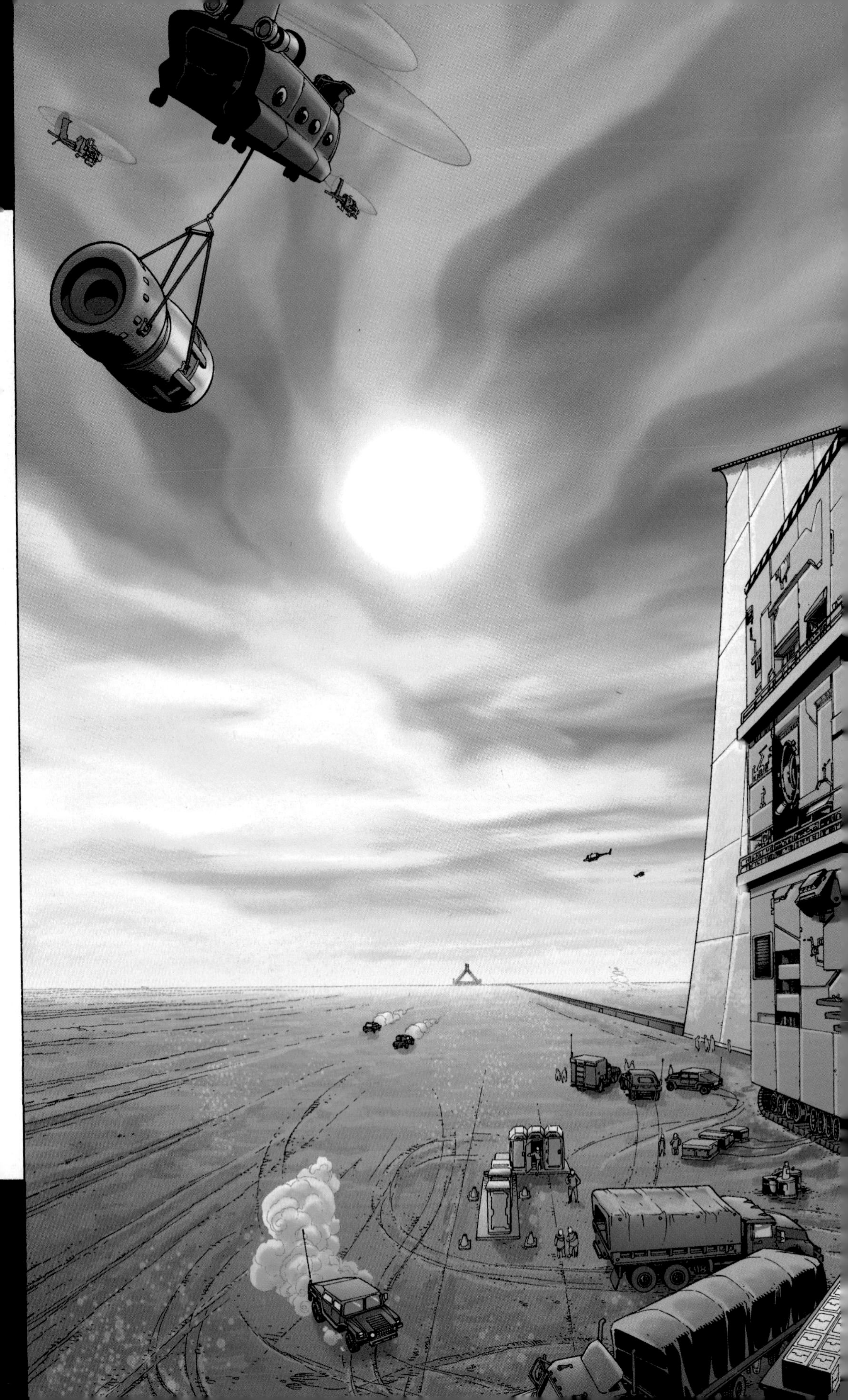

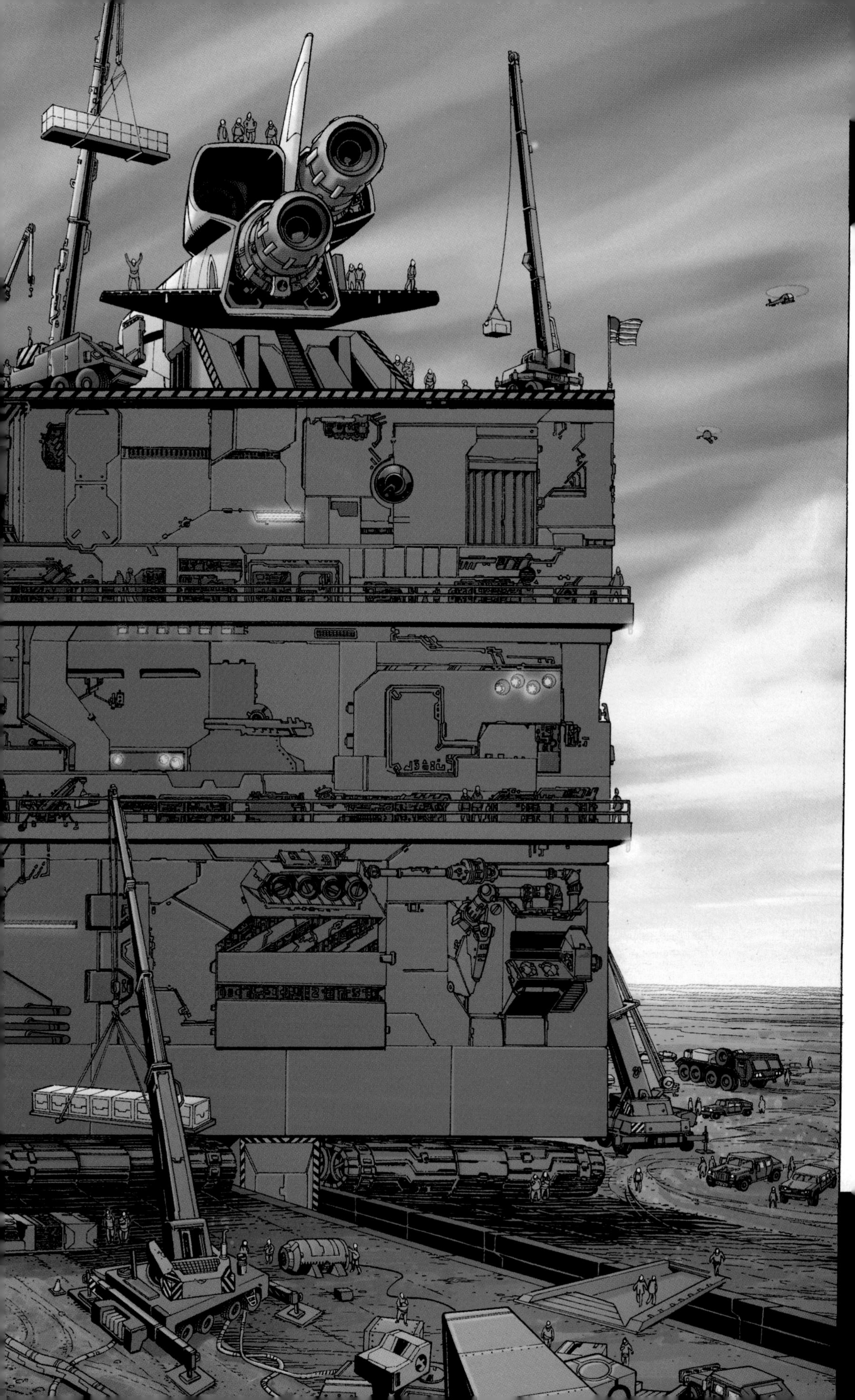

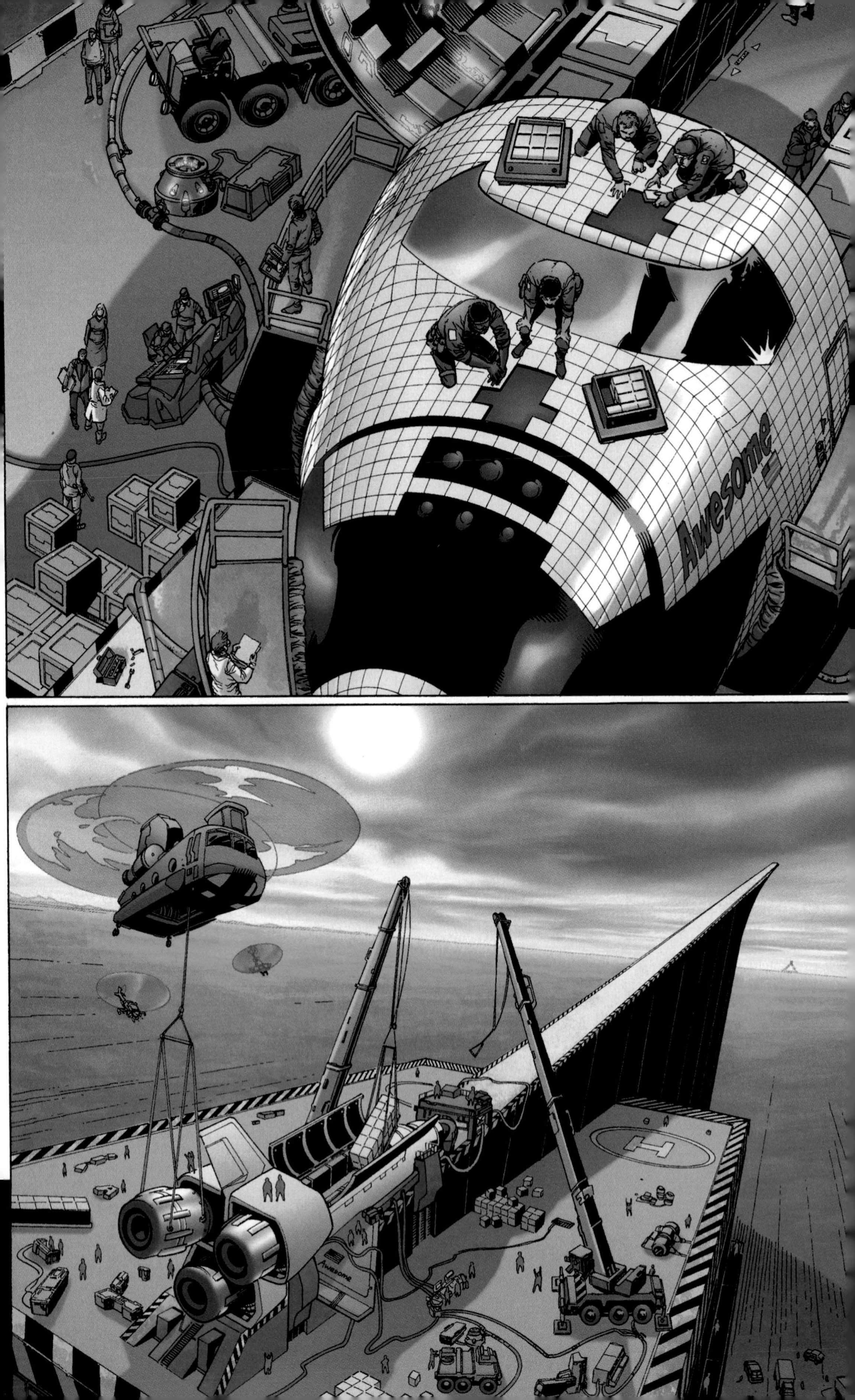
Awesome

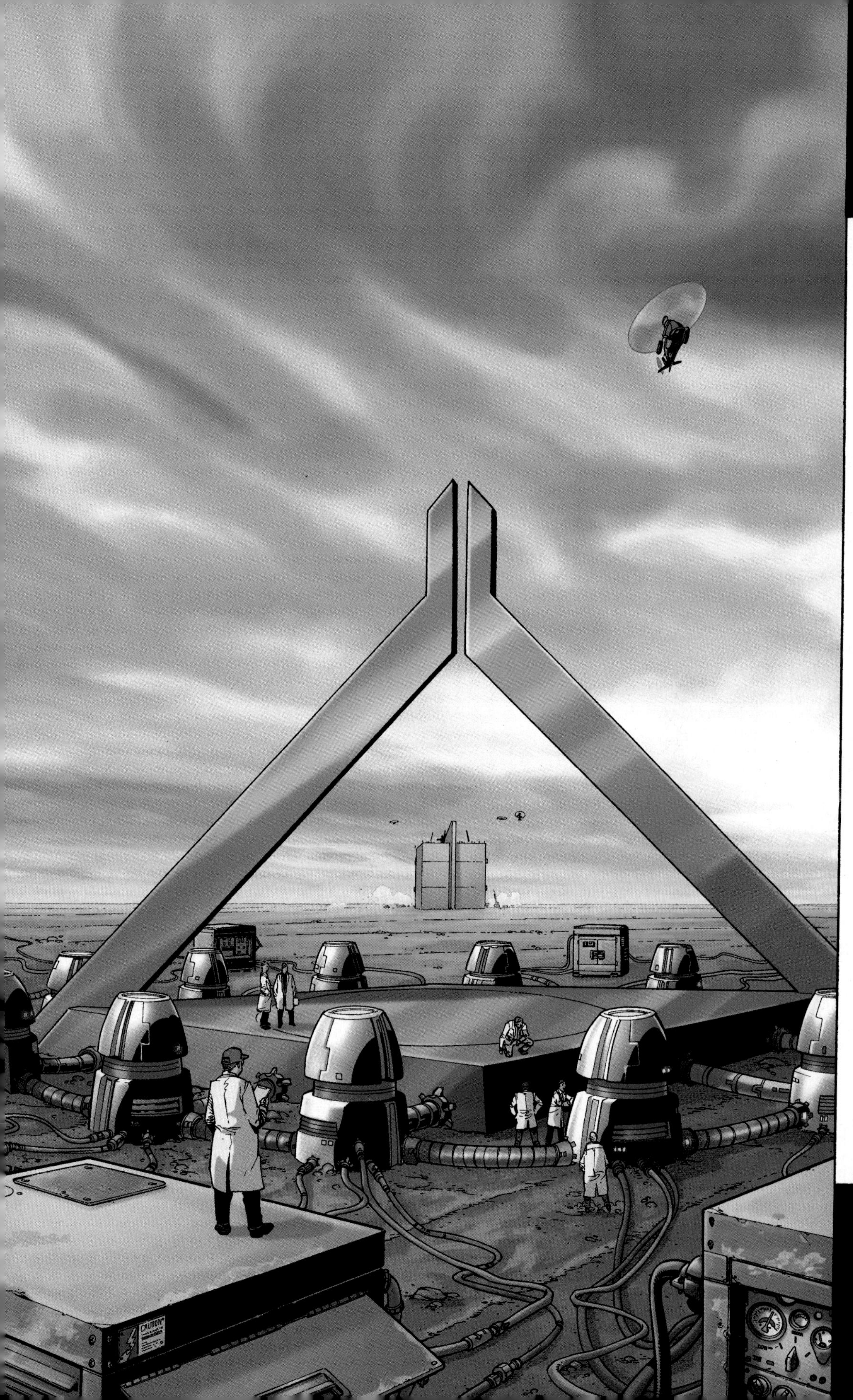
CAUTION

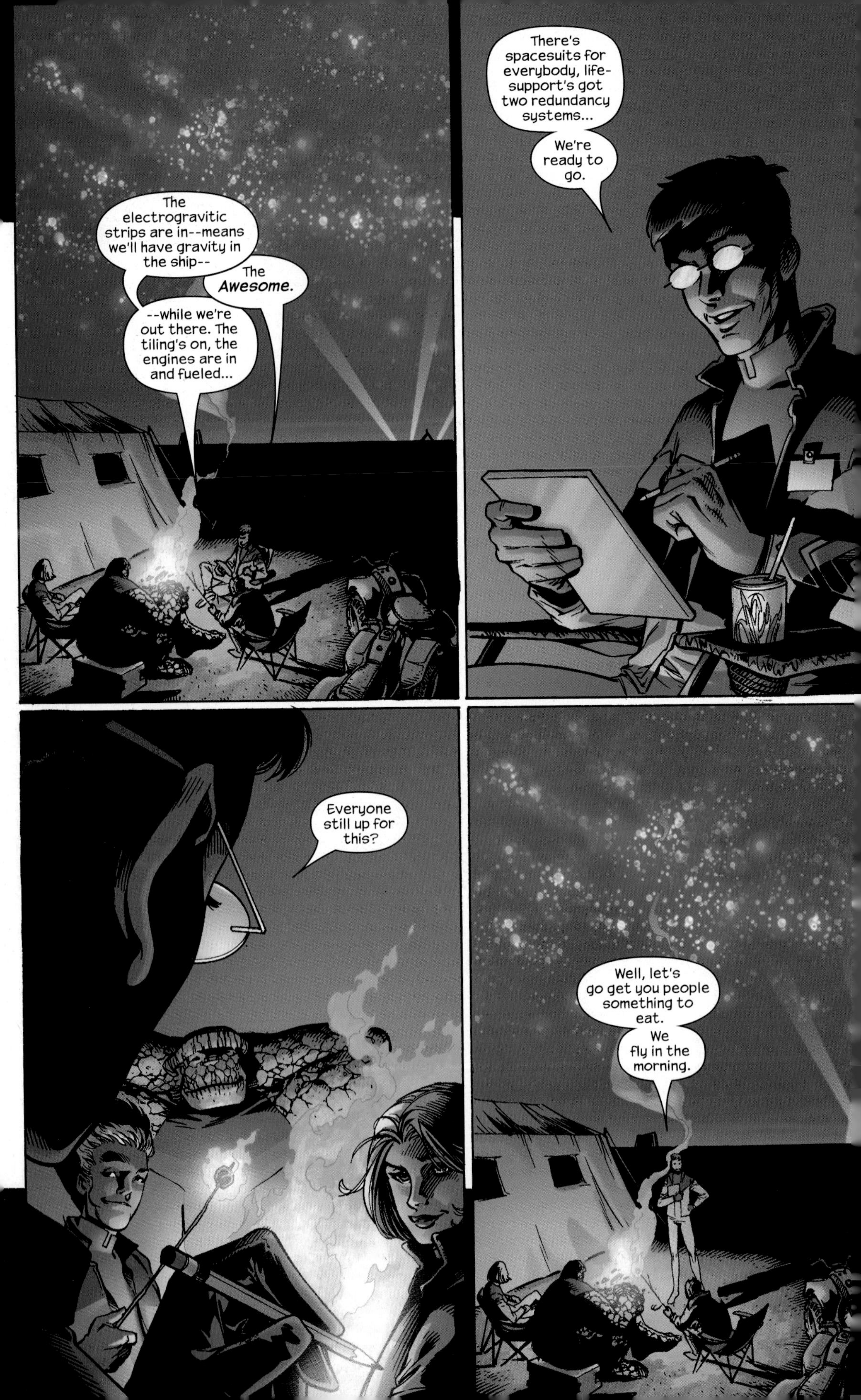
The electrogravitic strips are in--means we'll have gravity in the ship--
The *Awesome.*
--while we're out there. The tiling's on, the engines are in and fueled...
There's spacesuits for everybody, life-support's got two redundancy systems...
We're ready to go.
Everyone still up for this?
Well, let's go get you people something to eat.
We fly in the morning.

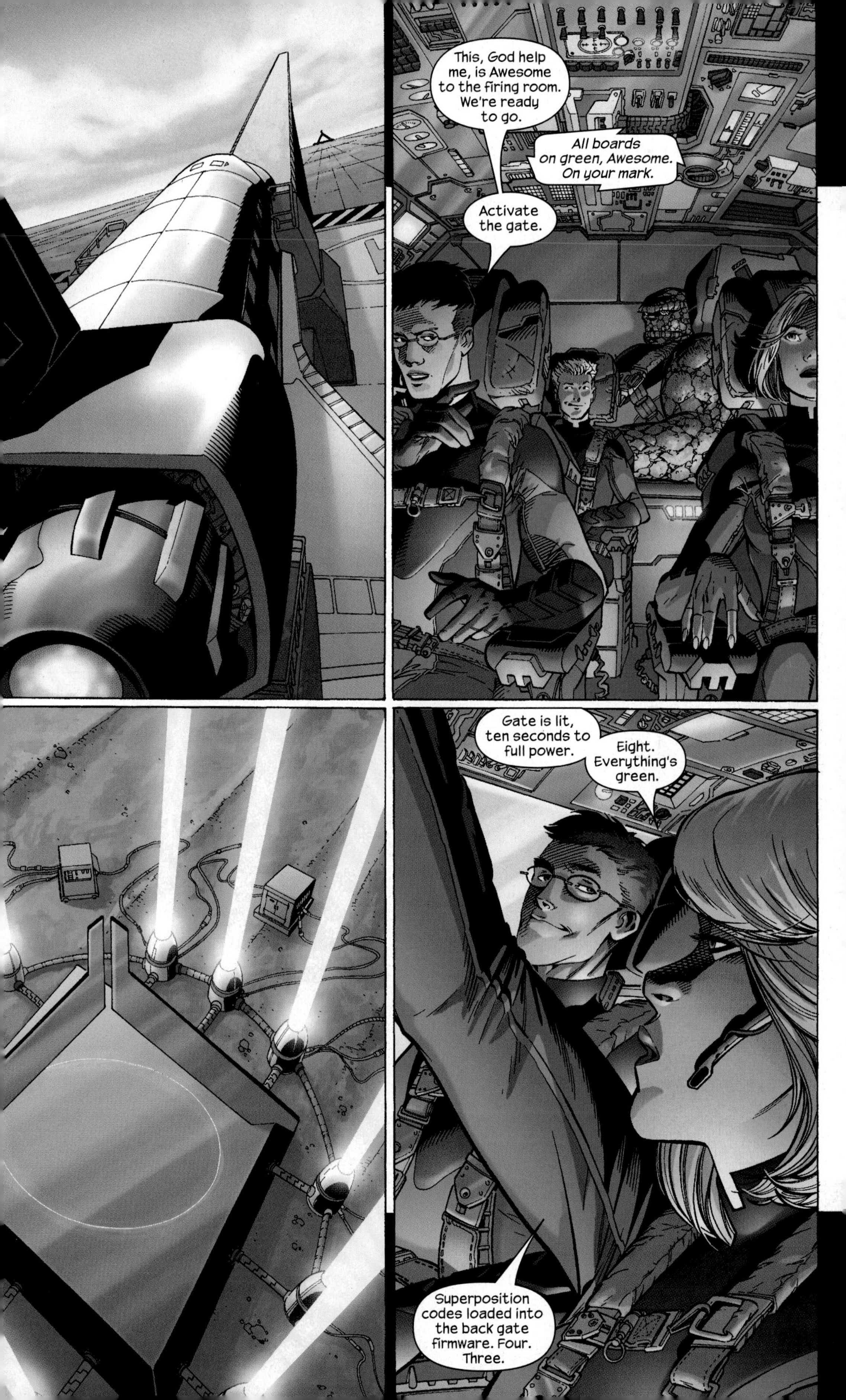
This, God help me, is Awesome to the firing room. We're ready to go.
All boards on green, Awesome. On your mark.
Activate the gate.
Gate is lit, ten seconds to full power.
Eight. Everything's green.
Superposition codes loaded into the back gate firmware. Four. Three.

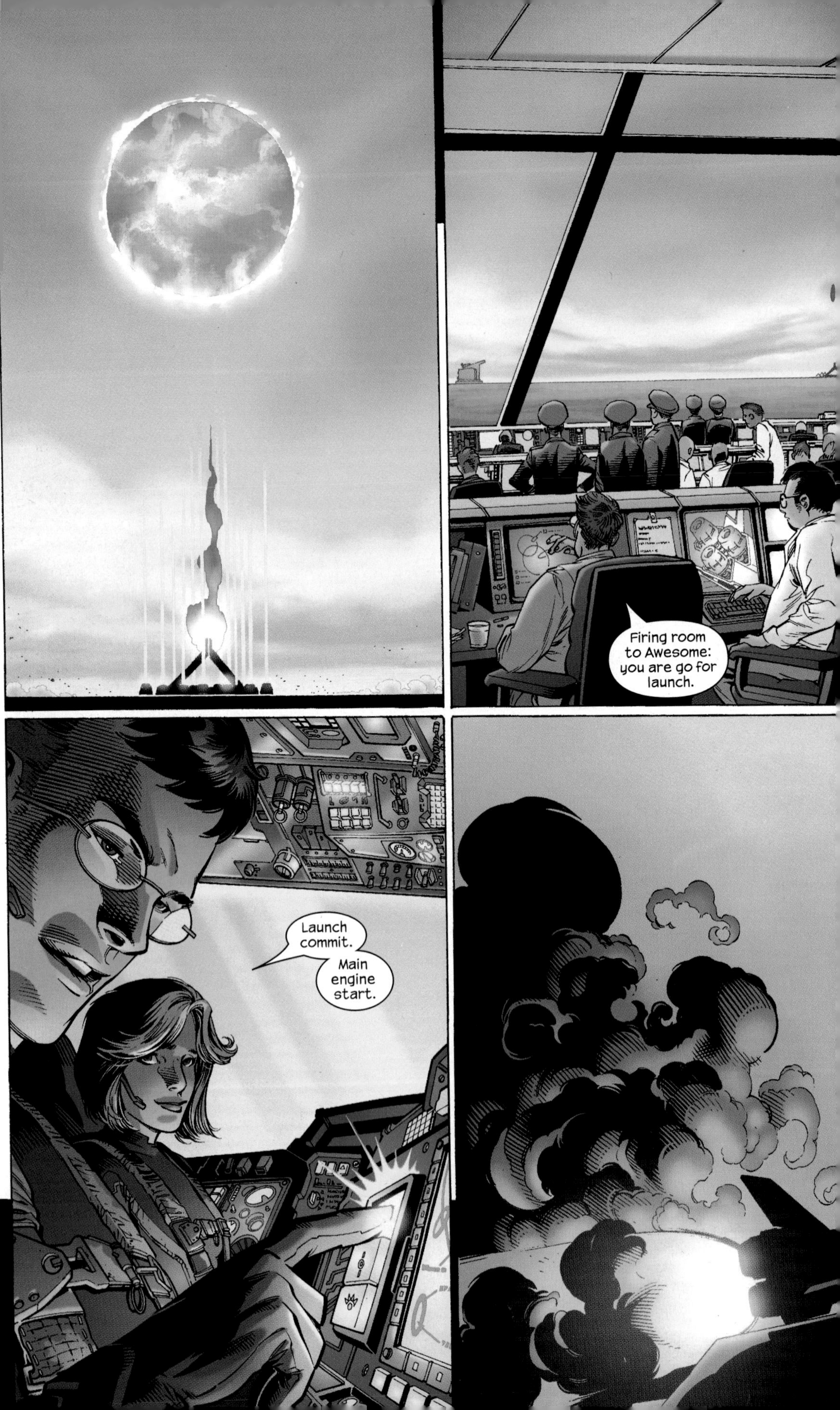
Firing room to Awesome: you are go for launch.
Launch commit.
Main engine start.

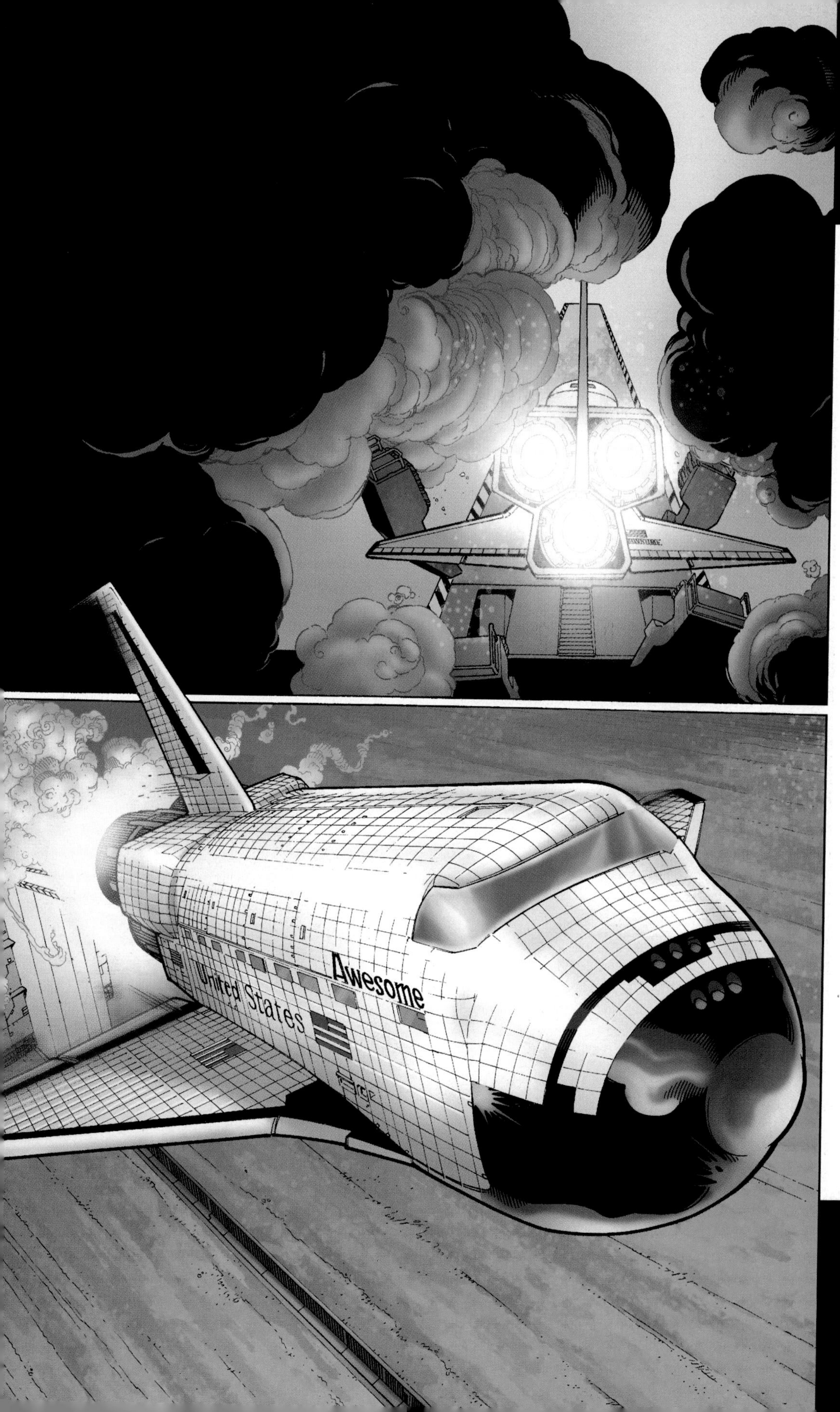
Awesome
United States

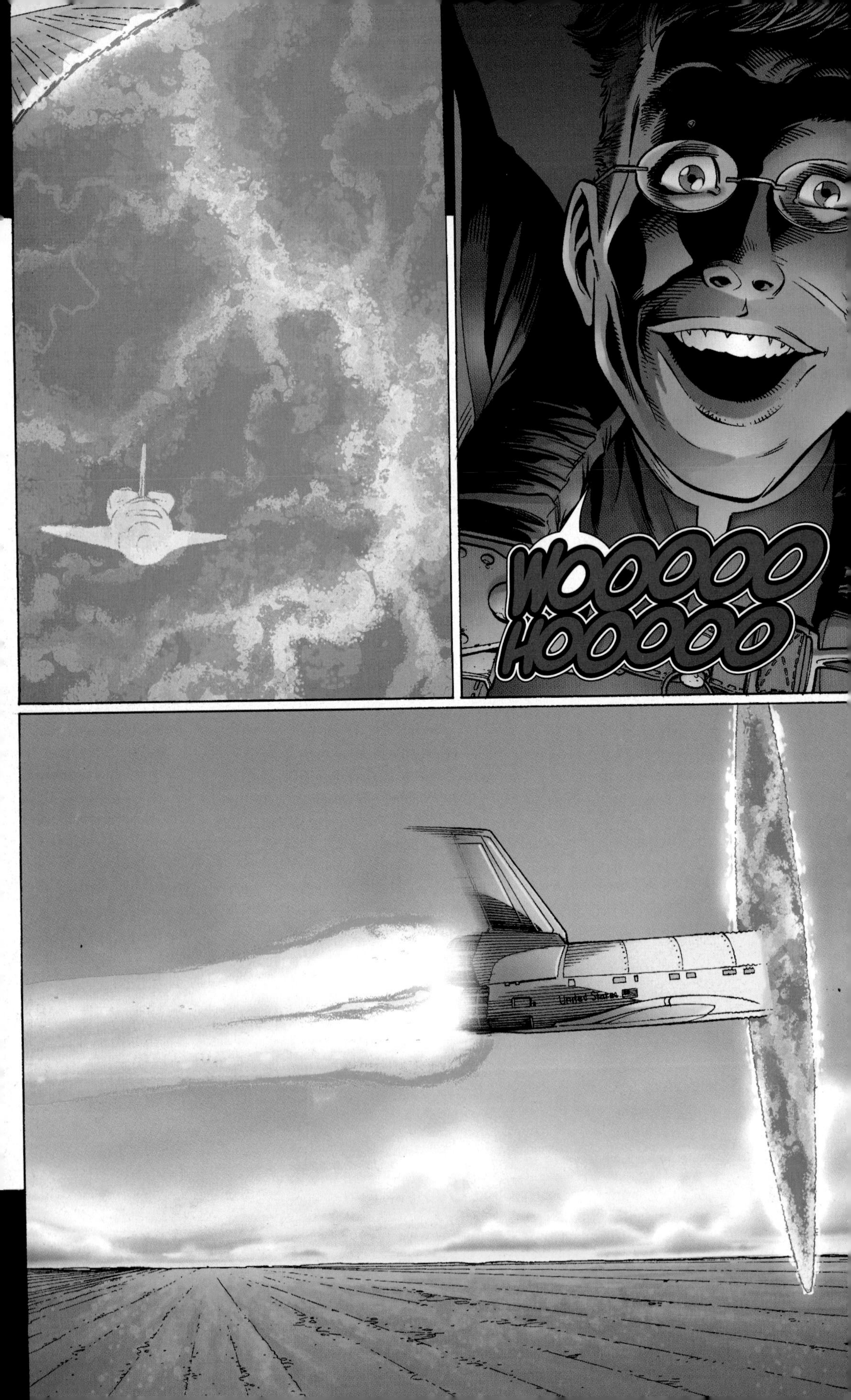
WOOOOO
HOOOOO
United States

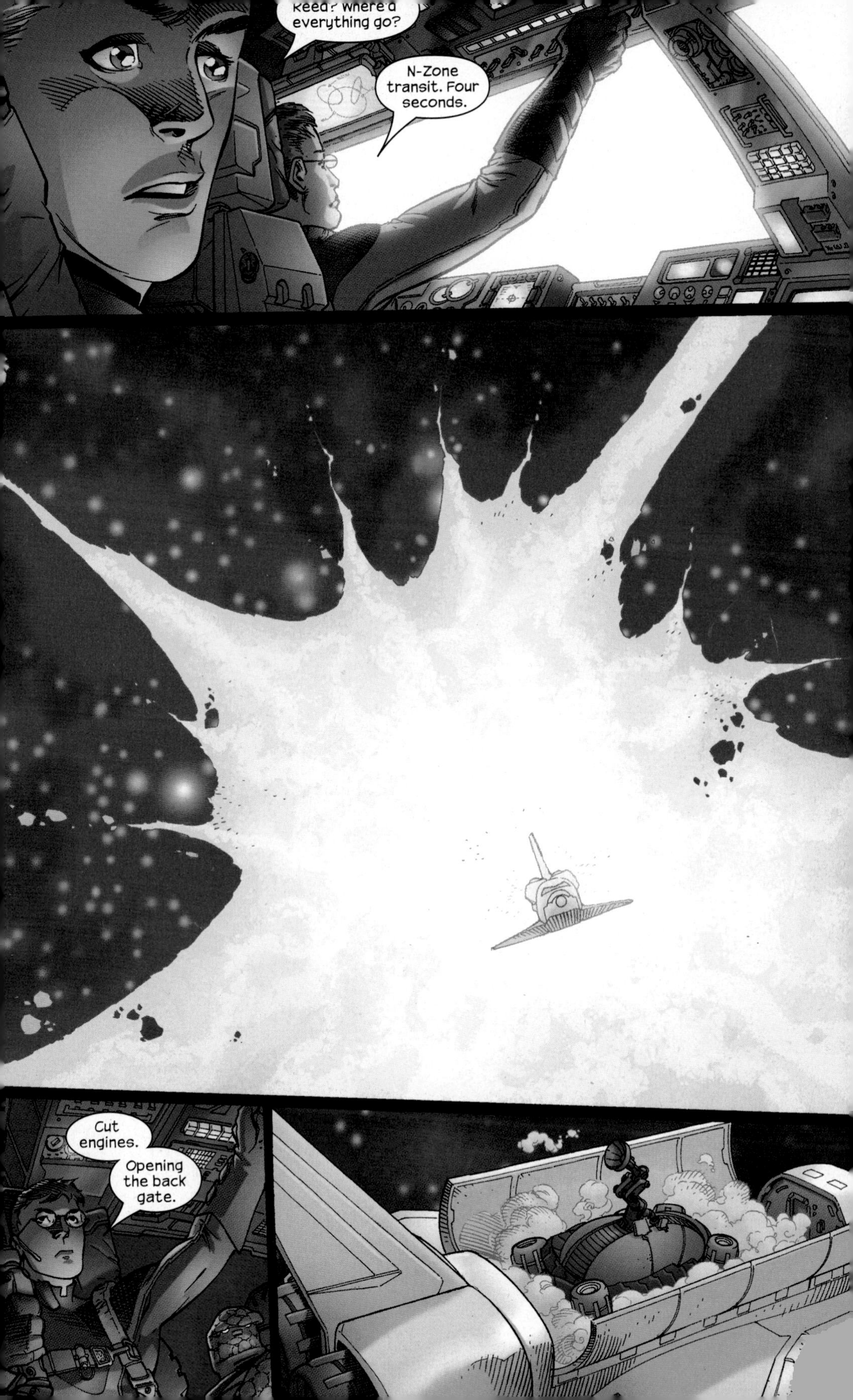
Reed? Where'd everything go?
N-Zone transit. Four seconds.
Cut engines.
Opening the back gate.

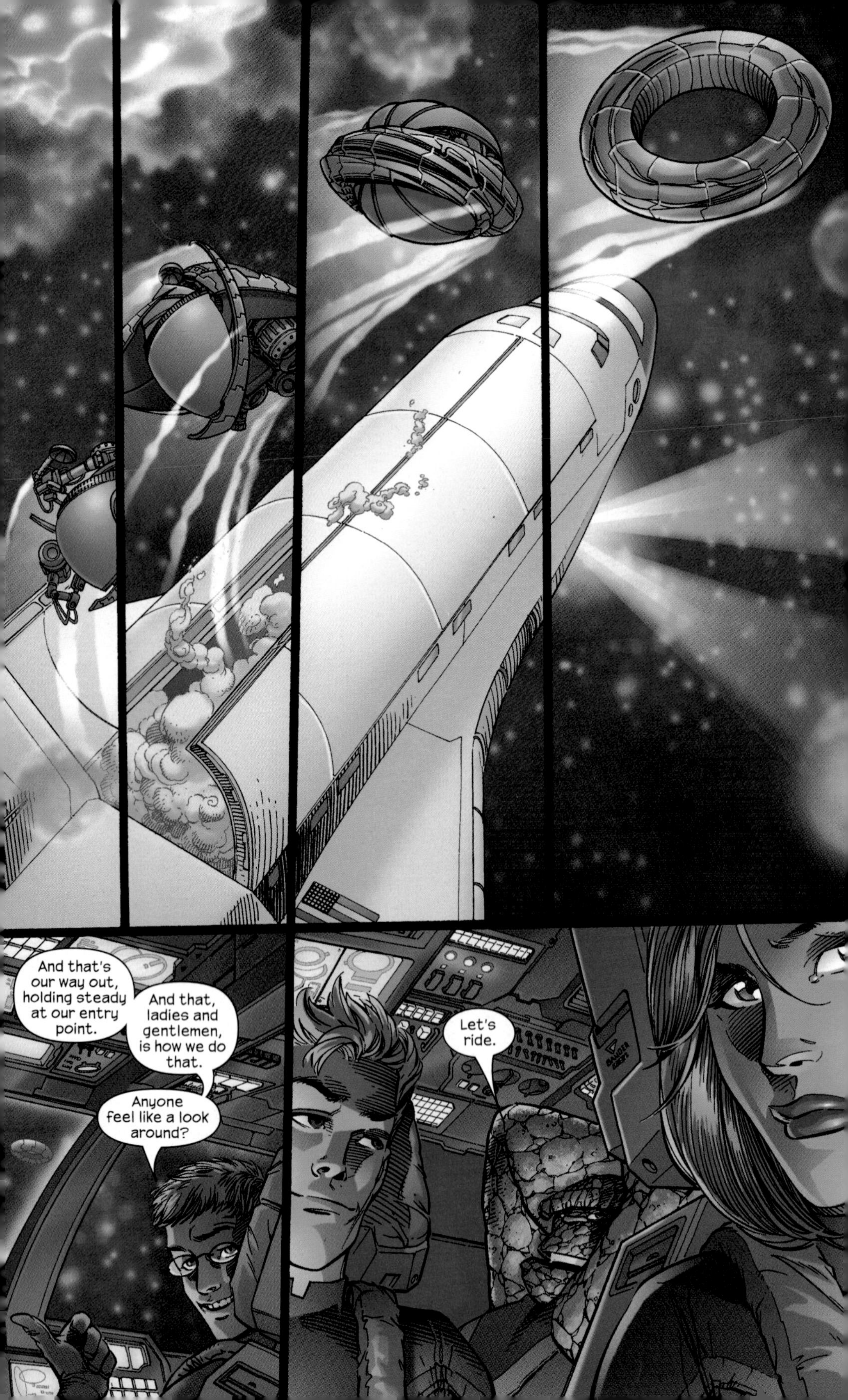
And that's our way out, holding steady at our entry point.
And that, ladies and gentlemen, is how we do that.
Anyone feel like a look around?
Let's ride.

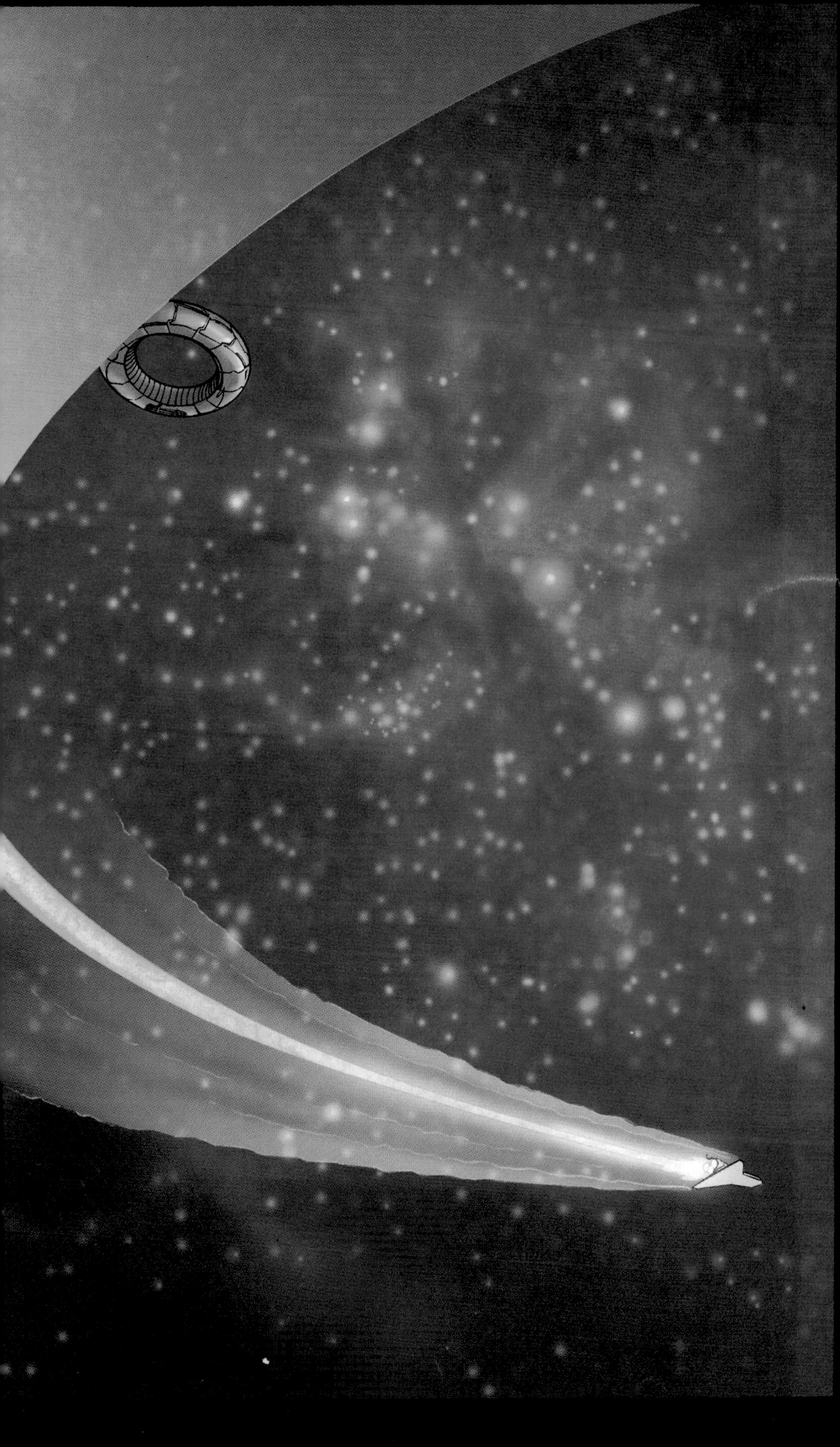

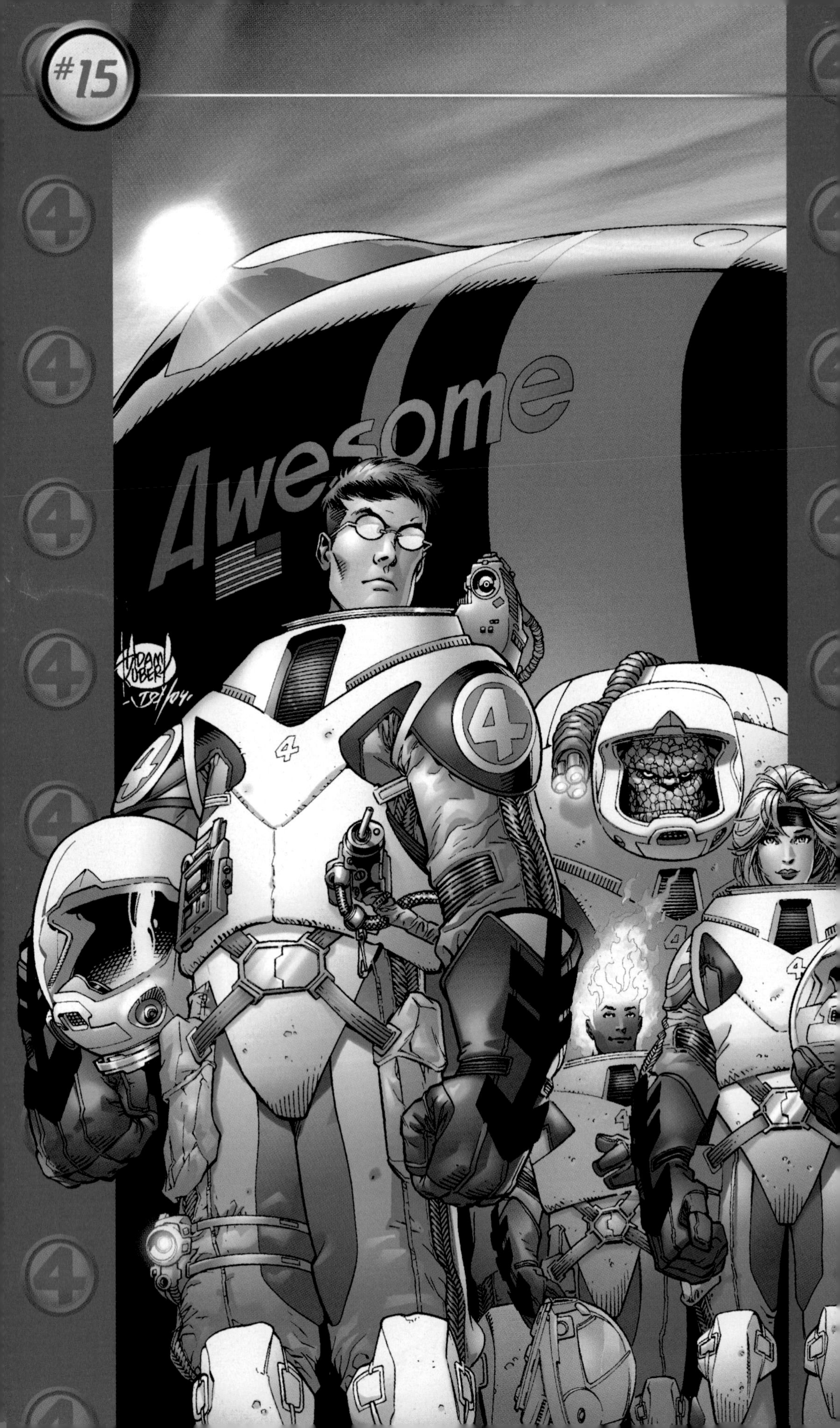
#15
Awesome

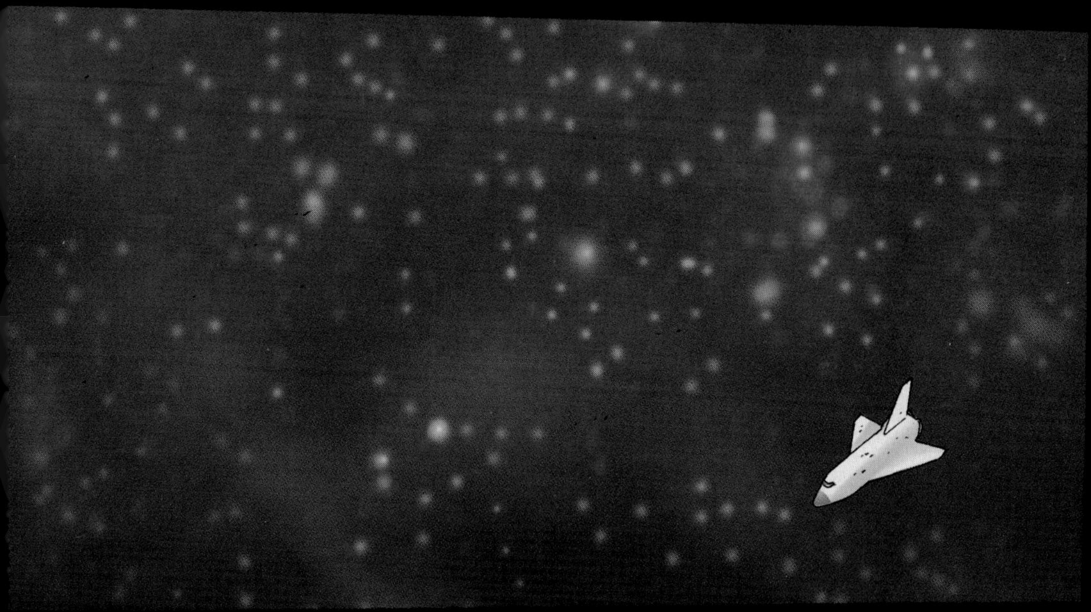

N-ZONE THREE of SIX

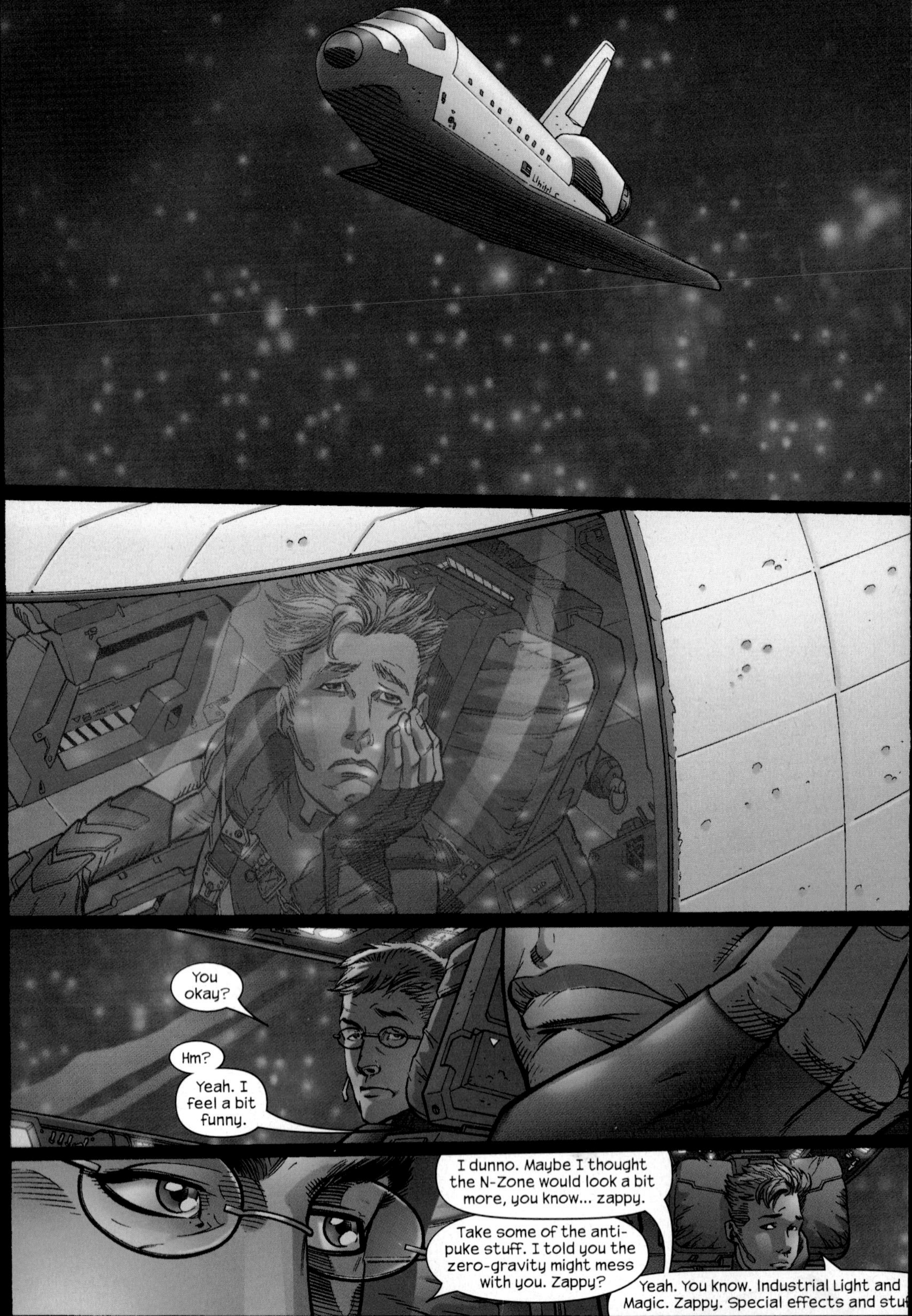

You okay?
Hm?
Yeah. I feel a bit funny.
I dunno. Maybe I thought the N-Zone would look a bit more, you know... zappy.
Take some of the anti-puke stuff. I told you the zero-gravity might mess with you. Zappy?
Yeah. You know. Industrial Light and Magic. Zappy. Special effects and stu

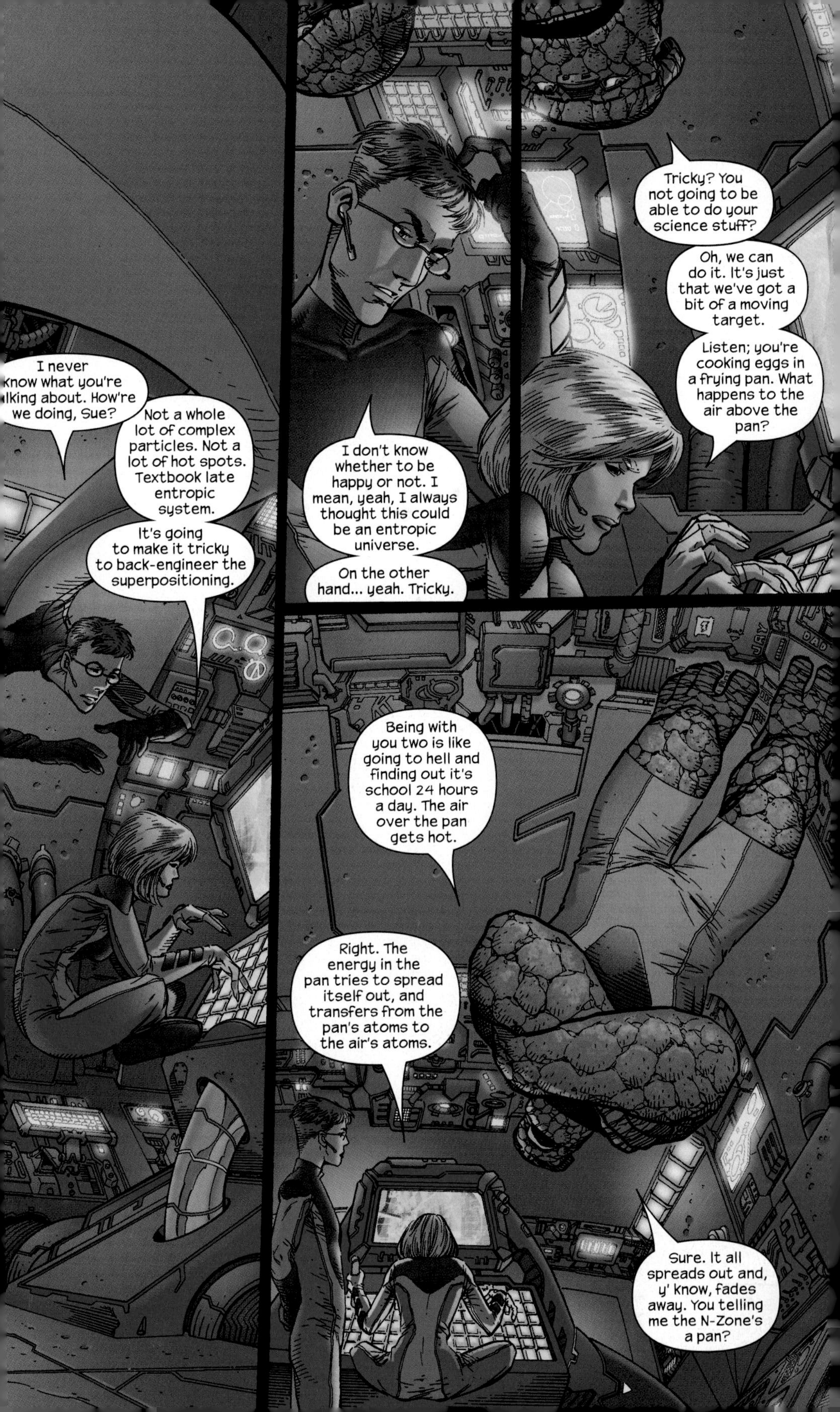
I never know what you're alking about. How're we doing, Sue?
Not a whole lot of complex particles. Not a lot of hot spots. Textbook late entropic system.
It's going to make it tricky to back-engineer the superpositioning.
I don't know whether to be happy or not. I mean, yeah, I always thought this could be an entropic universe.
On the other hand... yeah. Tricky.
Tricky? You not going to be able to do your science stuff?
Oh, we can do it. It's just that we've got a bit of a moving target.
Listen; you're cooking eggs in a frying pan. What happens to the air above the pan?
Being with you two is like going to hell and finding out it's school 24 hours a day. The air over the pan gets hot.
Right. The energy in the pan tries to spread itself out, and transfers from the pan's atoms to the air's atoms.
Sure. It all spreads out and, y' know, fades away. You telling me the N-Zone's a pan?

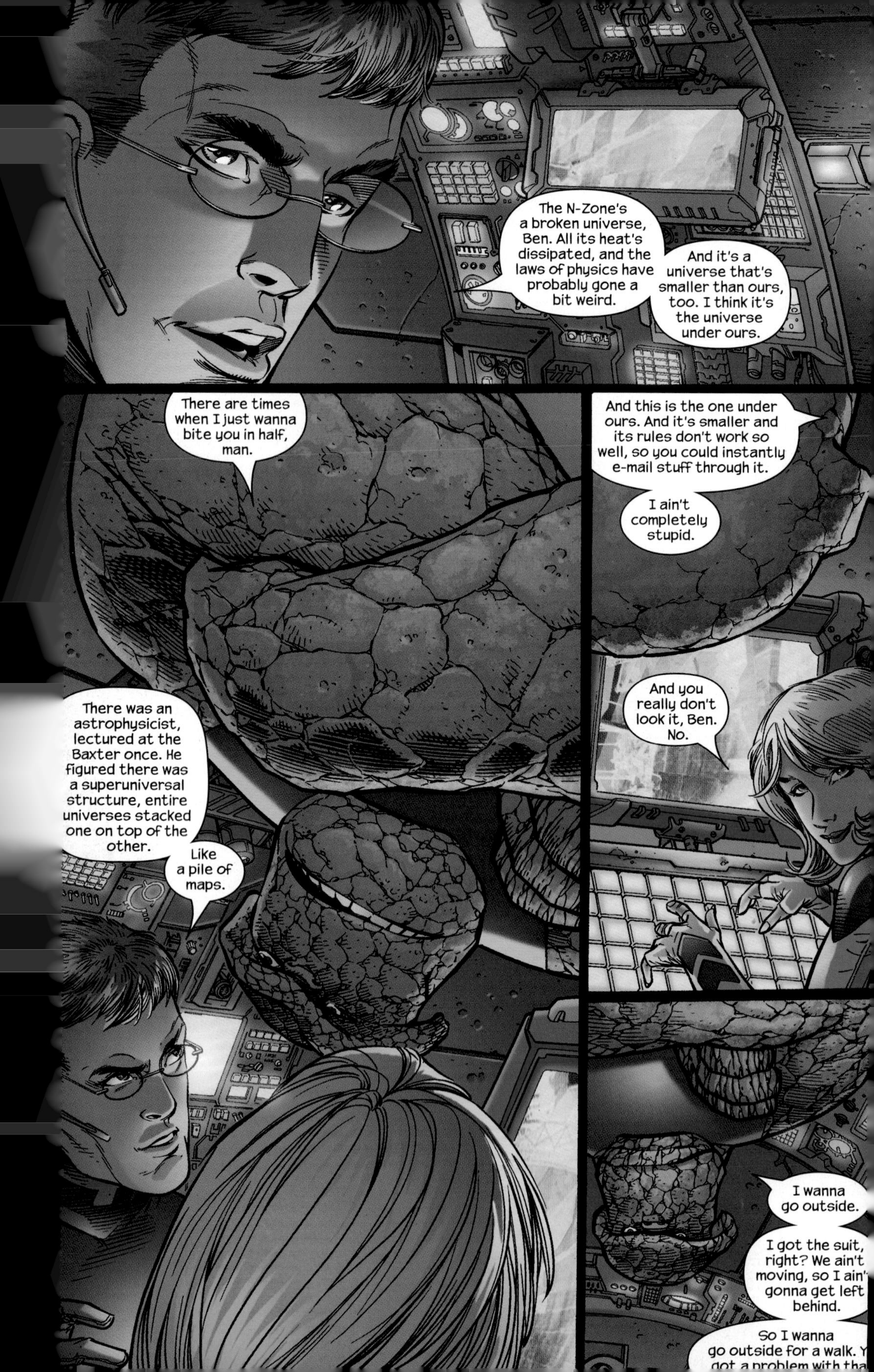
The N-Zone's a broken universe, Ben. All its heat's dissipated, and the laws of physics have probably gone a bit weird.
And it's a universe that's smaller than ours, too. I think it's the universe under ours.
There are times when I just wanna bite you in half, man.
There was an astrophysicist, lectured at the Baxter once. He figured there was a superuniversal structure, entire universes stacked one on top of the other.
Like a pile of maps.
And this is the one under ours. And it's smaller and its rules don't work so well, so you could instantly e-mail stuff through it.
I ain't completely stupid.
And you really don't look it, Ben. No.
I wanna go outside.
I got the suit, right? We ain't moving, so I ain't gonna get left behind.

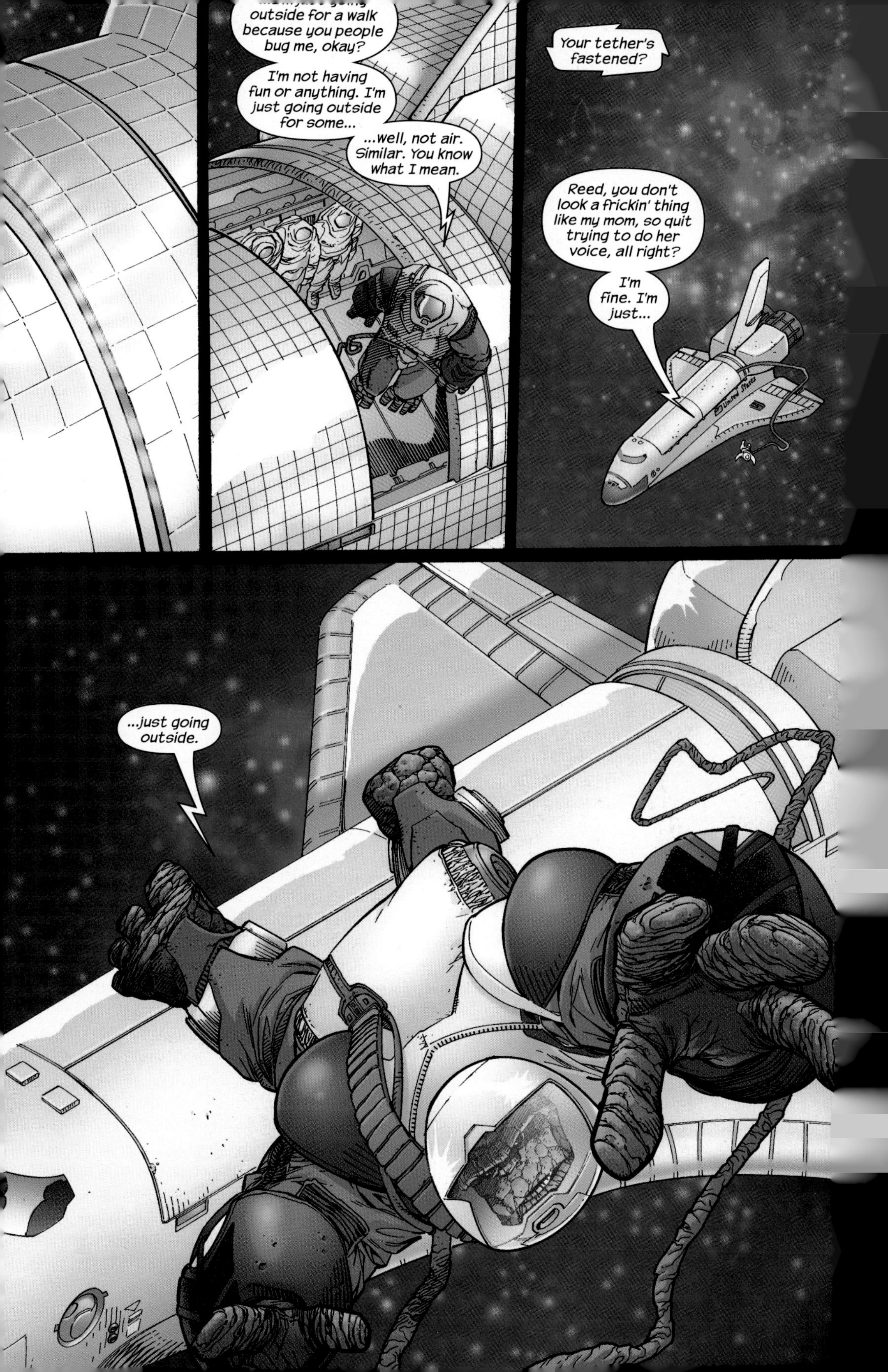
outside for a walk because you people bug me, okay?
I'm not having fun or anything. I'm just going outside for some...
...well, not air. Similar. You know what I mean.
Your tether's fastened?
Reed, you don't look a frickin' thing like my mom, so quit trying to do her voice, all right?
I'm fine. I'm just...
...just going outside.

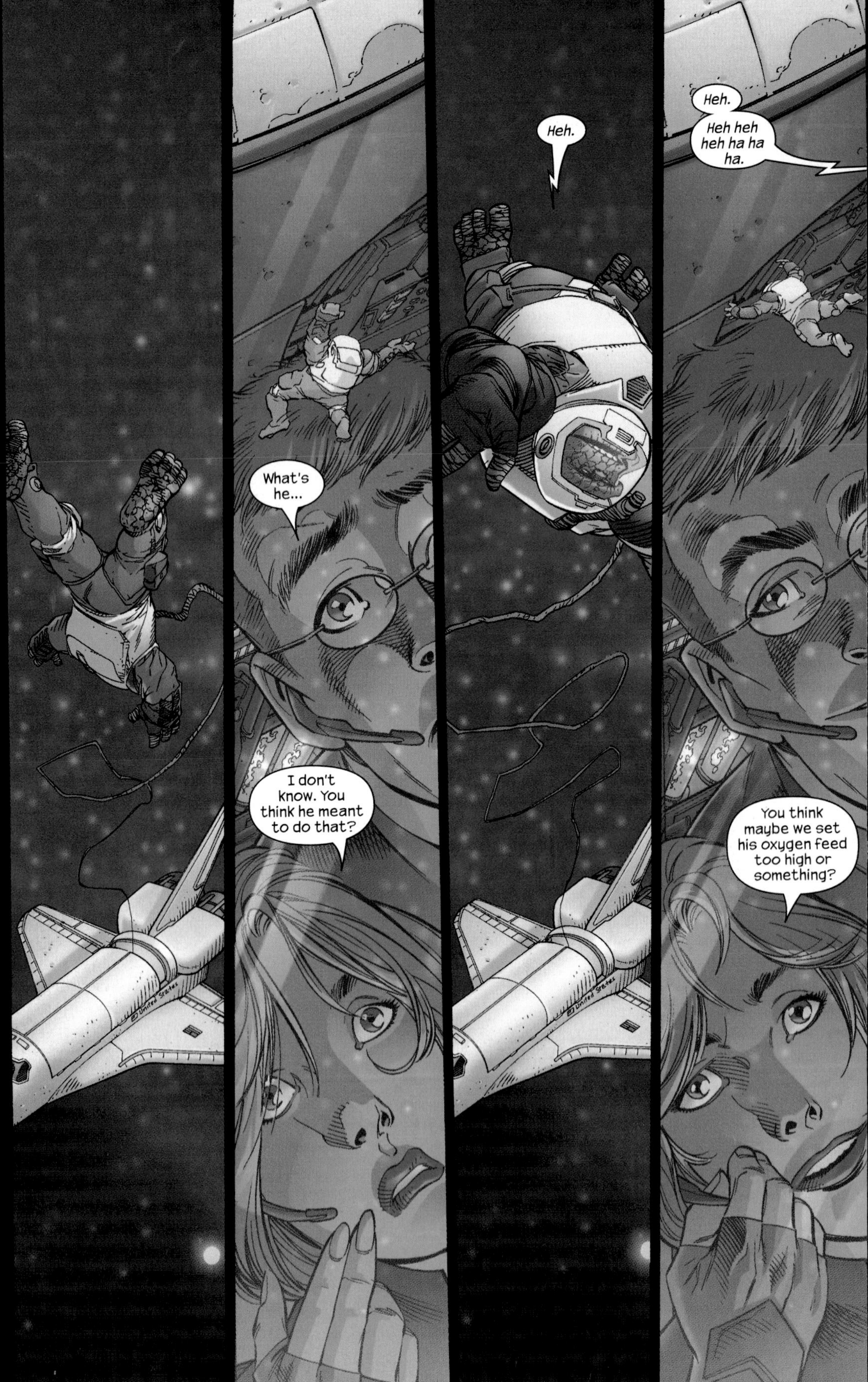
What's he...
I don't know. You think he meant to do that?
Heh.
Heh.
Heh heh heh ha ha ha.
You think maybe we set his oxygen feed too high or something?

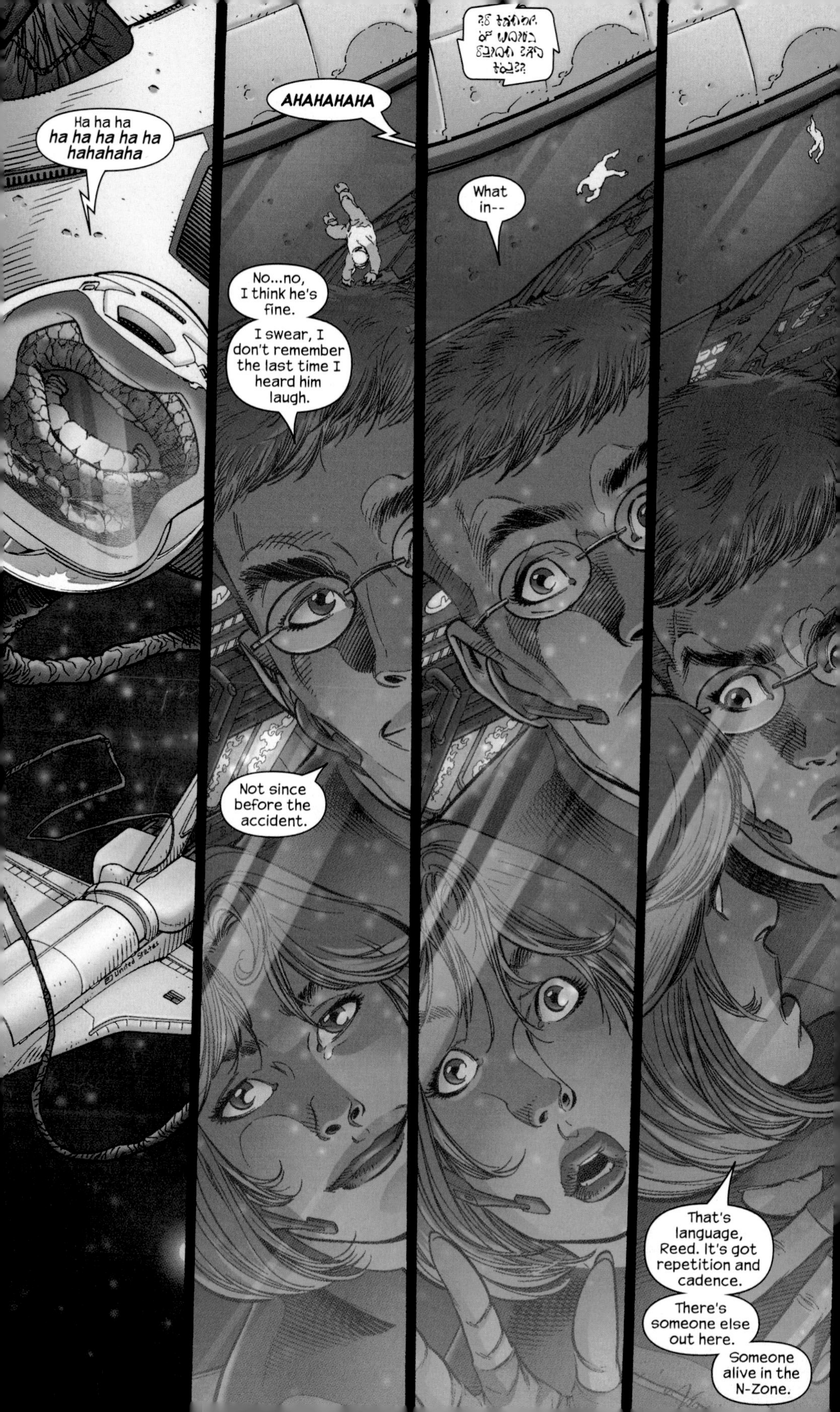
Ha ha ha
ha ha ha ha ha
hahahaha
AHAHAHAHA
No...no, I think he's fine.
I swear, I don't remember the last time I heard him laugh.
Not since before the accident.
What in--
That's language, Reed. It's got repetition and cadence.
There's someone else out here.
Someone alive in the N-Zone.

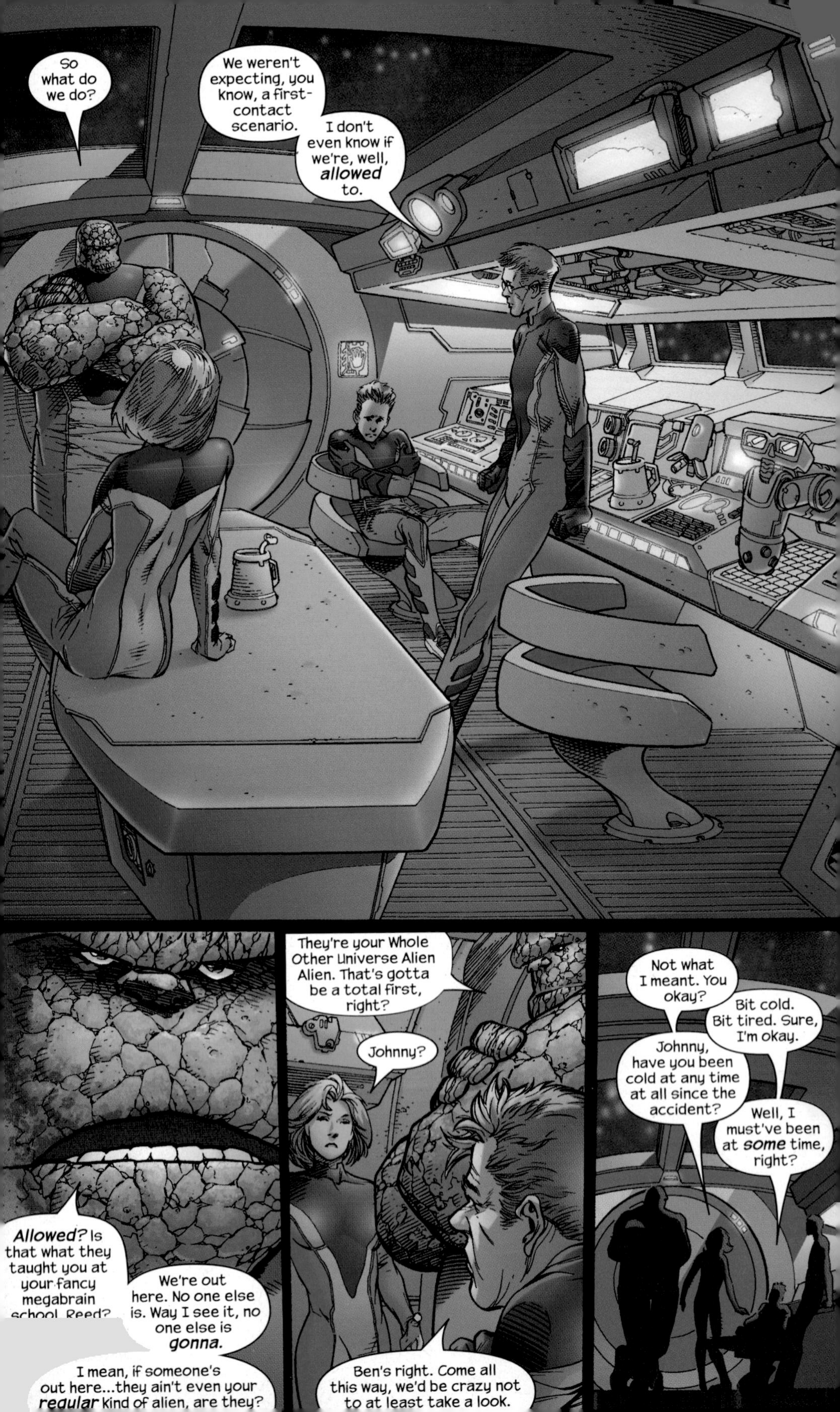

So what do we do?
We weren't expecting, you know, a first-contact scenario.
I don't even know if we're, well, *allowed* to.
Allowed? Is that what they taught you at your fancy megabrain school, Reed?
We're out here. No one else is. Way I see it, no one else is *gonna.*
I mean, if someone's out here...they ain't even your *regular* kind of alien, are they?
They're your Whole Other Universe Alien Alien. That's gotta be a total first, right?
Johnny?
Ben's right. Come all this way, we'd be crazy not to at least take a look.
Not what I meant. You okay?
Bit cold. Bit tired. Sure, I'm okay.
Johnny, have you been cold at any time at all since the accident?
Well, I must've been at *some* time, right?

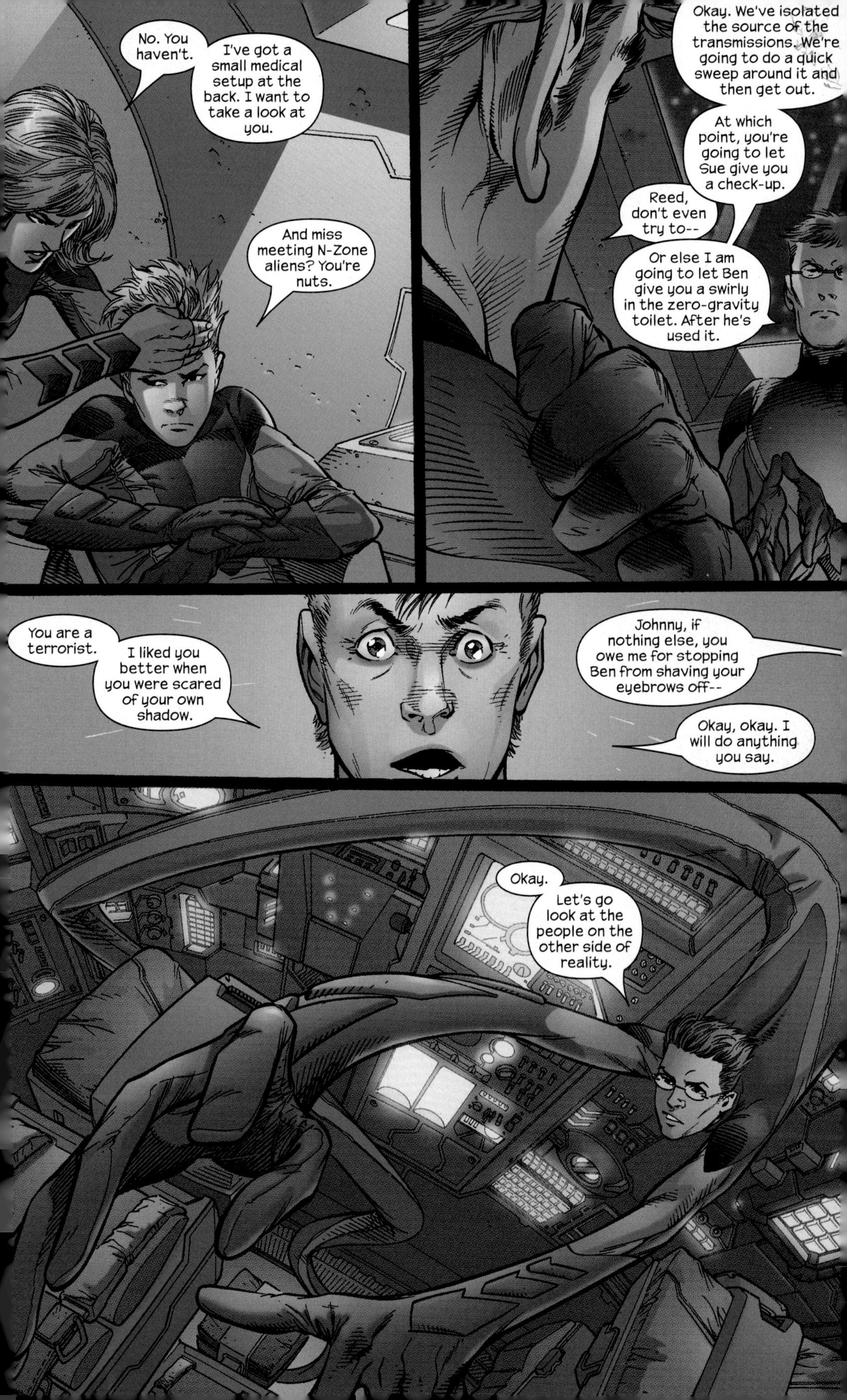
No. You haven't.
I've got a small medical setup at the back. I want to take a look at you.
And miss meeting N-Zone aliens? You're nuts.
Okay. We've isolated the source of the transmissions. We're going to do a quick sweep around it and then get out.
At which point, you're going to let Sue give you a check-up.
Reed, don't even try to--
Or else I am going to let Ben give you a swirly in the zero-gravity toilet. After he's used it.
You are a terrorist.
I liked you better when you were scared of your own shadow.
Johnny, if nothing else, you owe me for stopping Ben from shaving your eyebrows off--
Okay, okay. I will do anything you say.
Okay.
Let's go look at the people on the other side of reality.

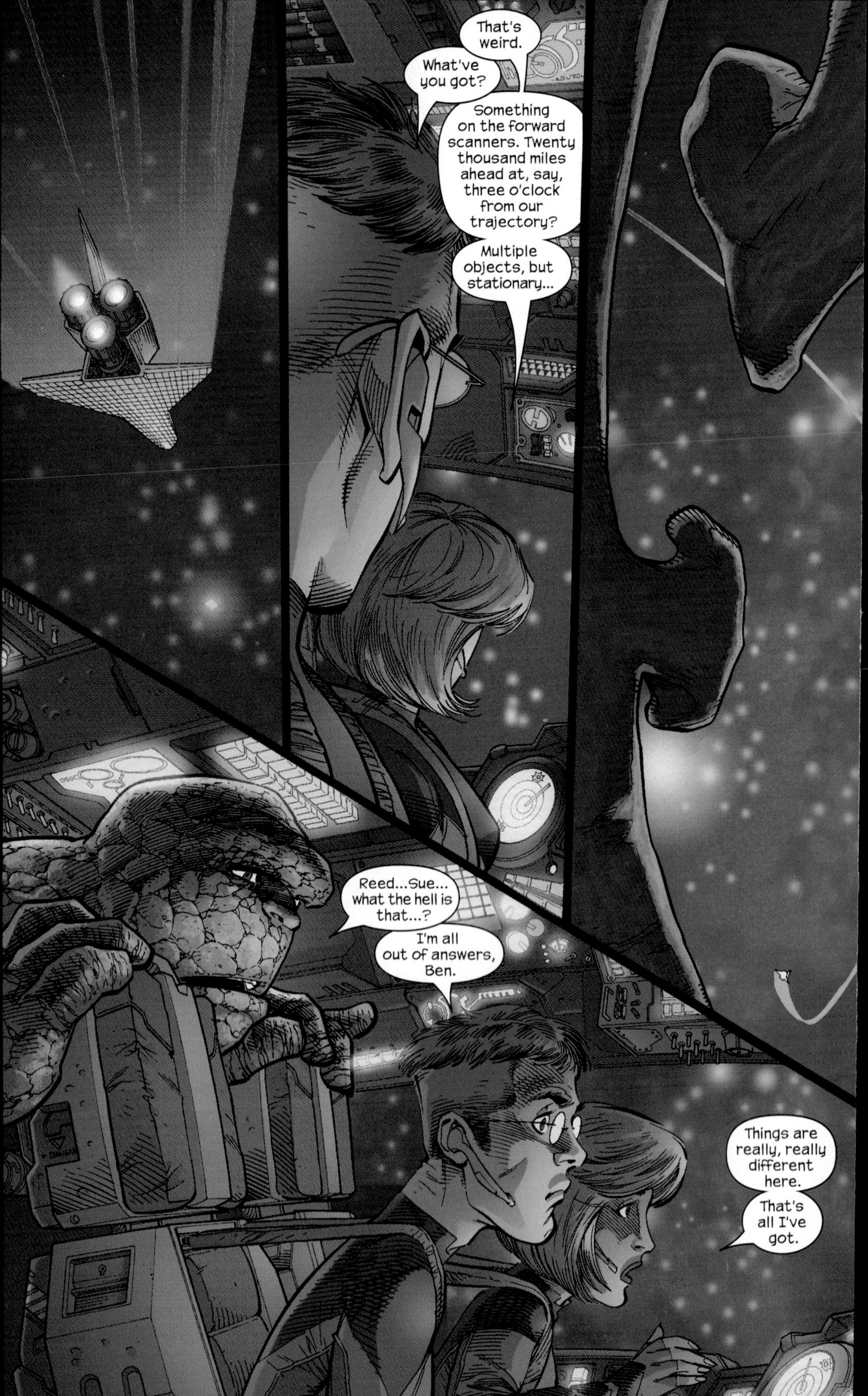
That's weird.
What've you got?
Something on the forward scanners. Twenty thousand miles ahead at, say, three o'clock from our trajectory?
Multiple objects, but stationary...
Reed...Sue... what the hell is that...?
I'm all out of answers, Ben.
Things are really, really different here.
That's all I've got.

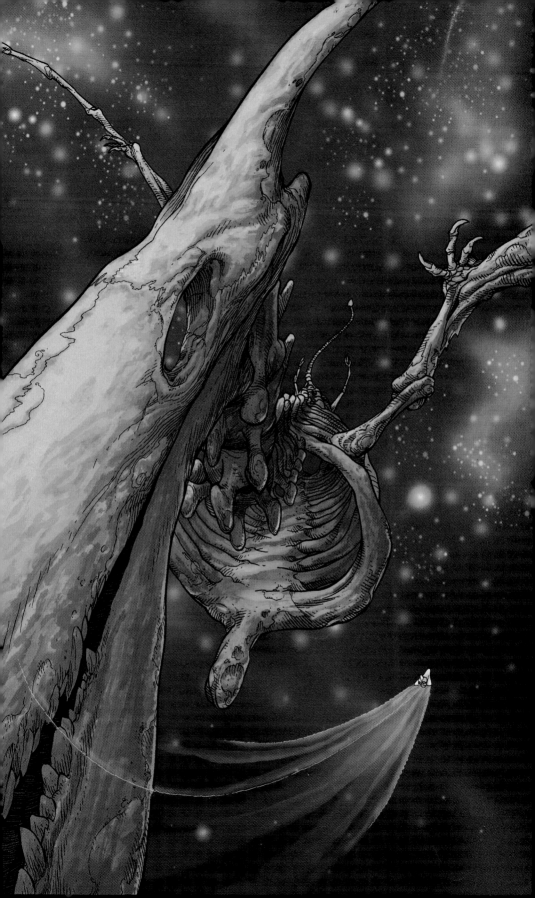

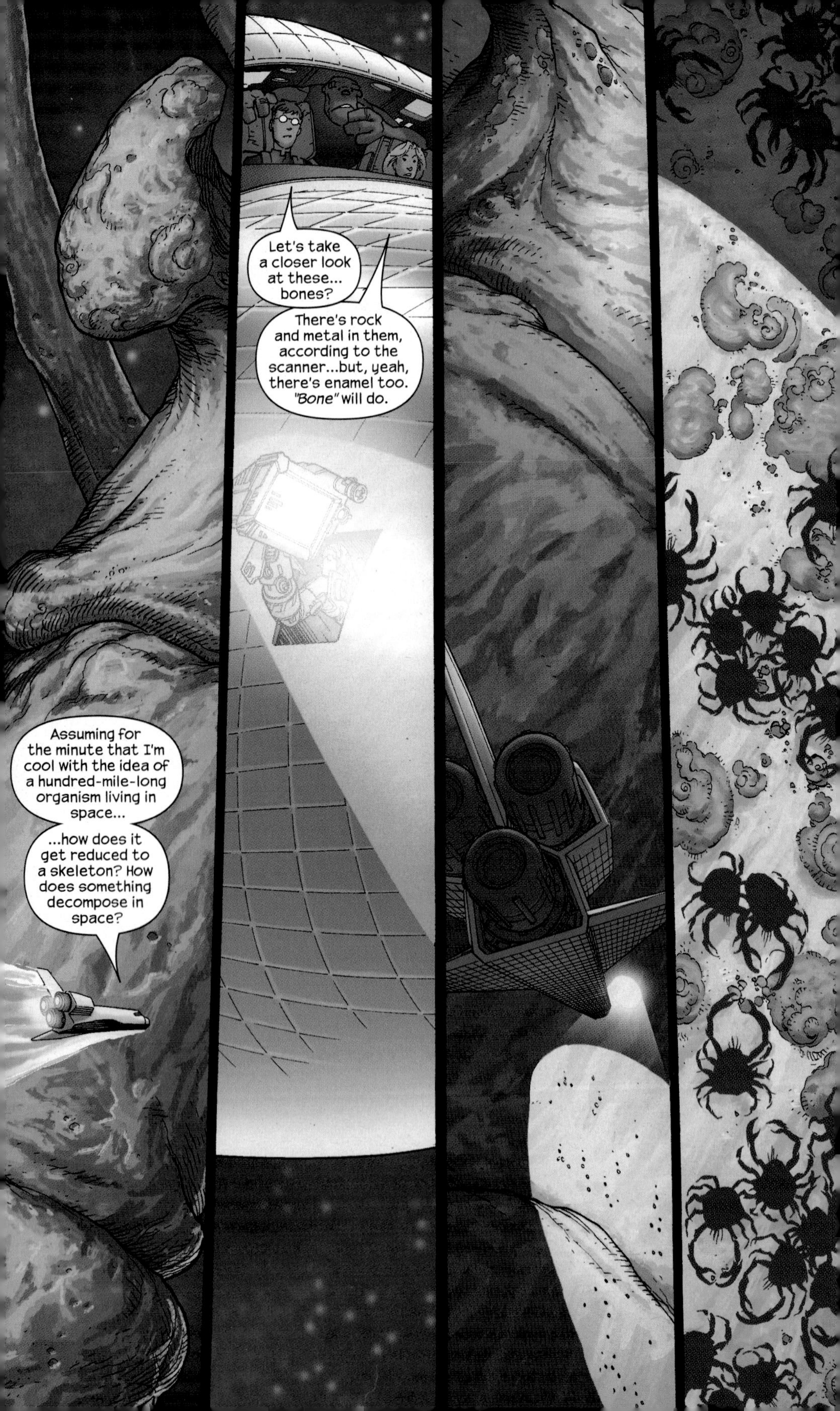
Let's take a closer look at these... bones?
There's rock and metal in them, according to the scanner...but, yeah, there's enamel too. "Bone" will do.
Assuming for the minute that I'm cool with the idea of a hundred-mile-long organism living in space...
...how does it get reduced to a skeleton? How does something decompose in space?

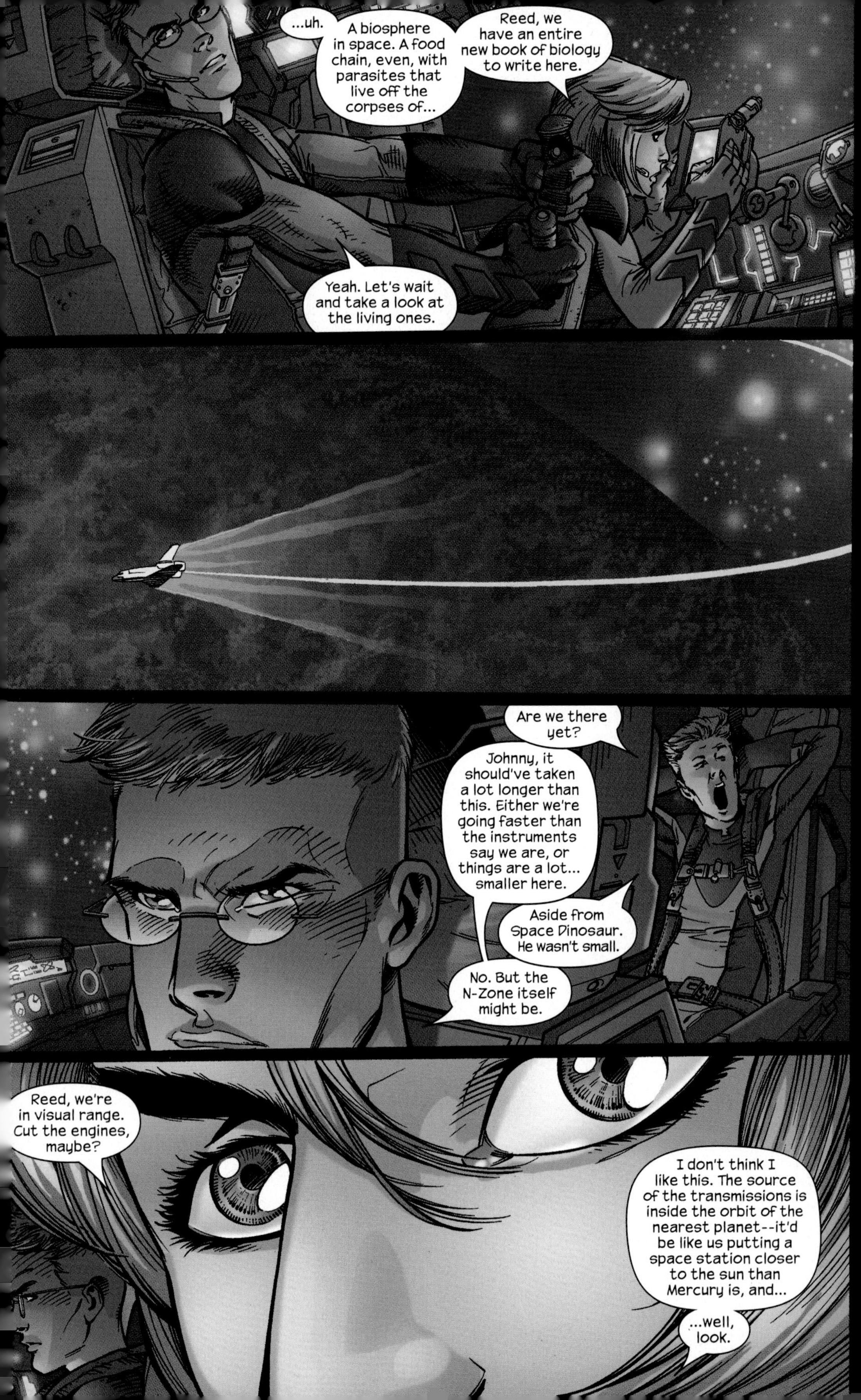

...uh.
A biosphere in space. A food chain, even, with parasites that live off the corpses of...
Reed, we have an entire new book of biology to write here.
Yeah. Let's wait and take a look at the living ones.
Are we there yet?
Johnny, it should've taken a lot longer than this. Either we're going faster than the instruments say we are, or things are a lot... smaller here.
Aside from Space Dinosaur. He wasn't small.
No. But the N-Zone itself might be.
Reed, we're in visual range. Cut the engines, maybe?
I don't think I like this. The source of the transmissions is inside the orbit of the nearest planet--it'd be like us putting a space station closer to the sun than Mercury is, and...
...well, look.

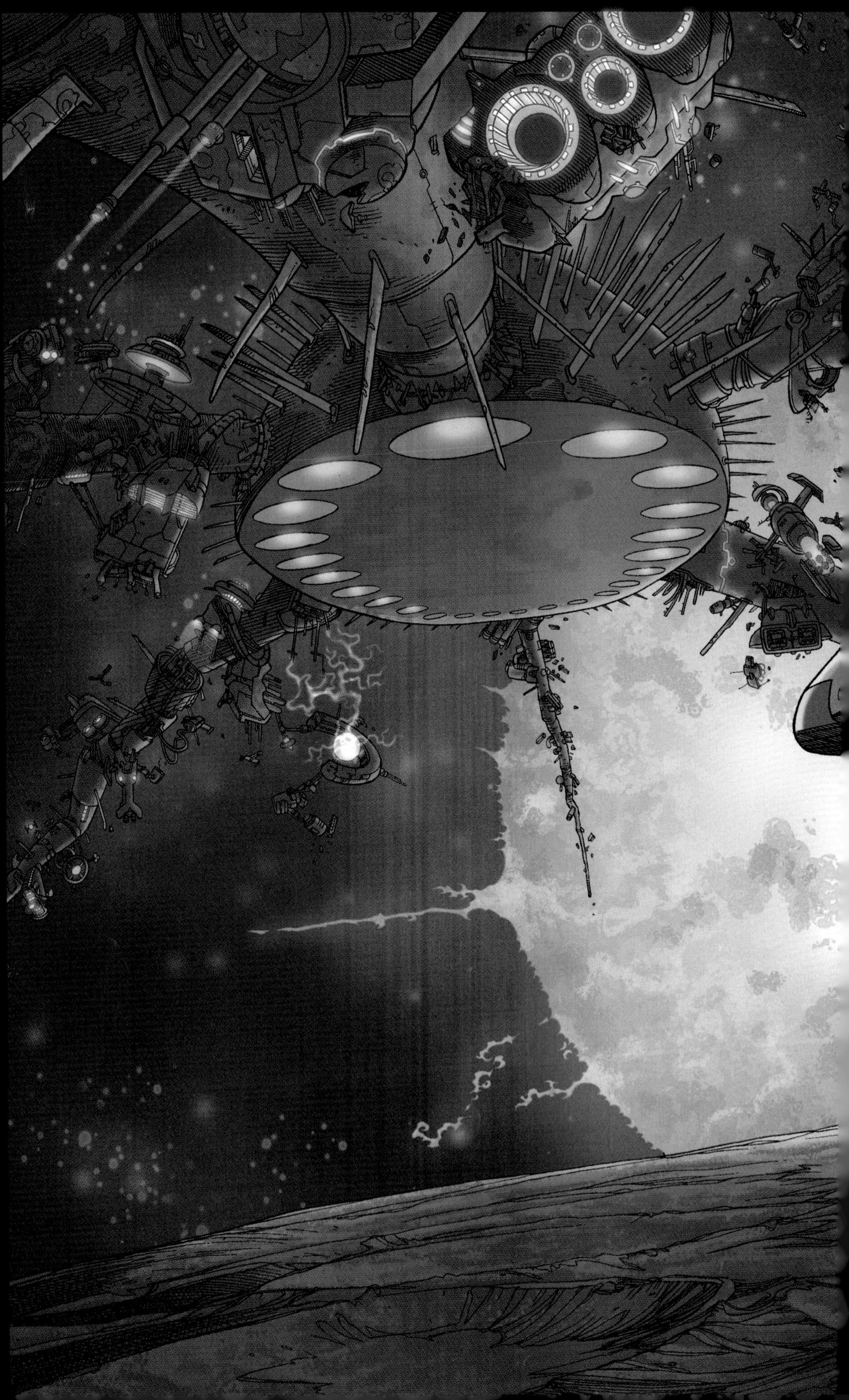

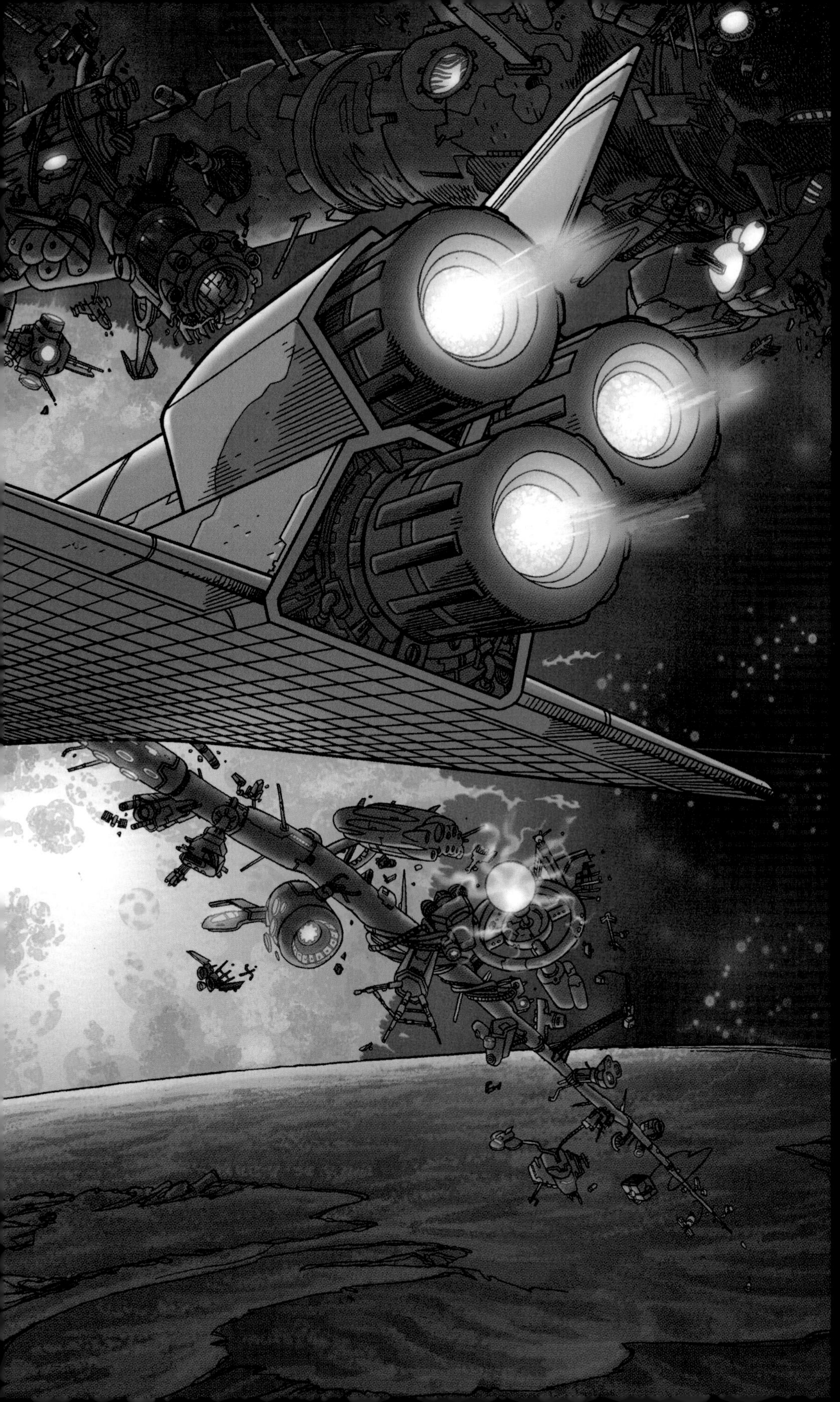

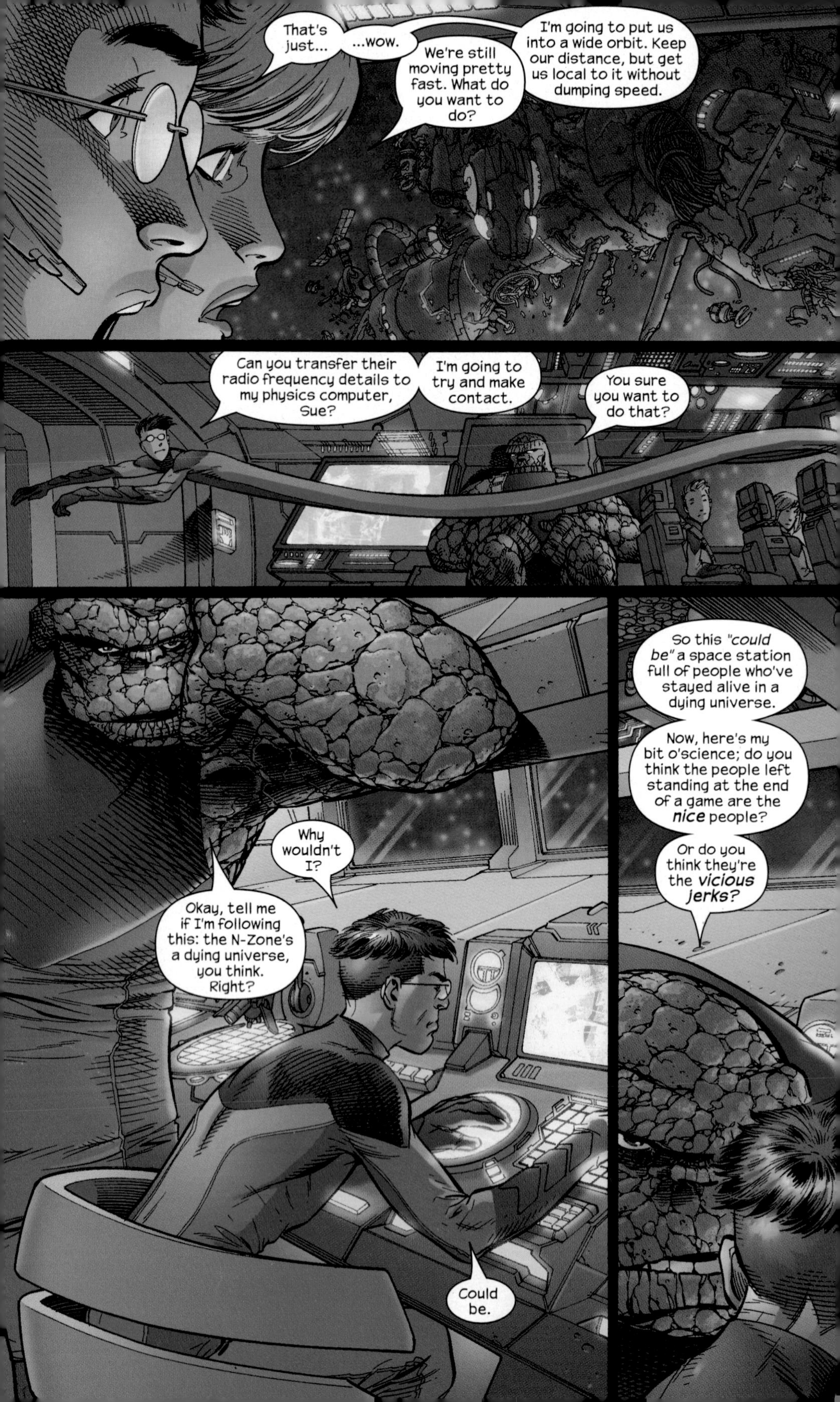
That's just...
...wow.
We're still moving pretty fast. What do you want to do?
I'm going to put us into a wide orbit. Keep our distance, but get us local to it without dumping speed.
Can you transfer their radio frequency details to my physics computer, Sue?
I'm going to try and make contact.
You sure you want to do that?
Why wouldn't I?
Okay, tell me if I'm following this: the N-Zone's a dying universe, you think. Right?
Could be.
So this "could be" a space station full of people who've stayed alive in a dying universe.
Now, here's my bit o'science; do you think the people left standing at the end of a game are the nice people?
Or do you think they're the vicious jerks?

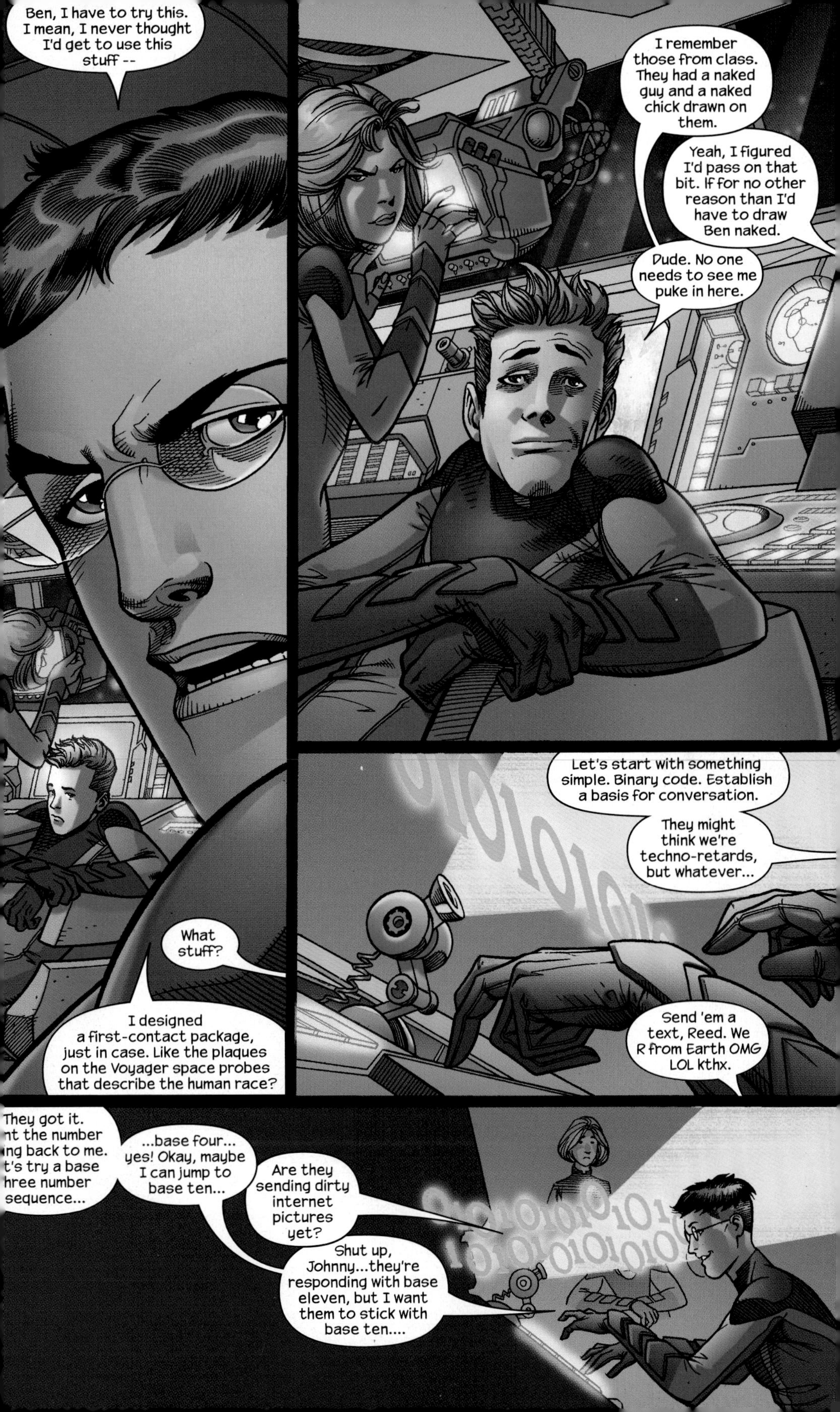
Ben, I have to try this. I mean, I never thought I'd get to use this stuff --
What stuff?
I designed a first-contact package, just in case. Like the plaques on the Voyager space probes that describe the human race?
I remember those from class. They had a naked guy and a naked chick drawn on them.
Yeah, I figured I'd pass on that bit. If for no other reason than I'd have to draw Ben naked.
Dude. No one needs to see me puke in here.
Let's start with something simple. Binary code. Establish a basis for conversation.
They might think we're techno-retards, but whatever...
Send 'em a text, Reed. We R from Earth OMG LOL kthx.
They got it. nt the number ng back to me. t's try a base hree number sequence...
...base four... yes! Okay, maybe I can jump to base ten...
Are they sending dirty internet pictures yet?
Shut up, Johnny...they're responding with base eleven, but I want them to stick with base ten....

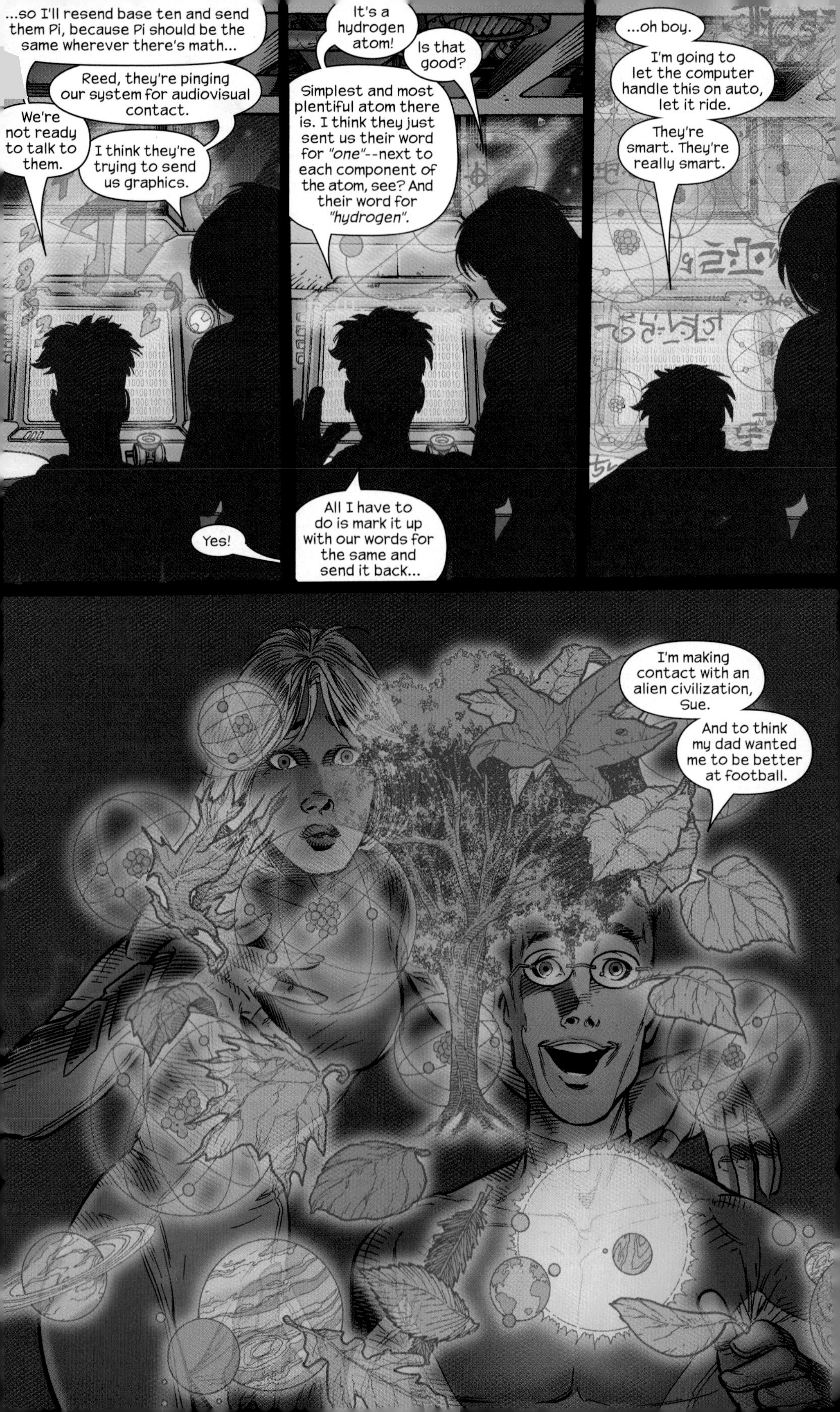
...so I'll resend base ten and send them Pi, because Pi should be the same wherever there's math...
Reed, they're pinging our system for audiovisual contact.
We're not ready to talk to them.
I think they're trying to send us graphics.
Yes!
It's a hydrogen atom!
Is that good?
Simplest and most plentiful atom there is. I think they just sent us their word for "one"--next to each component of the atom, see? And their word for "hydrogen".
All I have to do is mark it up with our words for the same and send it back...
...oh boy.
I'm going to let the computer handle this on auto, let it ride.
They're smart. They're really smart.
I'm making contact with an alien civilization, Sue.
And to think my dad wanted me to be better at football.

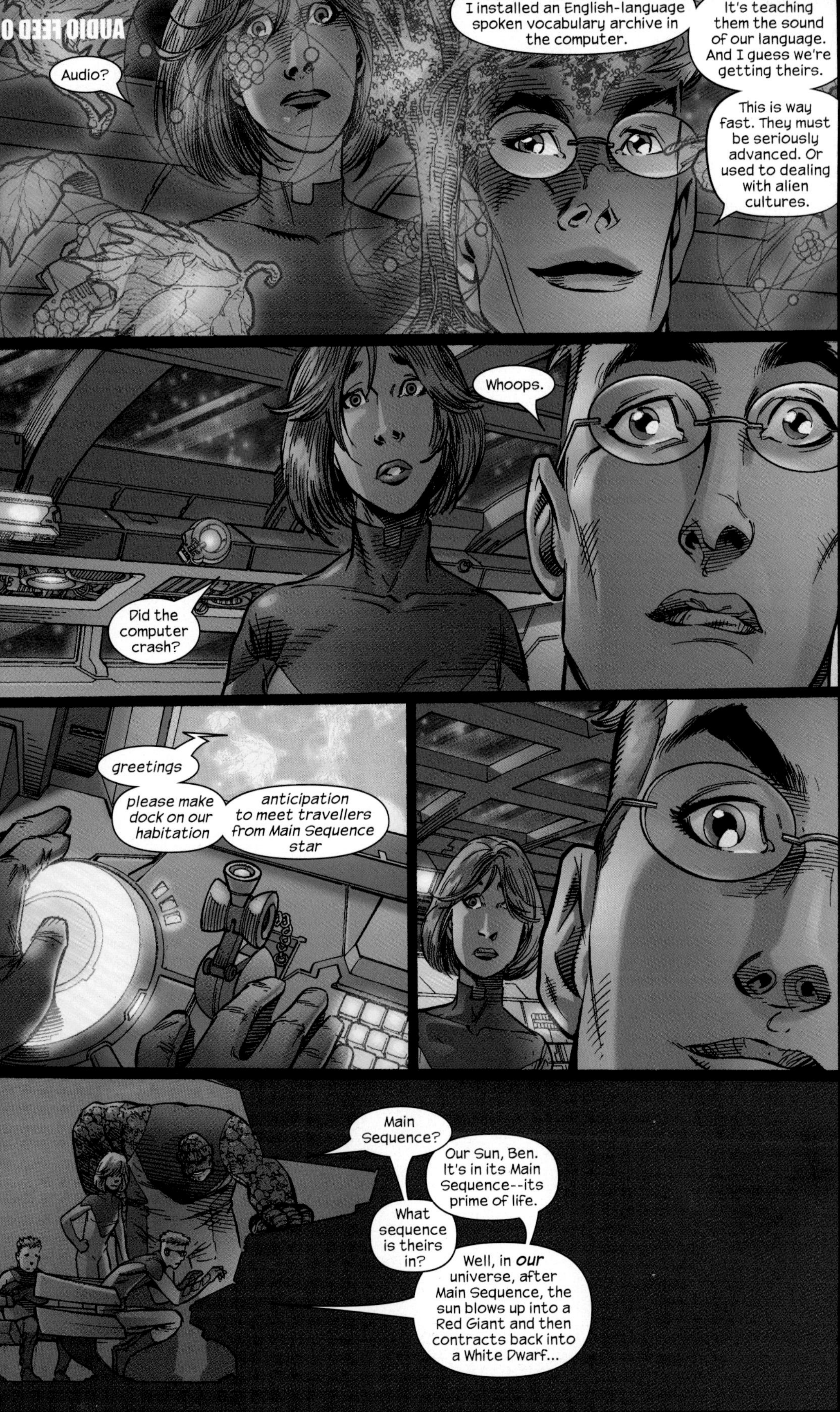
AUDIO FEED 0
I installed an English-language spoken vocabulary archive in the computer.
It's teaching them the sound of our language. And I guess we're getting theirs.
Audio?
This is way fast. They must be seriously advanced. Or used to dealing with alien cultures.
Whoops.
Did the computer crash?
greetings
please make dock on our habitation
anticipation to meet travellers from Main Sequence star
Main Sequence?
Our Sun, Ben. It's in its Main Sequence--its prime of life.
What sequence is theirs in?
Well, in *our* universe, after Main Sequence, the sun blows up into a Red Giant and then contracts back into a White Dwarf...

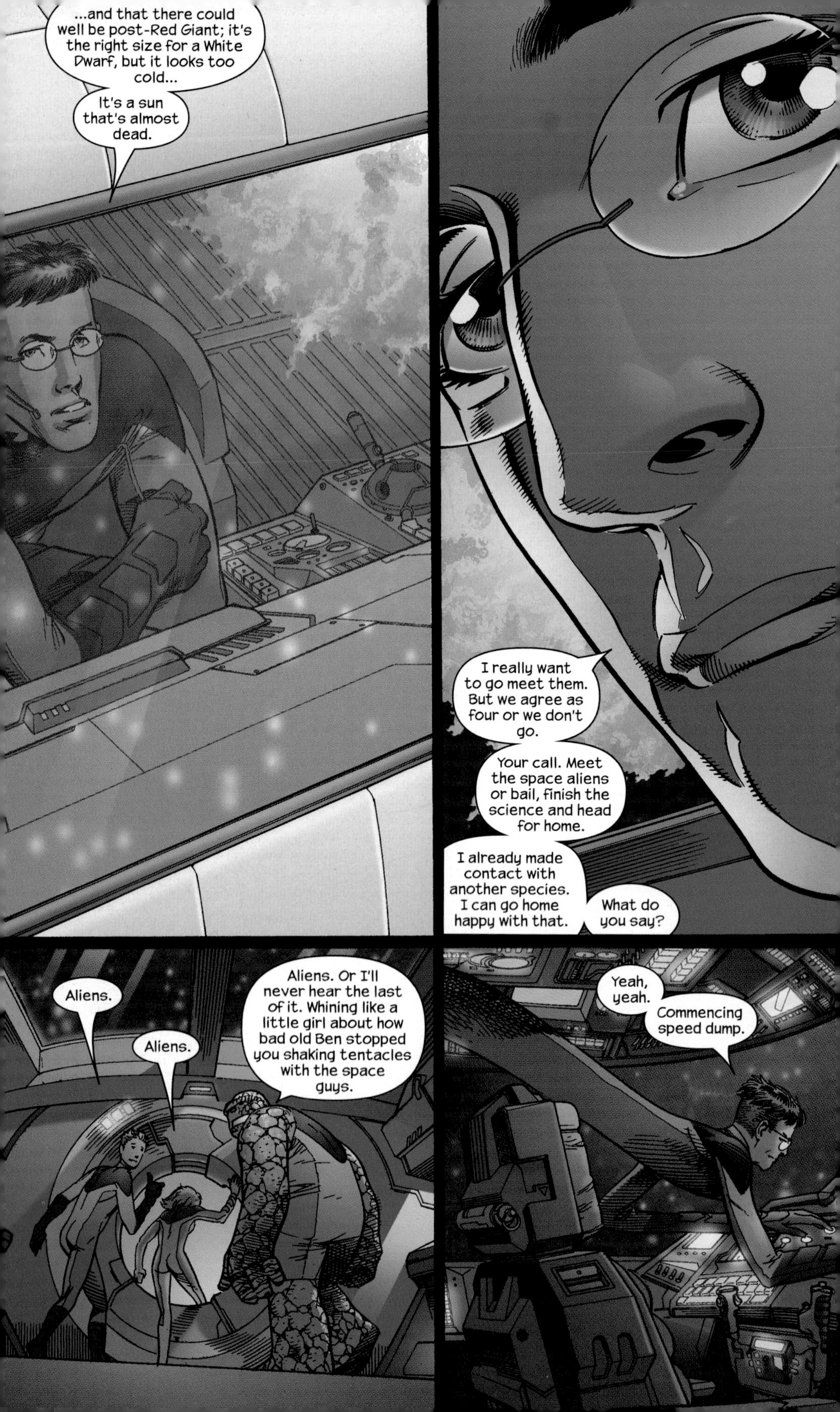
...and that there could well be post-Red Giant; it's the right size for a White Dwarf, but it looks too cold...
It's a sun that's almost dead.
I really want to go meet them. But we agree as four or we don't go.
Your call. Meet the space aliens or bail, finish the science and head for home.
I already made contact with another species. I can go home happy with that.
What do you say?
Aliens.
Aliens.
Aliens. Or I'll never hear the last of it. Whining like a little girl about how bad old Ben stopped you shaking tentacles with the space guys.
Yeah, yeah.
Commencing speed dump.

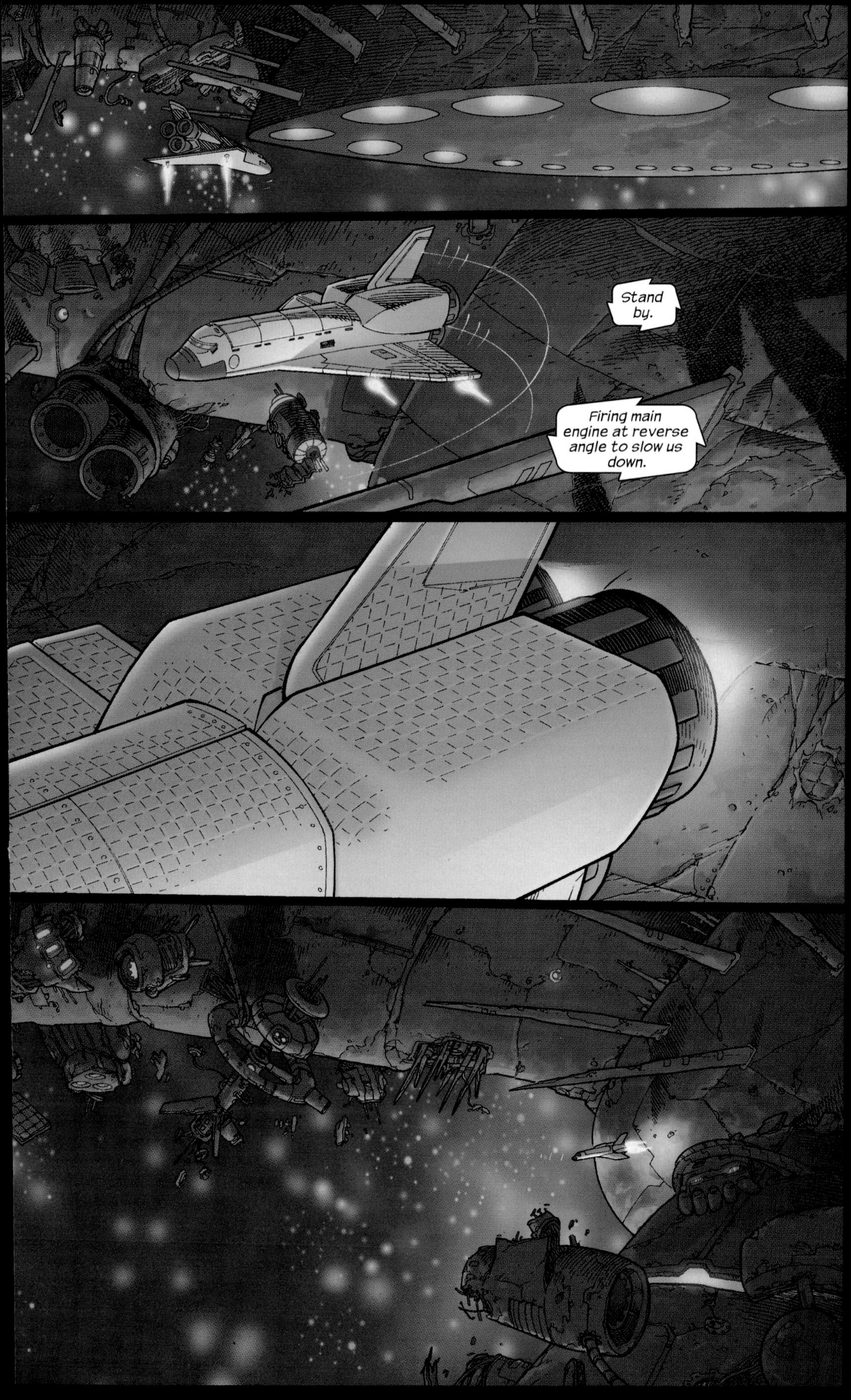
Stand by.
Firing main engine at reverse angle to slow us down.

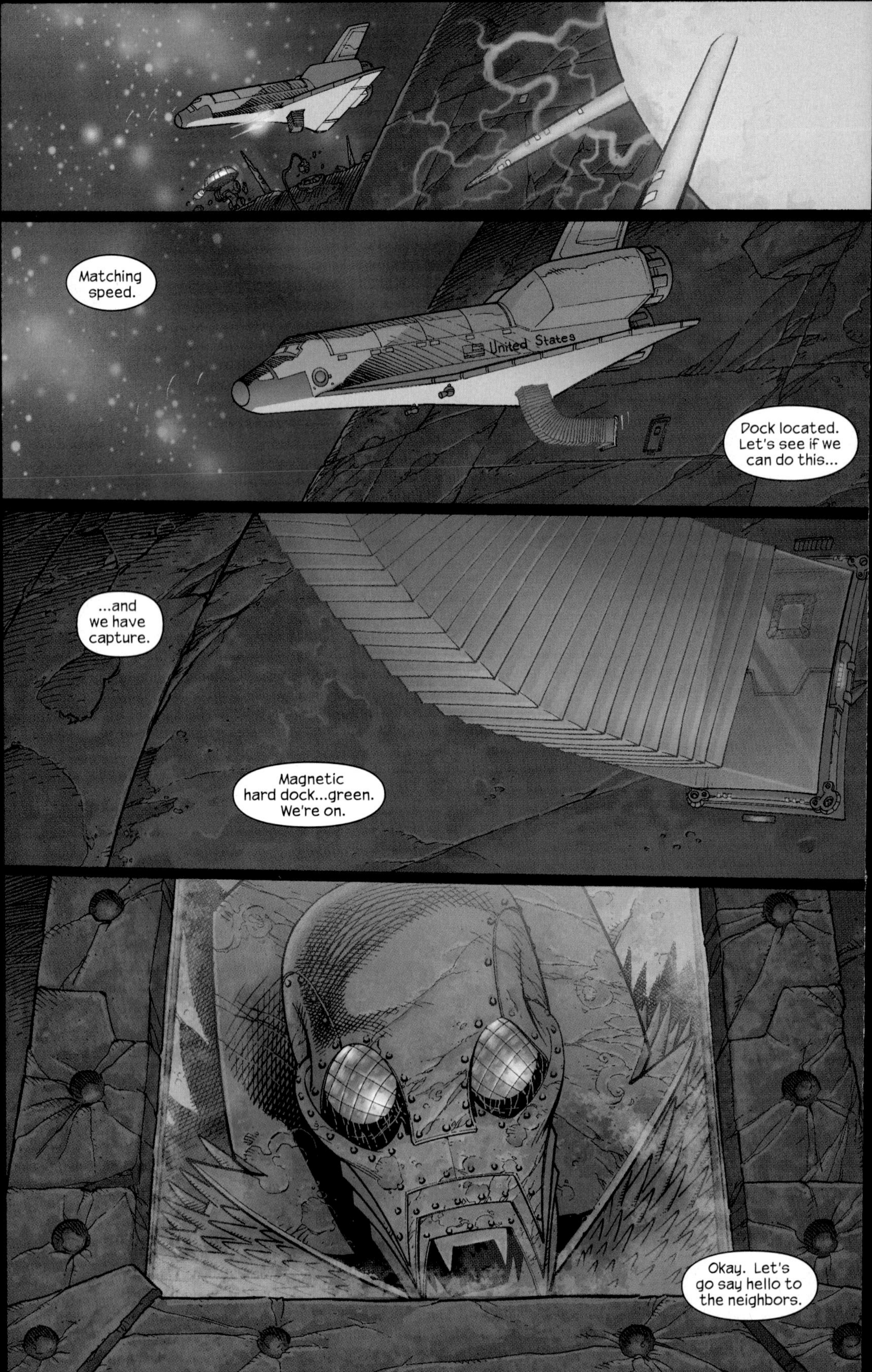
Matching speed.
United States
Dock located. Let's see if we can do this...
...and we have capture.
Magnetic hard dock...green. We're on.
Okay. Let's go say hello to the neighbors.

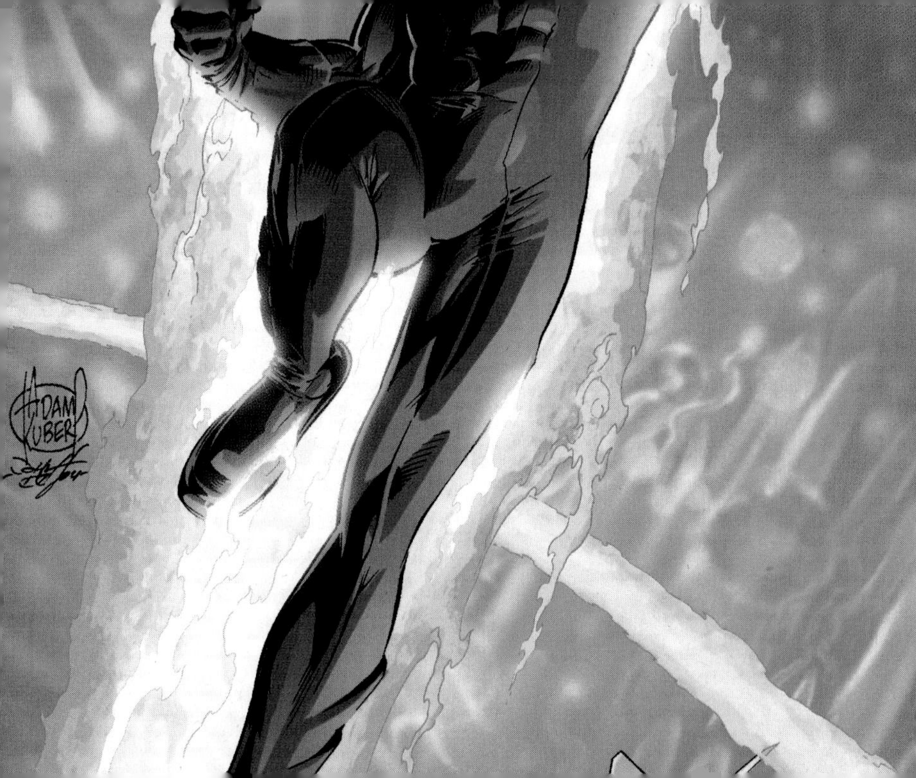

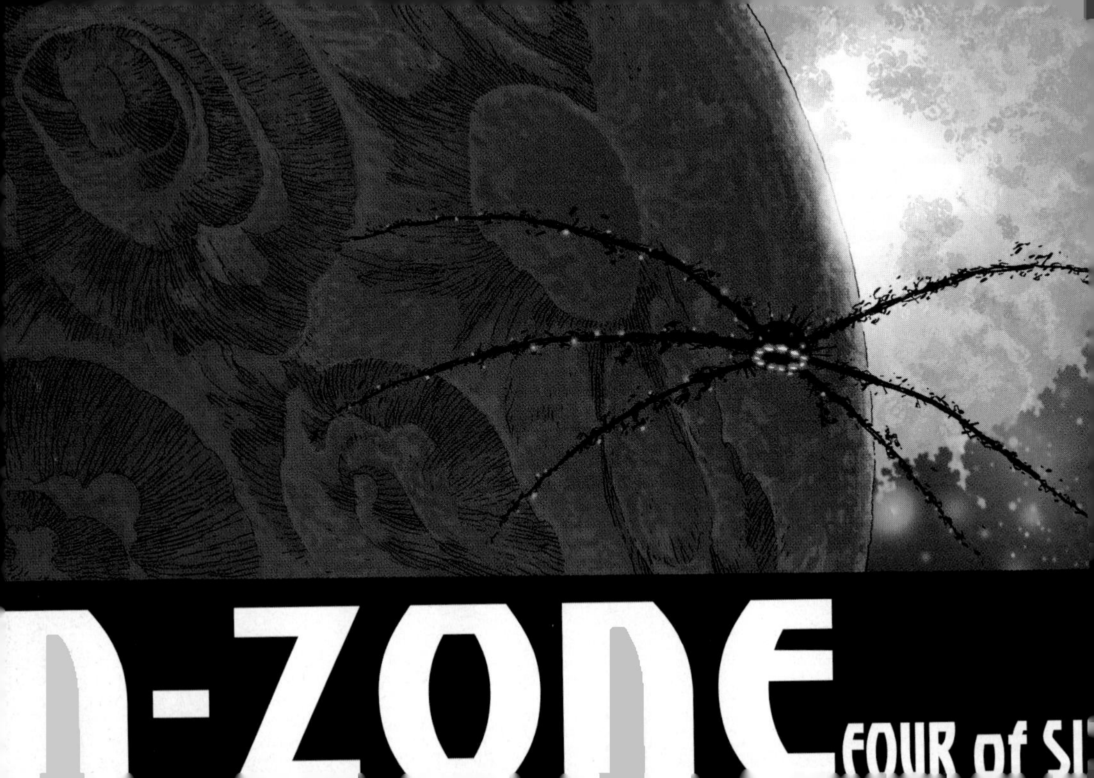

N-ZONE FOUR of SI

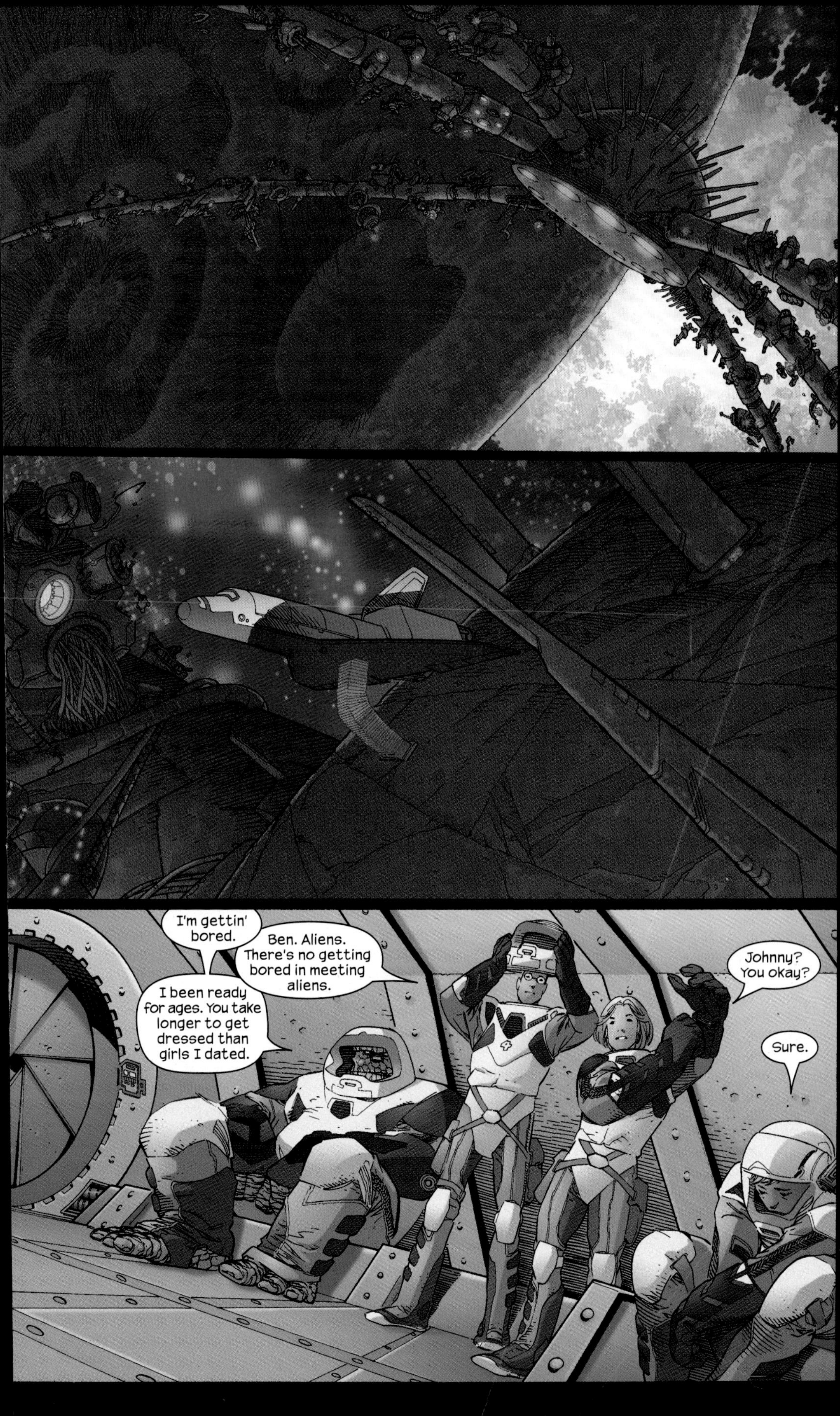
I'm gettin' bored.
I been ready for ages. You take longer to get dressed than girls I dated.
Ben. Aliens. There's no getting bored in meeting aliens.
Johnny? You okay?
Sure.

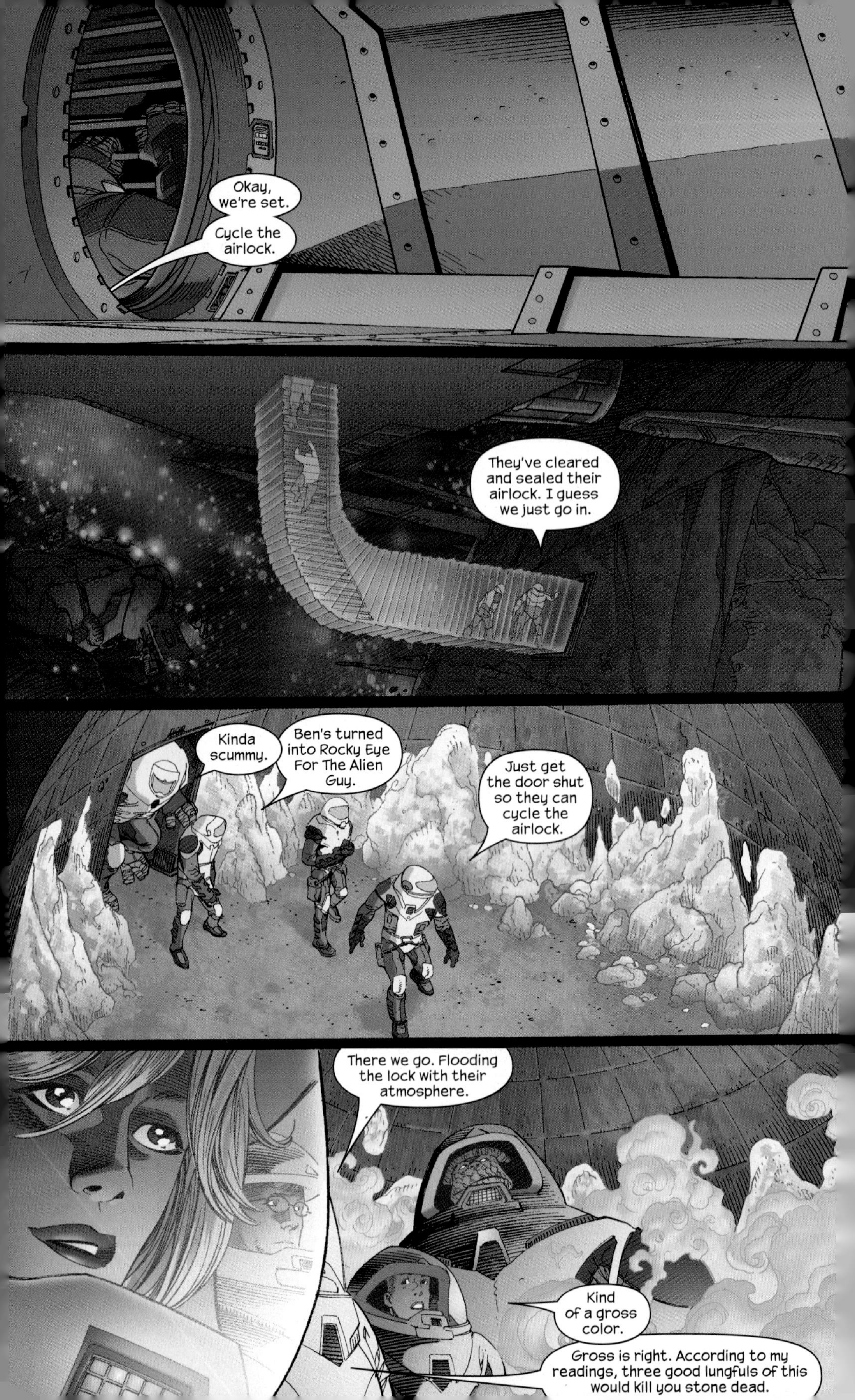
Okay, we're set.
Cycle the airlock.
They've cleared and sealed their airlock. I guess we just go in.
Kinda scummy.
Ben's turned into Rocky Eye For The Alien Guy.
Just get the door shut so they can cycle the airlock.
There we go. Flooding the lock with their atmosphere.
Kind of a gross color.
Gross is right. According to my readings, three good lungfuls of this would kill you stone dead.

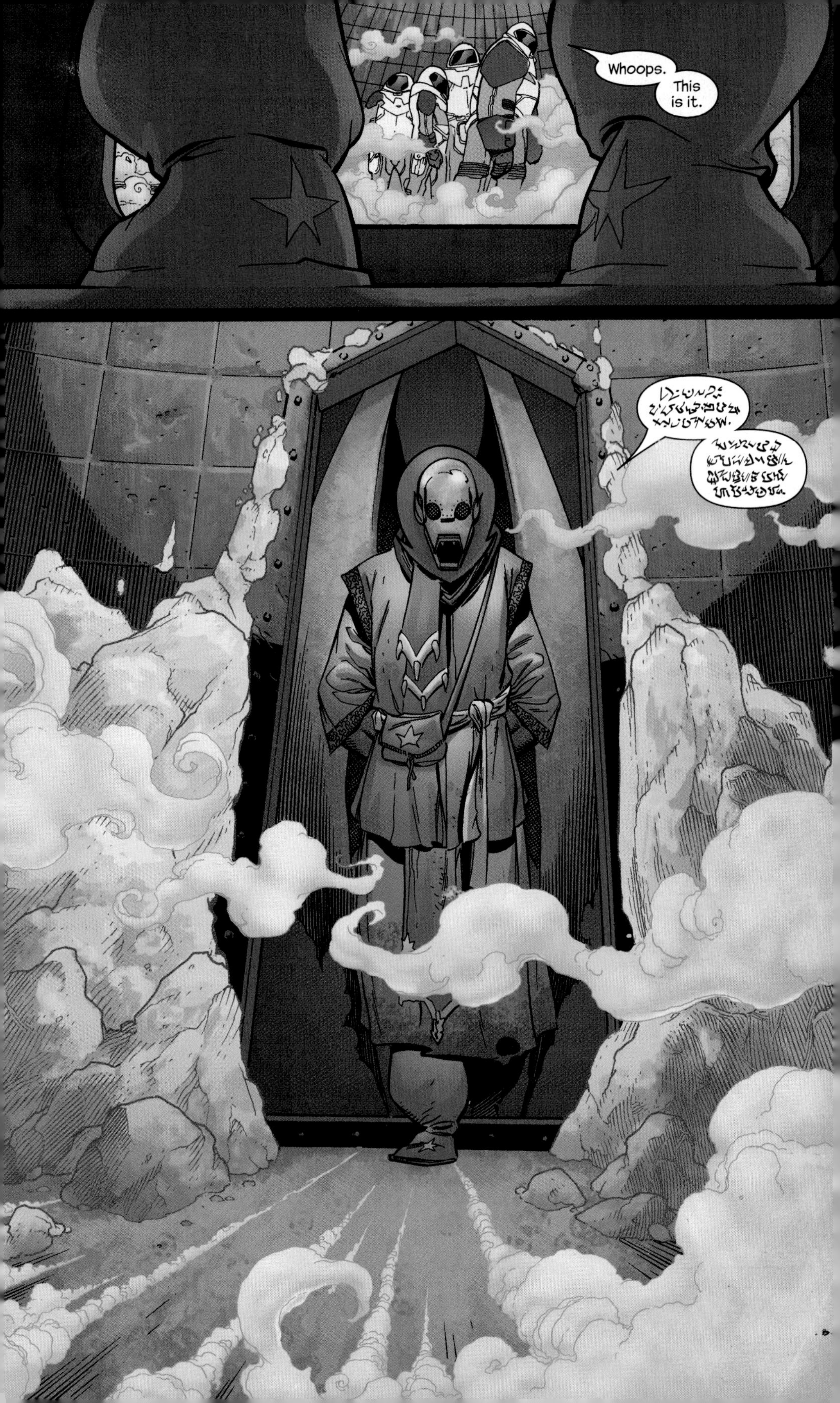
Whoops. This is it.

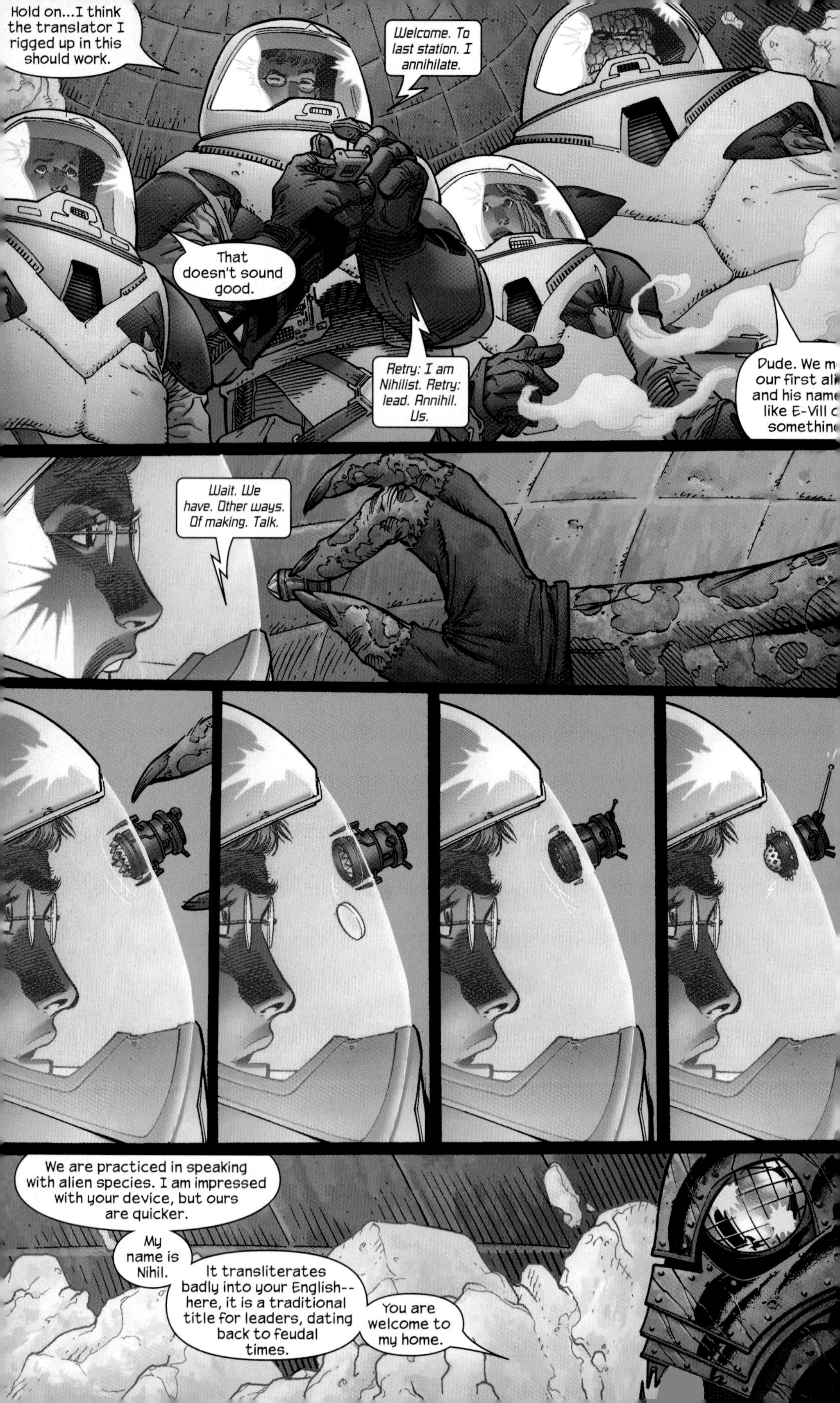

Hold on...I think the translator I rigged up in this should work.
Welcome. To last station. I annihilate.
That doesn't sound good.
Retry: I am Nihilist. Retry: lead. Annihil. Us.
Dude. We m our first ali and his name like E-Vill c somethin
Wait. We have. Other ways. Of making. Talk.
We are practiced in speaking with alien species. I am impressed with your device, but ours are quicker.
My name is Nihil.
It transliterates badly into your English-- here, it is a traditional title for leaders, dating back to feudal times.
You are welcome to my home.

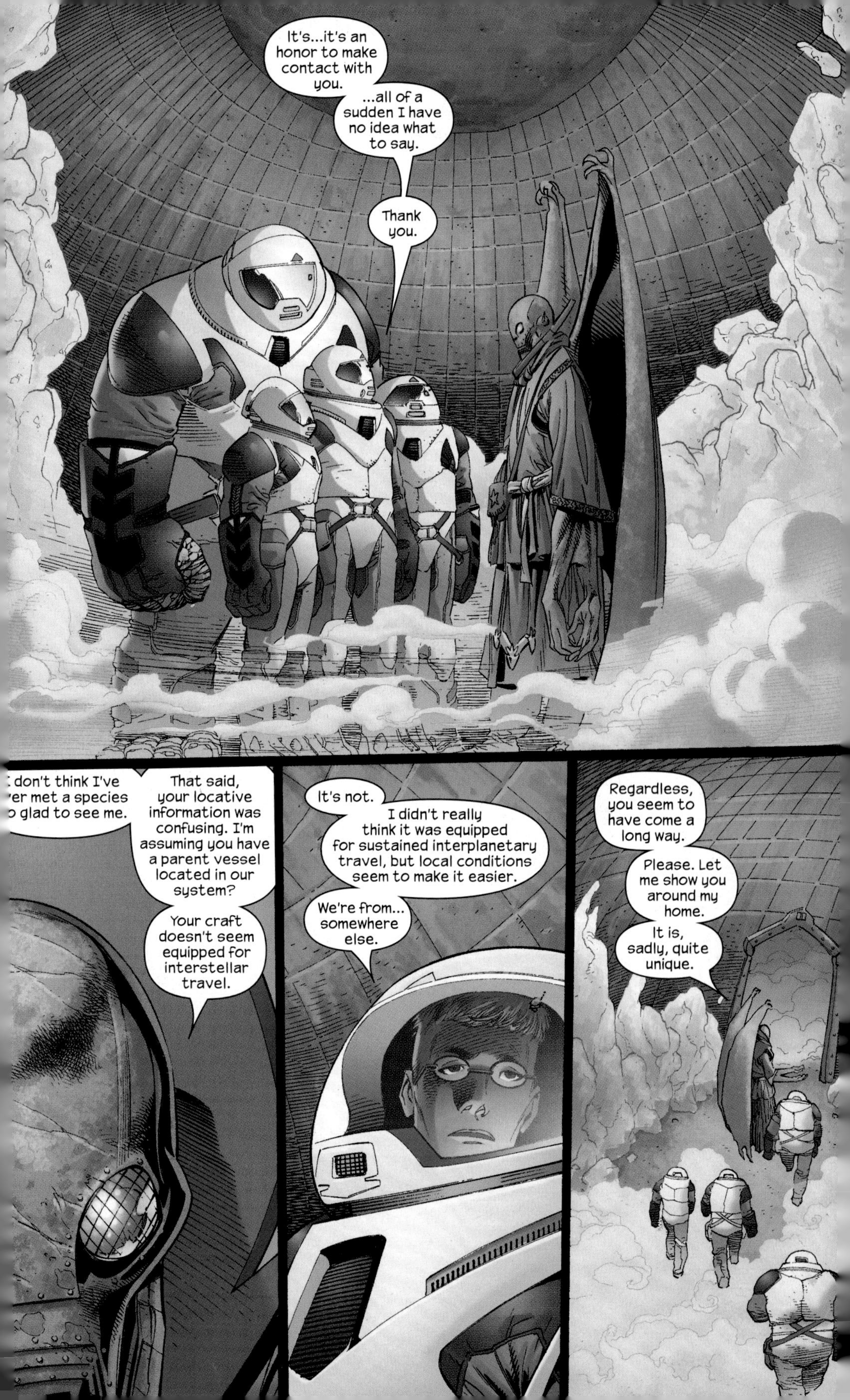
It's...it's an honor to make contact with you.
...all of a sudden I have no idea what to say.
Thank you.
don't think I've
ver met a species
o glad to see me.
That said, your locative information was confusing. I'm assuming you have a parent vessel located in our system?
Your craft doesn't seem equipped for interstellar travel.
It's not.
I didn't really think it was equipped for sustained interplanetary travel, but local conditions seem to make it easier.
We're from... somewhere else.
Regardless, you seem to have come a long way.
Please. Let me show you around my home.
It is, sadly, quite unique.

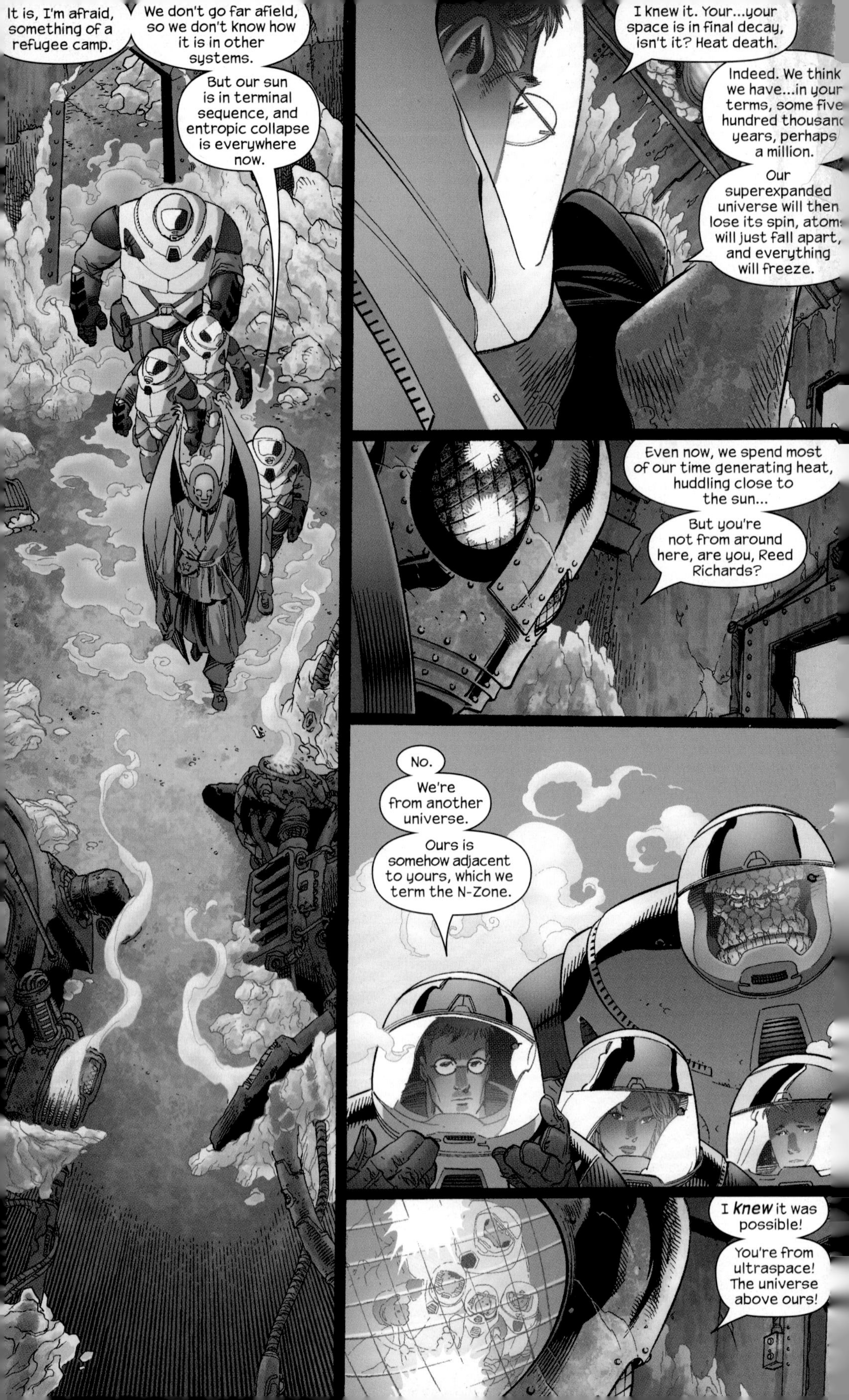
It is, I'm afraid, something of a refugee camp.
We don't go far afield, so we don't know how it is in other systems.
But our sun is in terminal sequence, and entropic collapse is everywhere now.
I knew it. Your...your space is in final decay, isn't it? Heat death.
Indeed. We think we have...in your terms, some five hundred thousand years, perhaps a million.
Our superexpanded universe will then lose its spin, atoms will just fall apart, and everything will freeze.
Even now, we spend most of our time generating heat, huddling close to the sun...
But you're not from around here, are you, Reed Richards?
No.
We're from another universe.
Ours is somehow adjacent to yours, which we term the N-Zone.
I *knew* it was possible!
You're from ultraspace! The universe above ours!

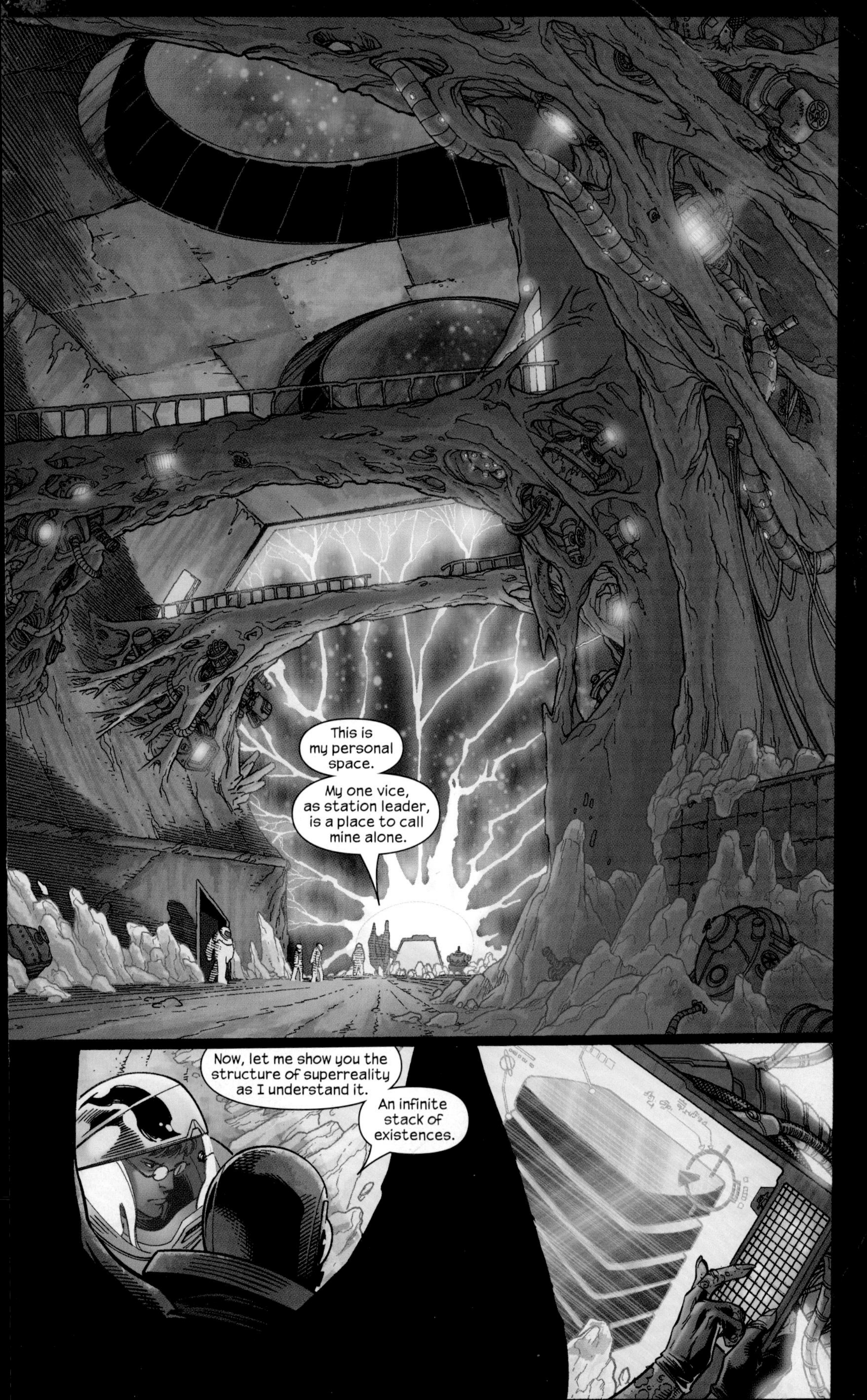
This is my personal space.
My one vice, as station leader, is a place to call mine alone.
Now, let me show you the structure of superreality as I understand it.
An infinite stack of existences.

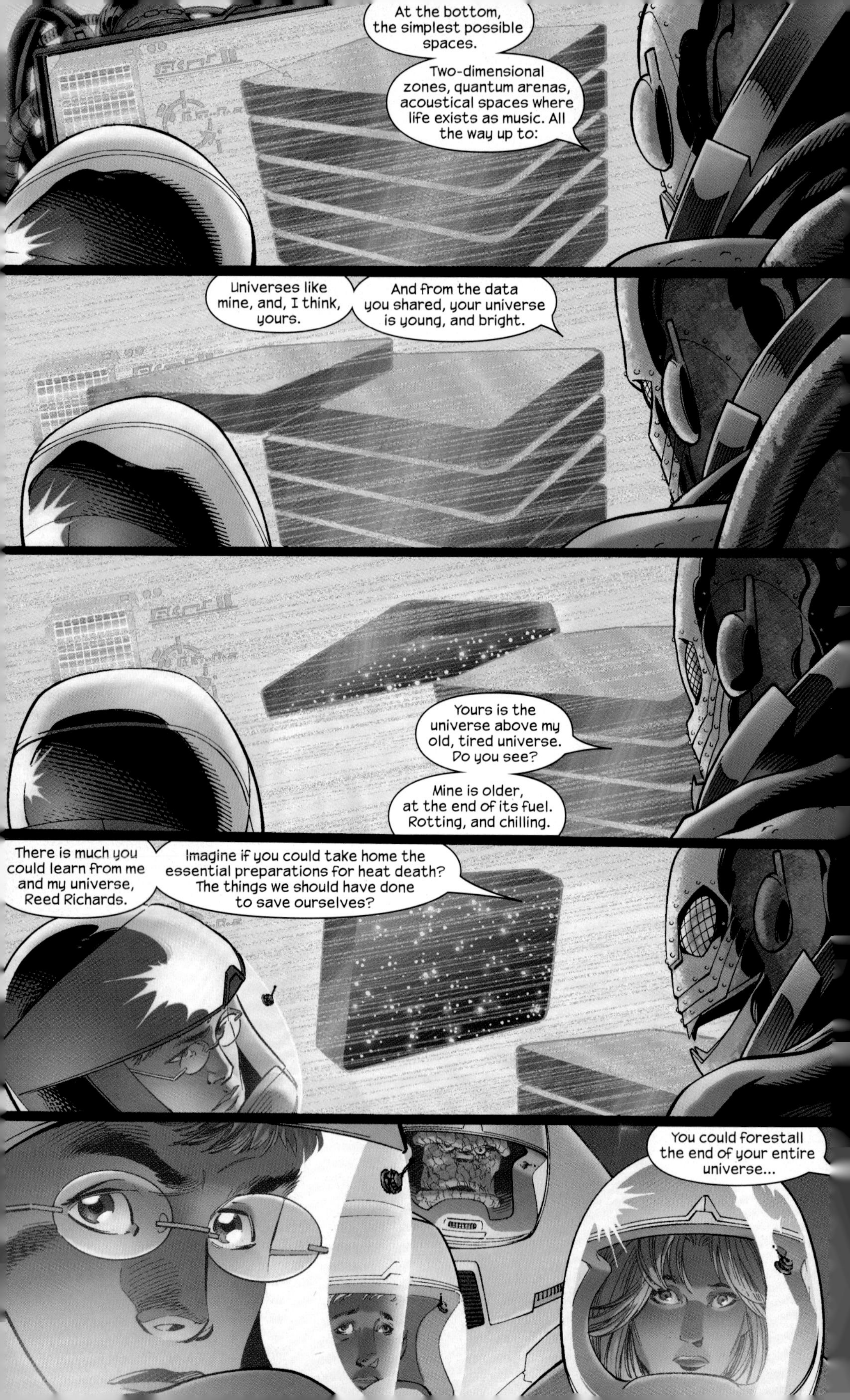
At the bottom, the simplest possible spaces.
Two-dimensional zones, quantum arenas, acoustical spaces where life exists as music. All the way up to:
Universes like mine, and, I think, yours.
And from the data you shared, your universe is young, and bright.
Yours is the universe above my old, tired universe. Do you see?
Mine is older, at the end of its fuel. Rotting, and chilling.
There is much you could learn from me and my universe, Reed Richards.
Imagine if you could take home the essential preparations for heat death? The things we should have done to save ourselves?
You could forestall the end of your entire universe...

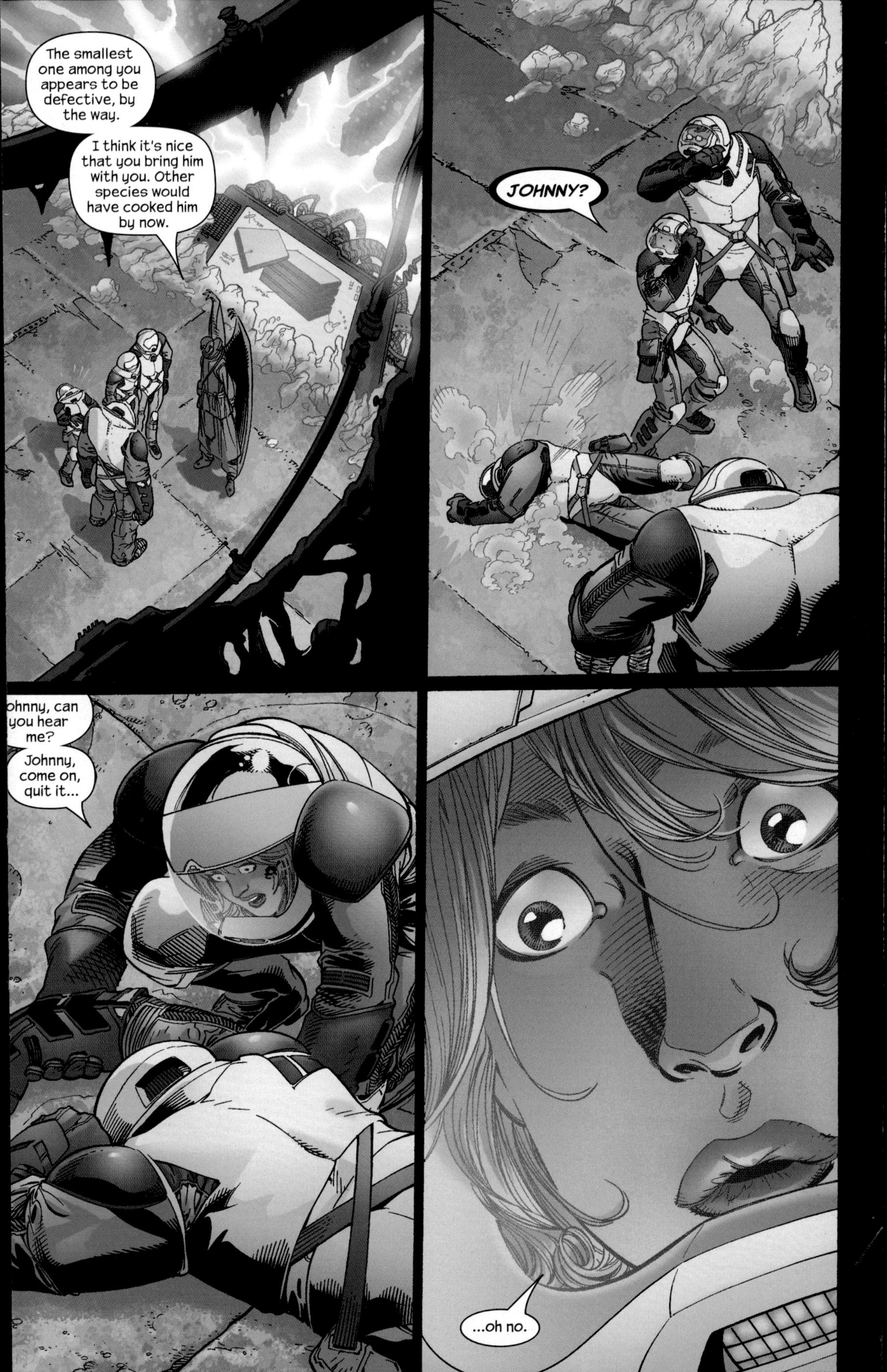
The smallest one among you appears to be defective, by the way.
I think it's nice that you bring him with you. Other species would have cooked him by now.
JOHNNY?
Johnny, can you hear me?
Johnny, come on, quit it...
...oh no.

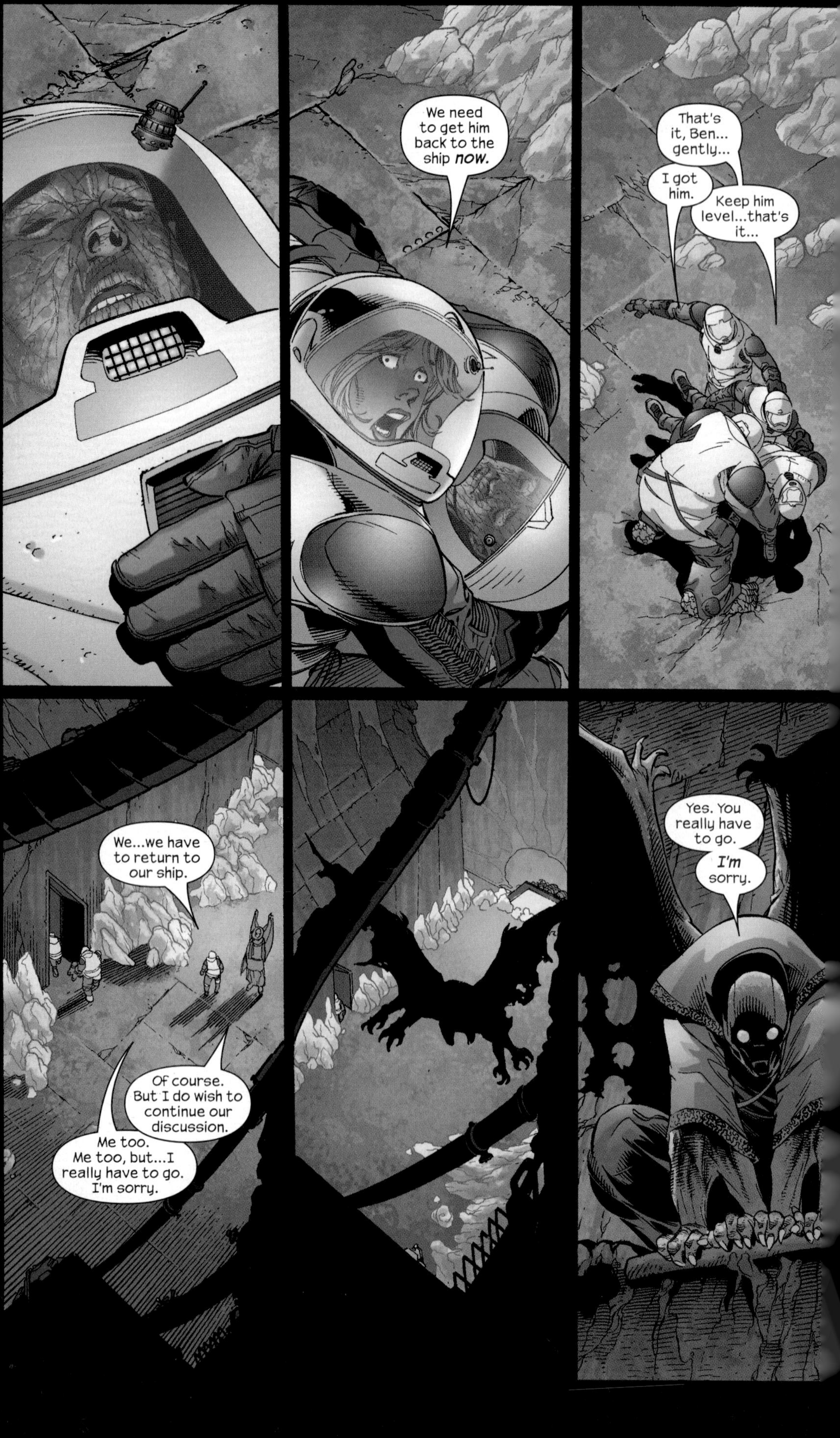
We need to get him back to the ship *now.*
That's it, Ben... gently...
I got him.
Keep him level...that's it...
We...we have to return to our ship.
Of course. But I do wish to continue our discussion.
Me too. Me too, but...I really have to go. I'm sorry.
Yes. You really have to go.
I'm sorry.

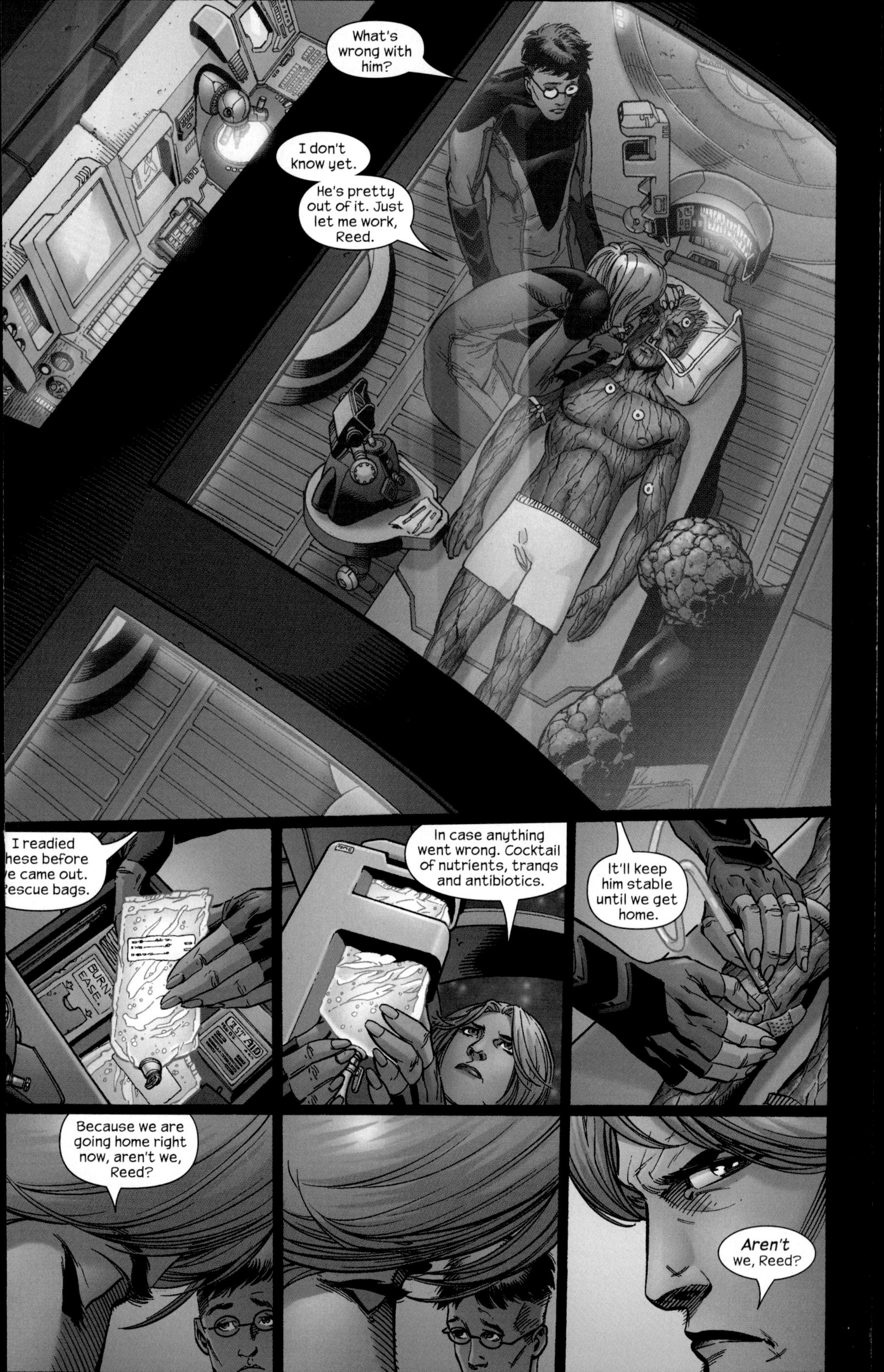
What's wrong with him?
I don't know yet.
He's pretty out of it. Just let me work, Reed.
I readied hese before e came out. escue bags.
BURN EASE.
1ST AID
In case anything went wrong. Cocktail of nutrients, tranqs and antibiotics.
It'll keep him stable until we get home.
Because we are going home right now, aren't we, Reed?
Aren't we, Reed?

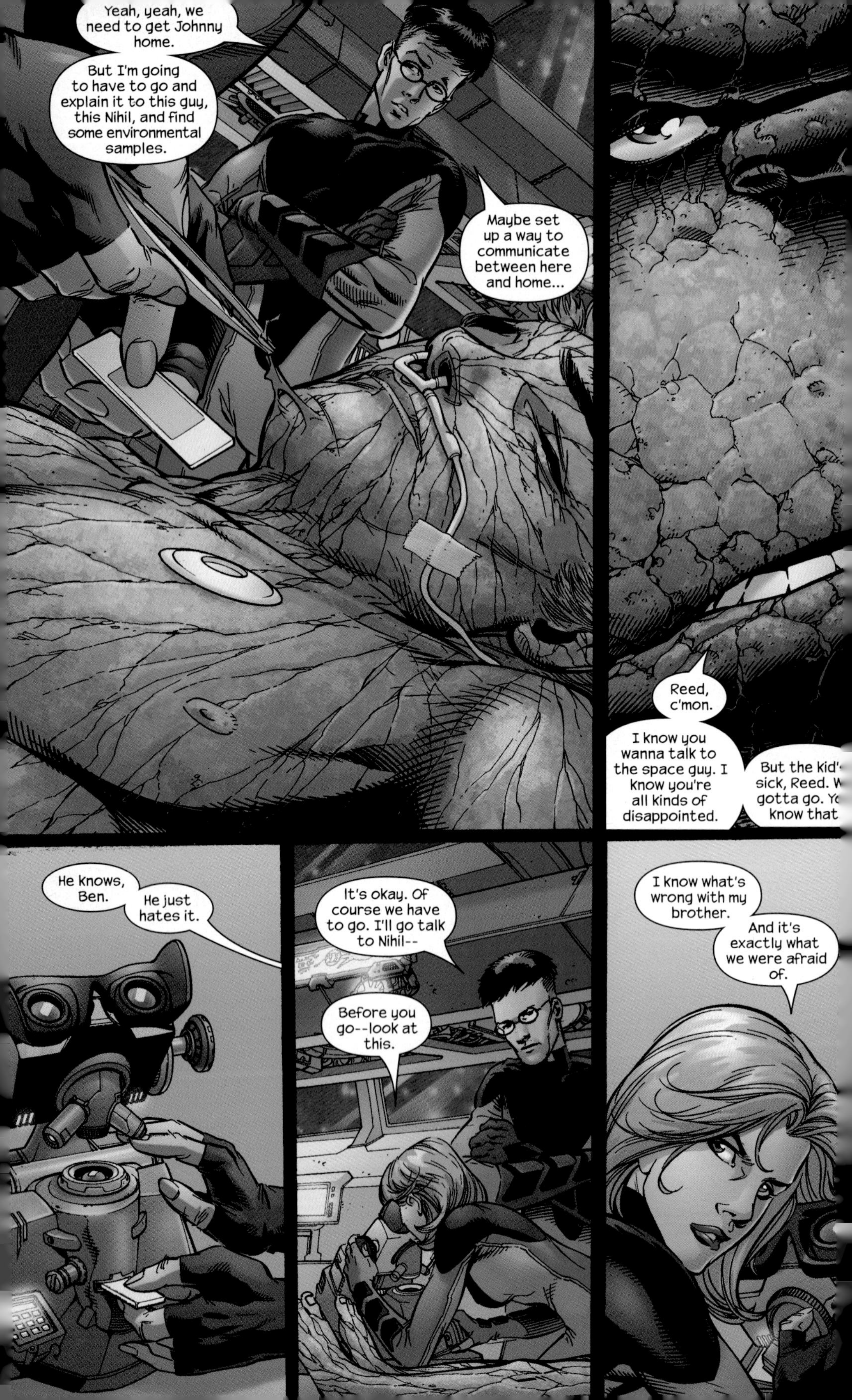
Yeah, yeah, we need to get Johnny home.
But I'm going to have to go and explain it to this guy, this Nihil, and find some environmental samples.
Maybe set up a way to communicate between here and home...
Reed, c'mon.
I know you wanna talk to the space guy. I know you're all kinds of disappointed.
He knows, Ben.
He just hates it.
It's okay. Of course we have to go. I'll go talk to Nihil--
Before you go--look at this.
I know what's wrong with my brother.
And it's exactly what we were afraid of.

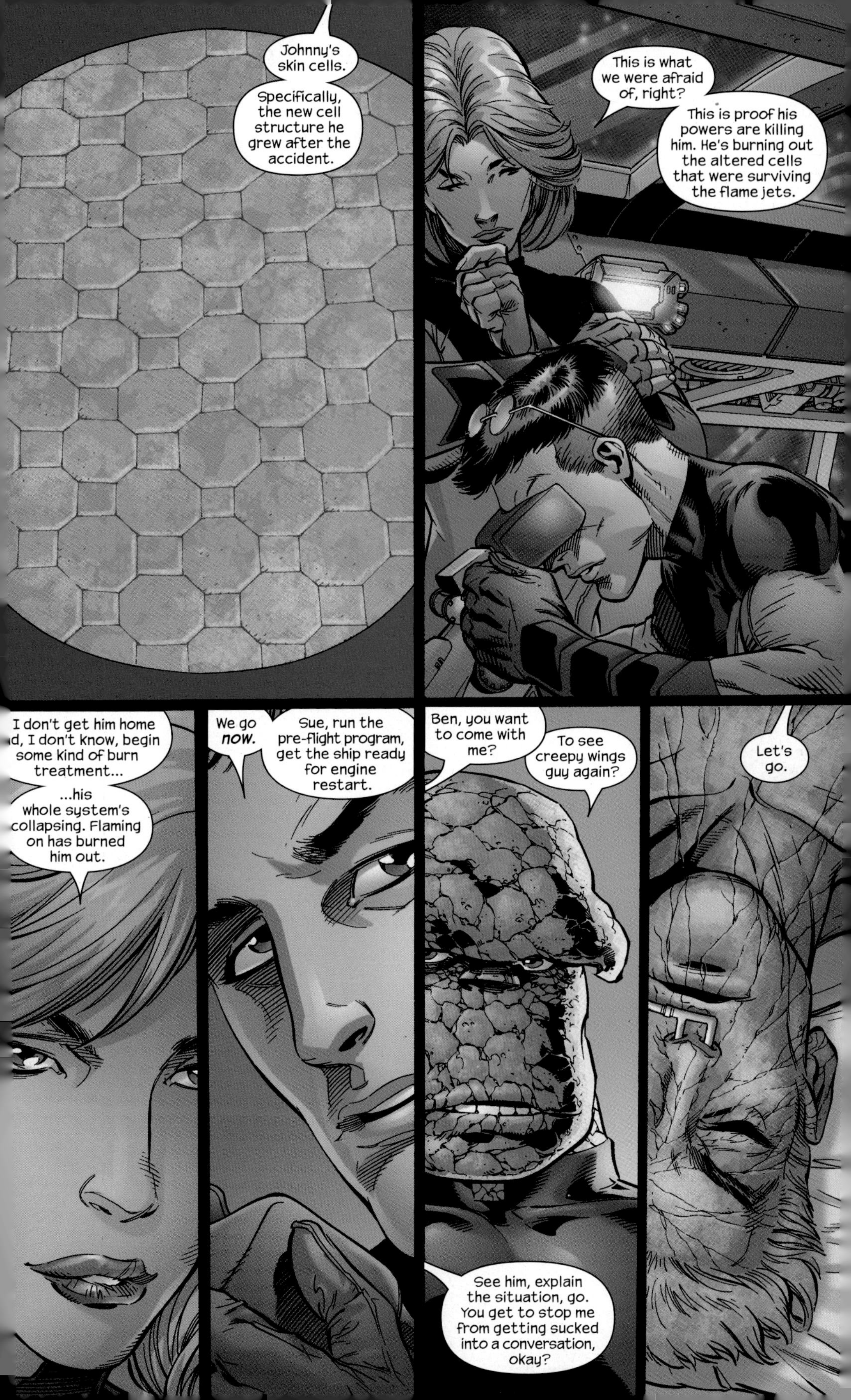
Johnny's skin cells.
Specifically, the new cell structure he grew after the accident.
This is what we were afraid of, right?
This is proof his powers are killing him. He's burning out the altered cells that were surviving the flame jets.
I don't get him home ...d, I don't know, begin some kind of burn treatment...
...his whole system's collapsing. Flaming on has burned him out.
We go NOW.
Sue, run the pre-flight program, get the ship ready for engine restart.
Ben, you want to come with me?
To see creepy wings guy again?
See him, explain the situation, go. You get to stop me from getting sucked into a conversation, okay?
Let's go.

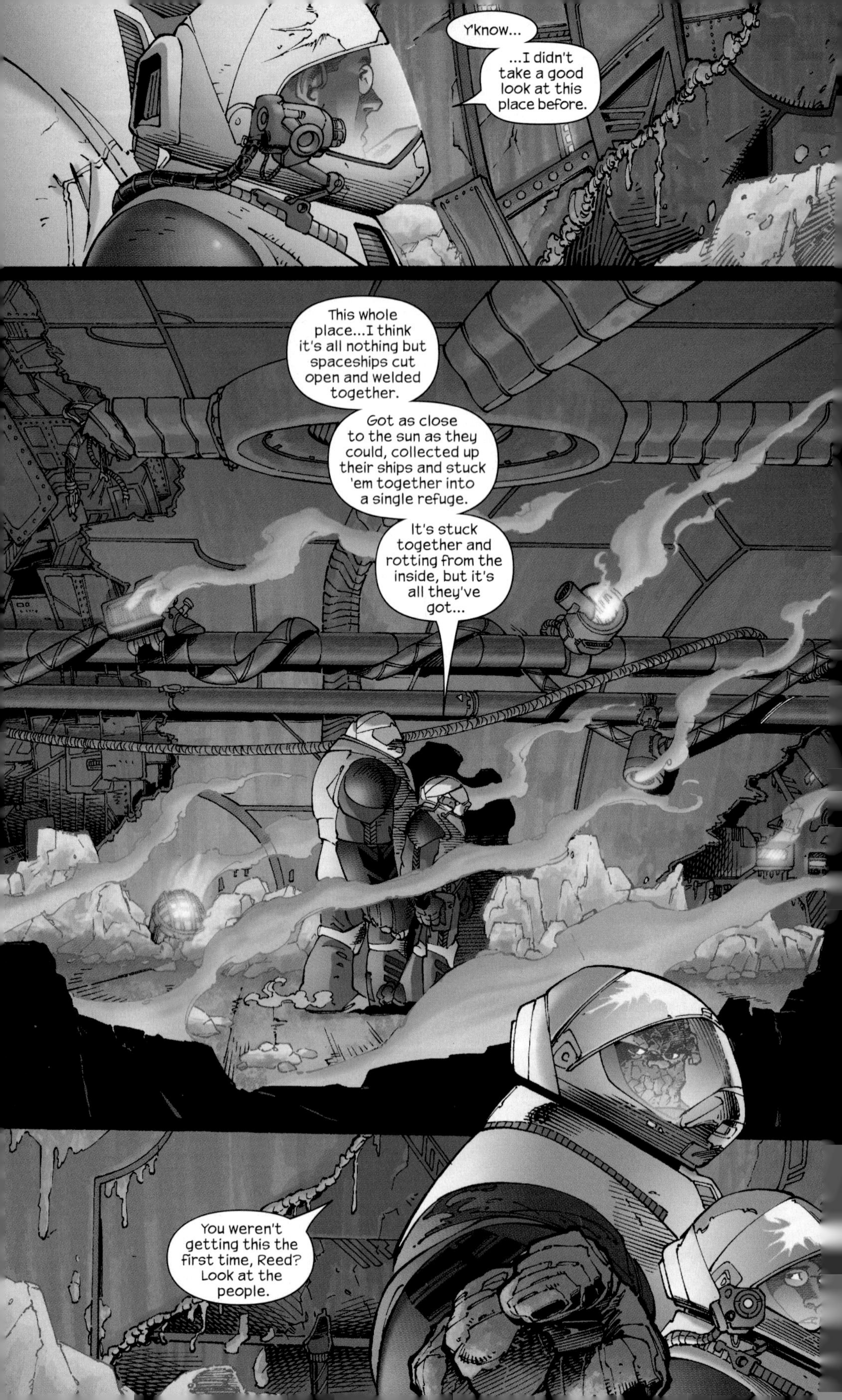
Y'know...
...I didn't take a good look at this place before.
This whole place...I think it's all nothing but spaceships cut open and welded together.
Got as close to the sun as they could, collected up their ships and stuck 'em together into a single refuge.
It's stuck together and rotting from the inside, but it's all they've got...
You weren't getting this the first time, Reed? Look at the people.

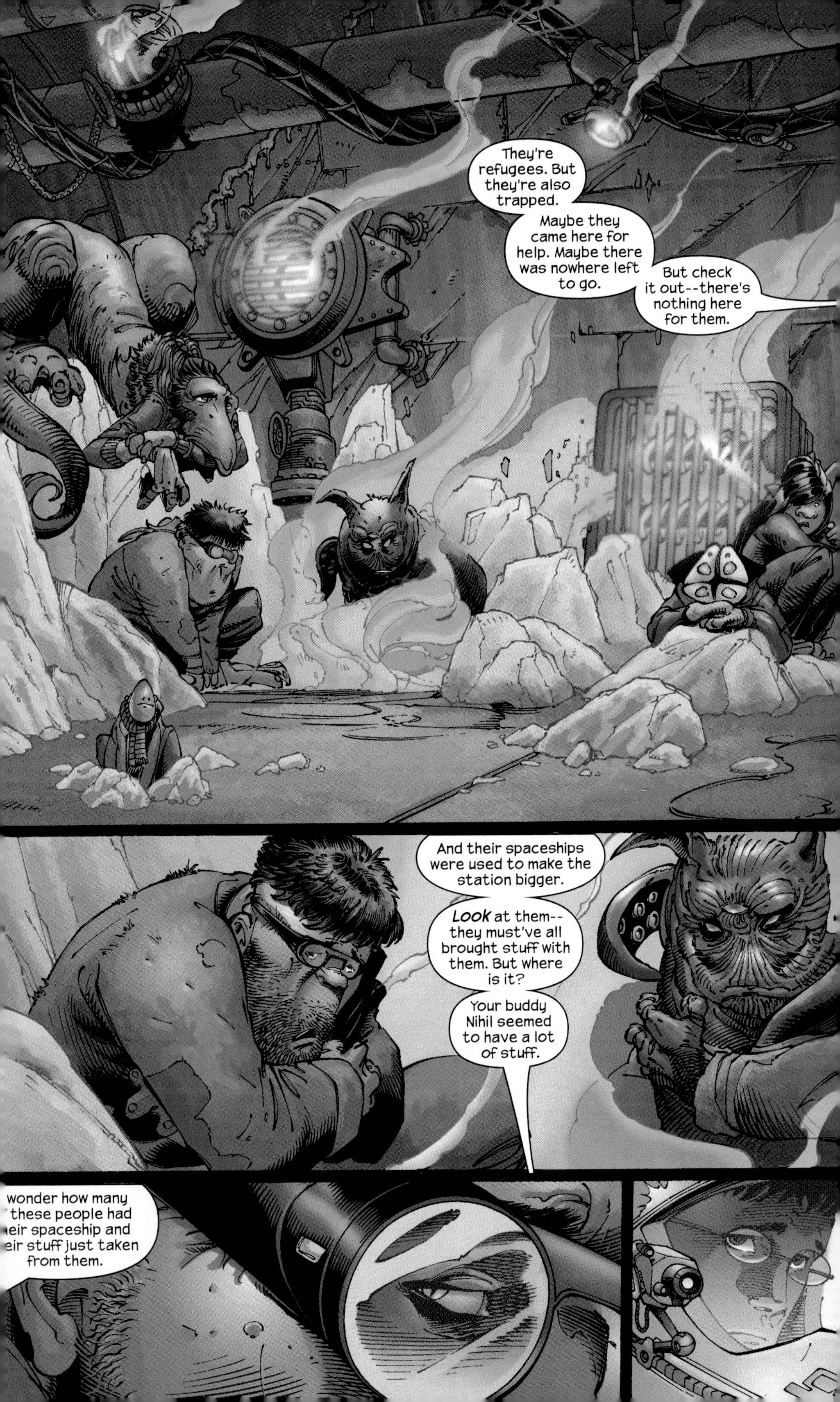
They're refugees. But they're also trapped.
Maybe they came here for help. Maybe there was nowhere left to go.
But check it out--there's nothing here for them.
And their spaceships were used to make the station bigger.
LOOK at them--they must've all brought stuff with them. But where is it?
Your buddy Nihil seemed to have a lot of stuff.
wonder how many these people had eir spaceship and eir stuff just taken from them.

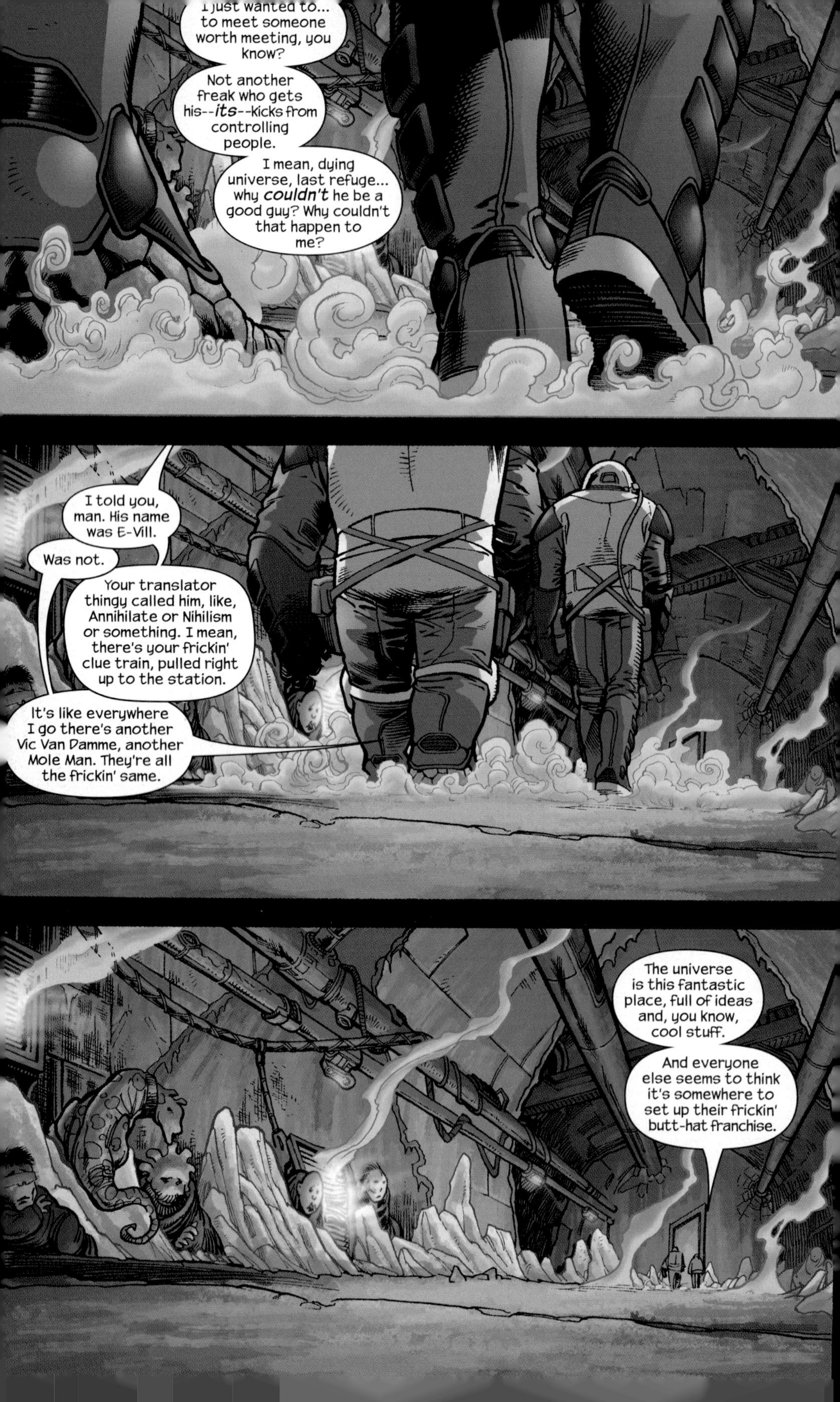
I just wanted to... to meet someone worth meeting, you know?
Not another freak who gets his--its--kicks from controlling people.
I mean, dying universe, last refuge... why couldn't he be a good guy? Why couldn't that happen to me?
I told you, man. His name was E-Vill.
Was not.
Your translator thingy called him, like, Annihilate or Nihilism or something. I mean, there's your frickin' clue train, pulled right up to the station.
It's like everywhere I go there's another Vic Van Damme, another Mole Man. They're all the frickin' same.
The universe is this fantastic place, full of ideas and, you know, cool stuff.
And everyone else seems to think it's somewhere to set up their frickin' butt-hat franchise.

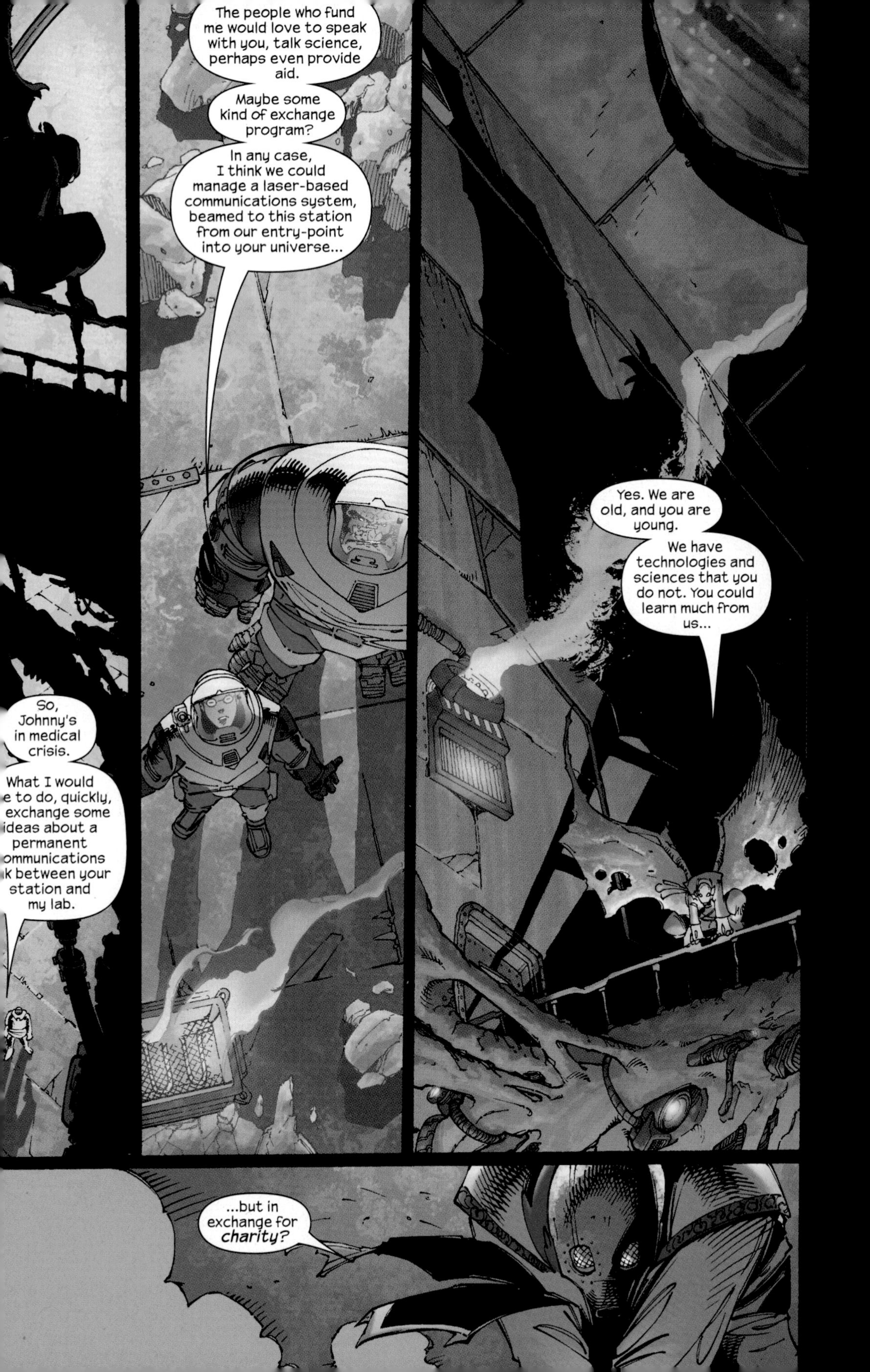

The people who fund me would love to speak with you, talk science, perhaps even provide aid.
Maybe some kind of exchange program?
In any case, I think we could manage a laser-based communications system, beamed to this station from our entry-point into your universe...
Yes. We are old, and you are young.
We have technologies and sciences that you do not. You could learn much from us...
So, Johnny's in medical crisis.
What I would e to do, quickly, exchange some ideas about a permanent ommunications k between your station and my lab.
...but in exchange for *charity?*

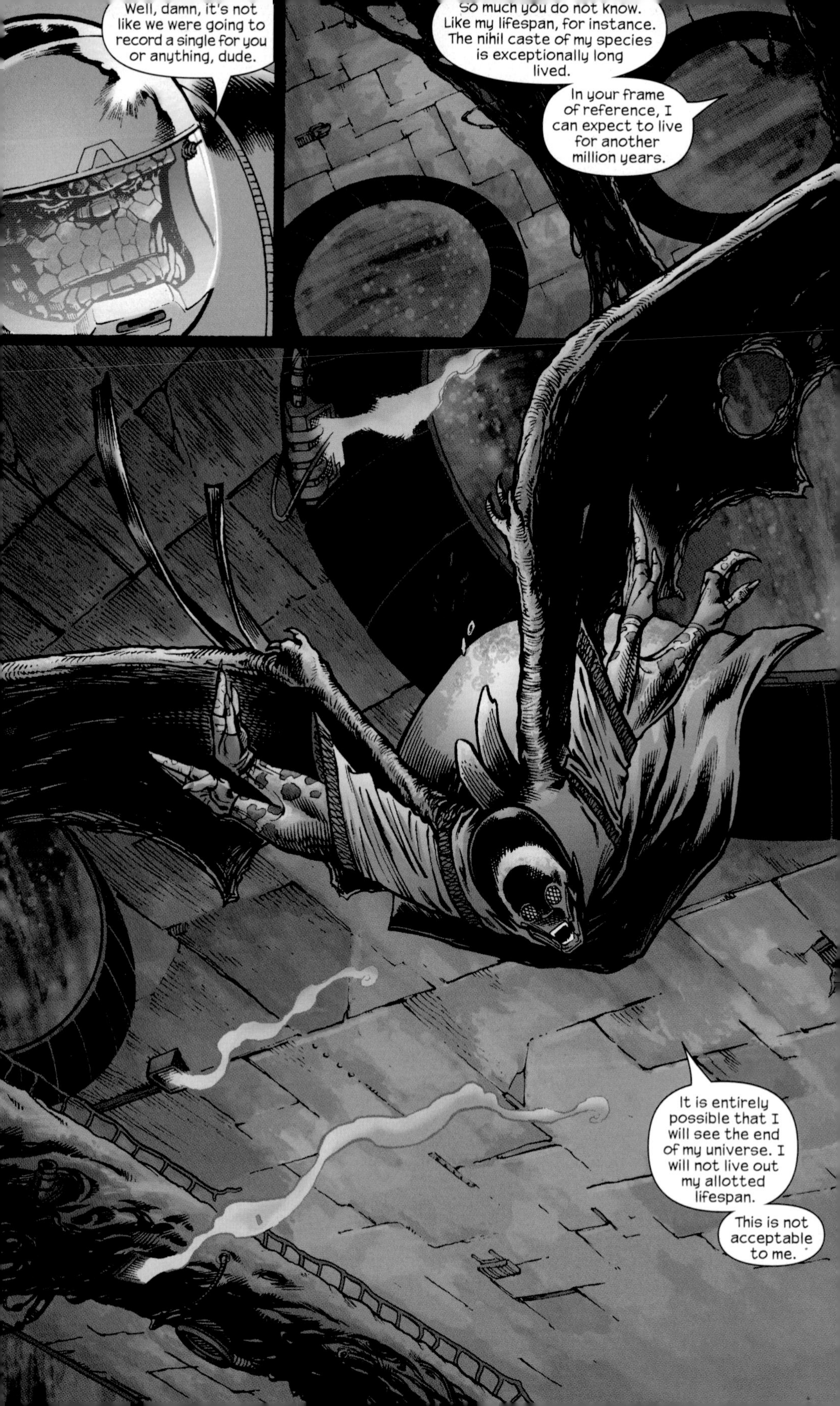
Well, damn, it's not like we were going to record a single for you or anything, dude.
So much you do not know. Like my lifespan, for instance. The nihil caste of my species is exceptionally long lived.
In your frame of reference, I can expect to live for another million years.
It is entirely possible that I will see the end of my universe. I will not live out my allotted lifespan.
This is not acceptable to me.

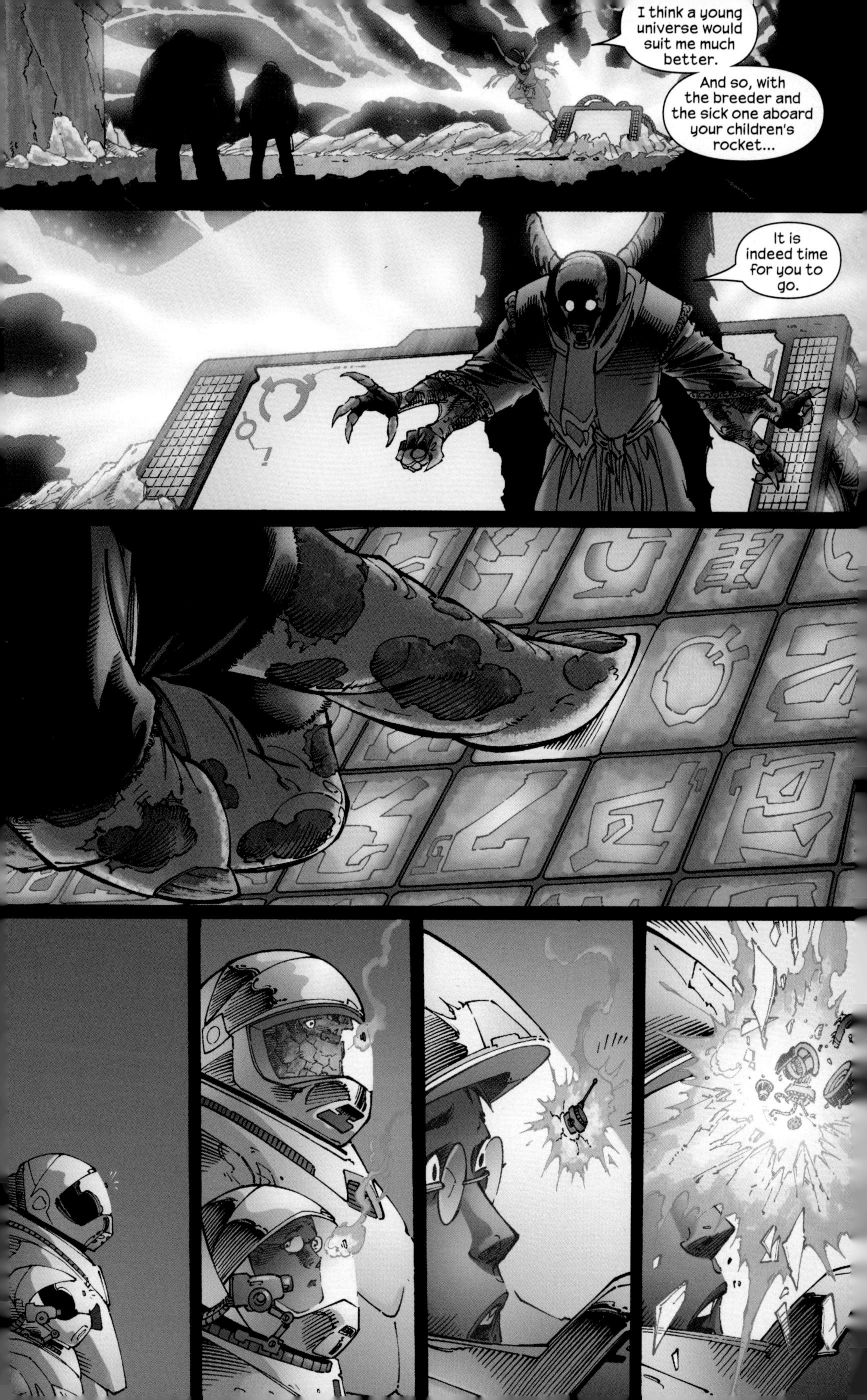
I think a young universe would suit me much better.
And so, with the breeder and the sick one aboard your children's rocket...
It is indeed time for you to go.

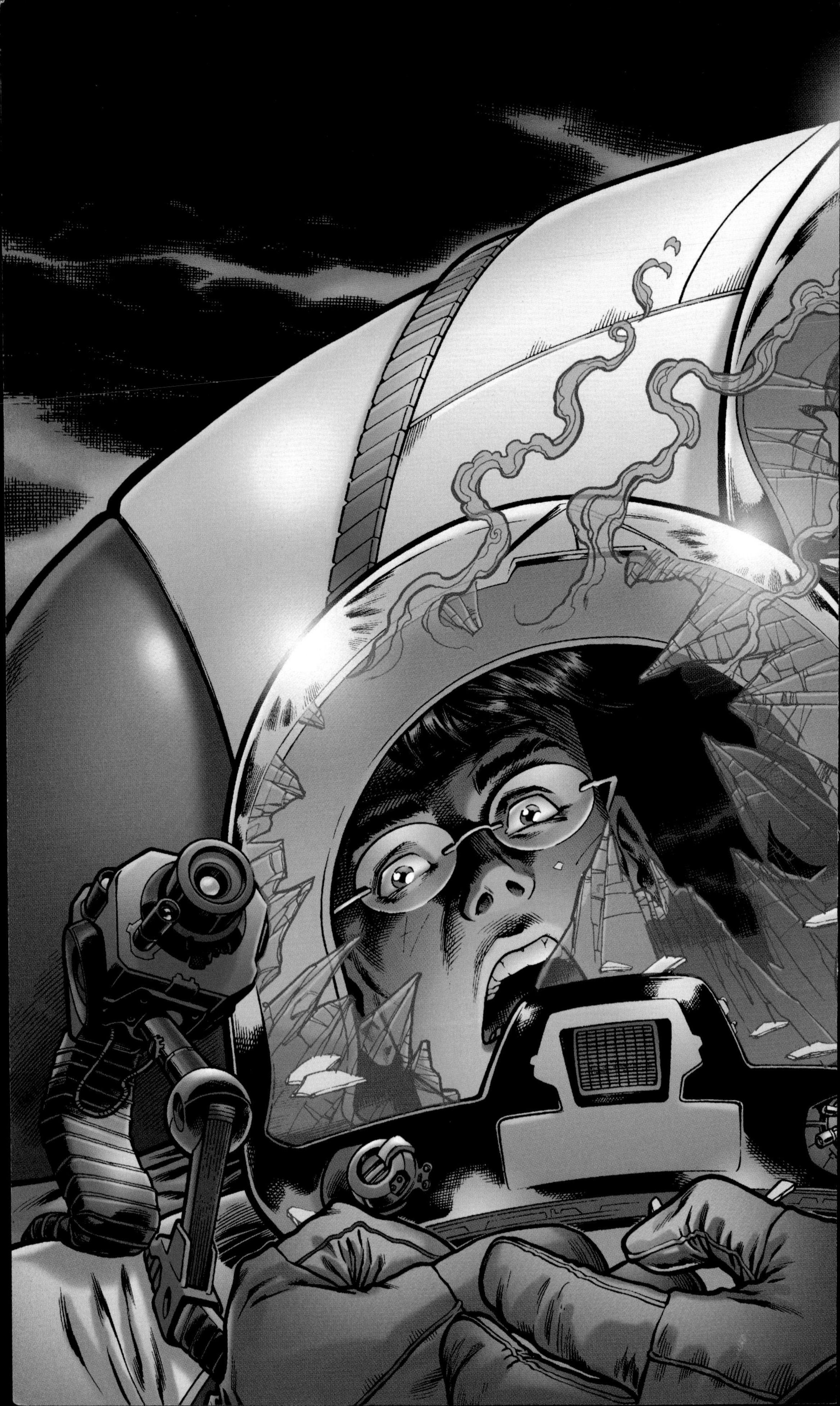

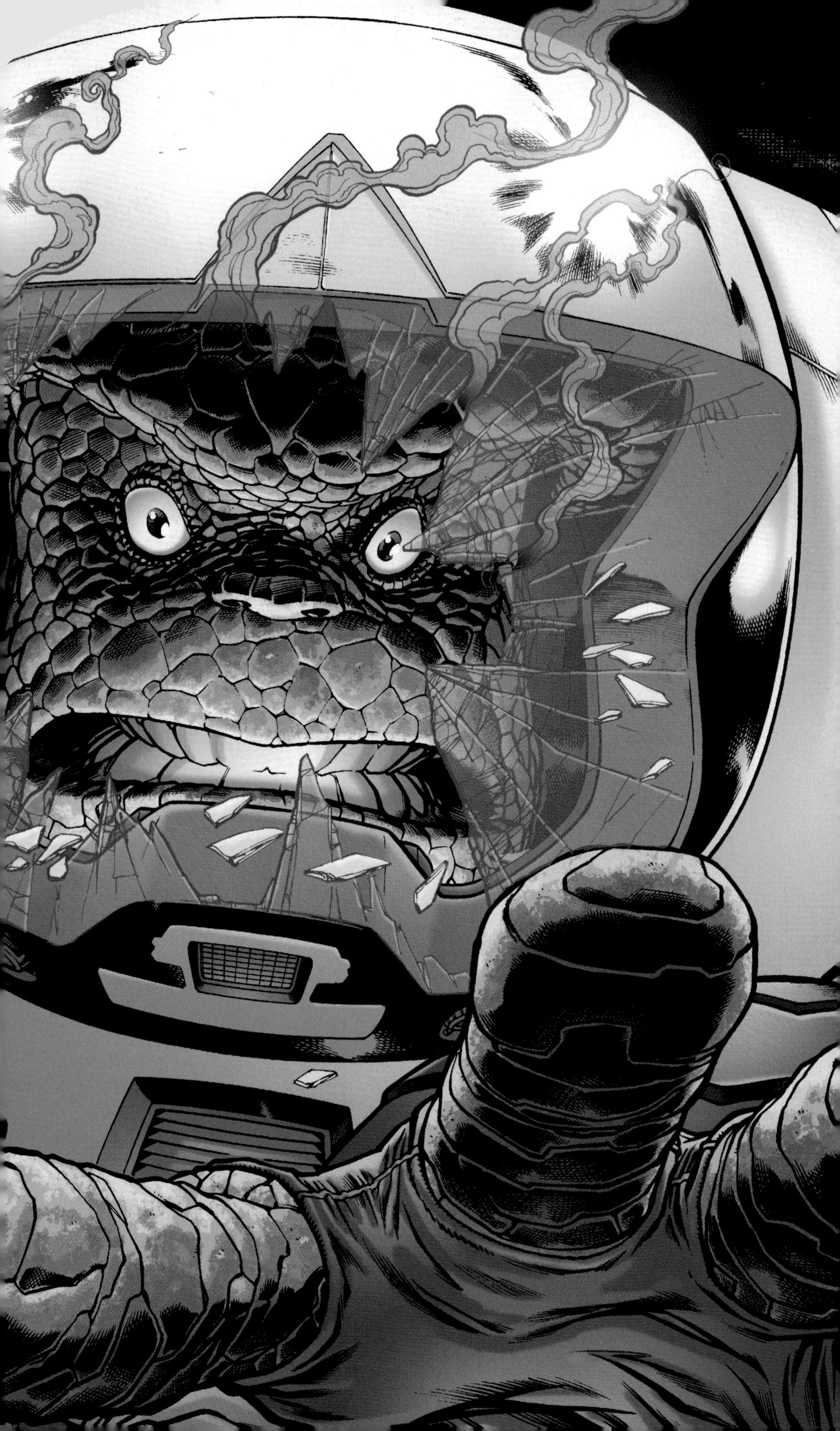

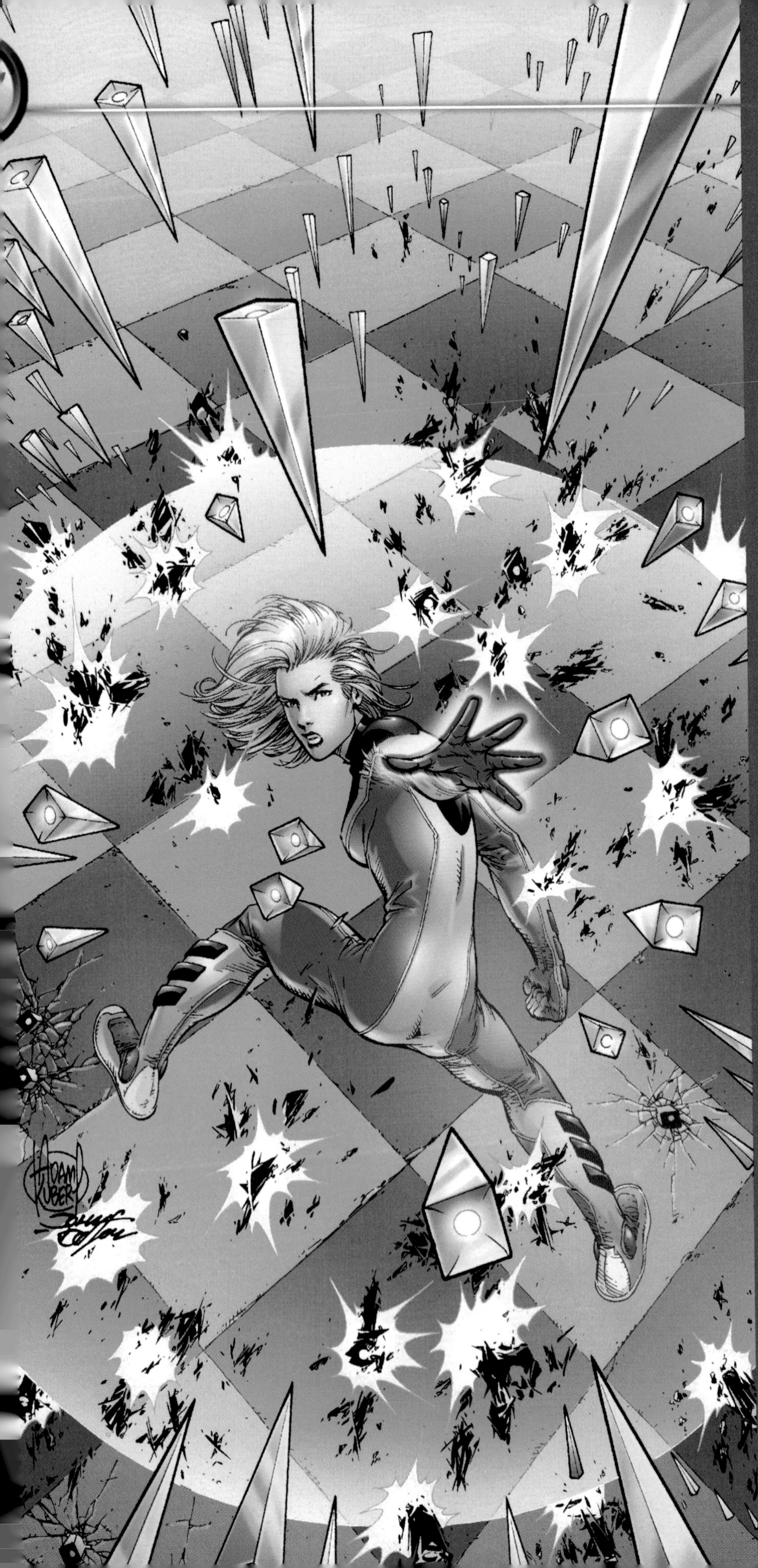
ADAM KUBERT

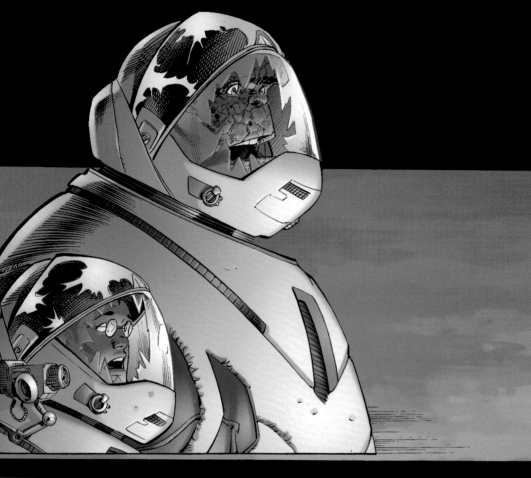

N-ZONE FIVE of SIX

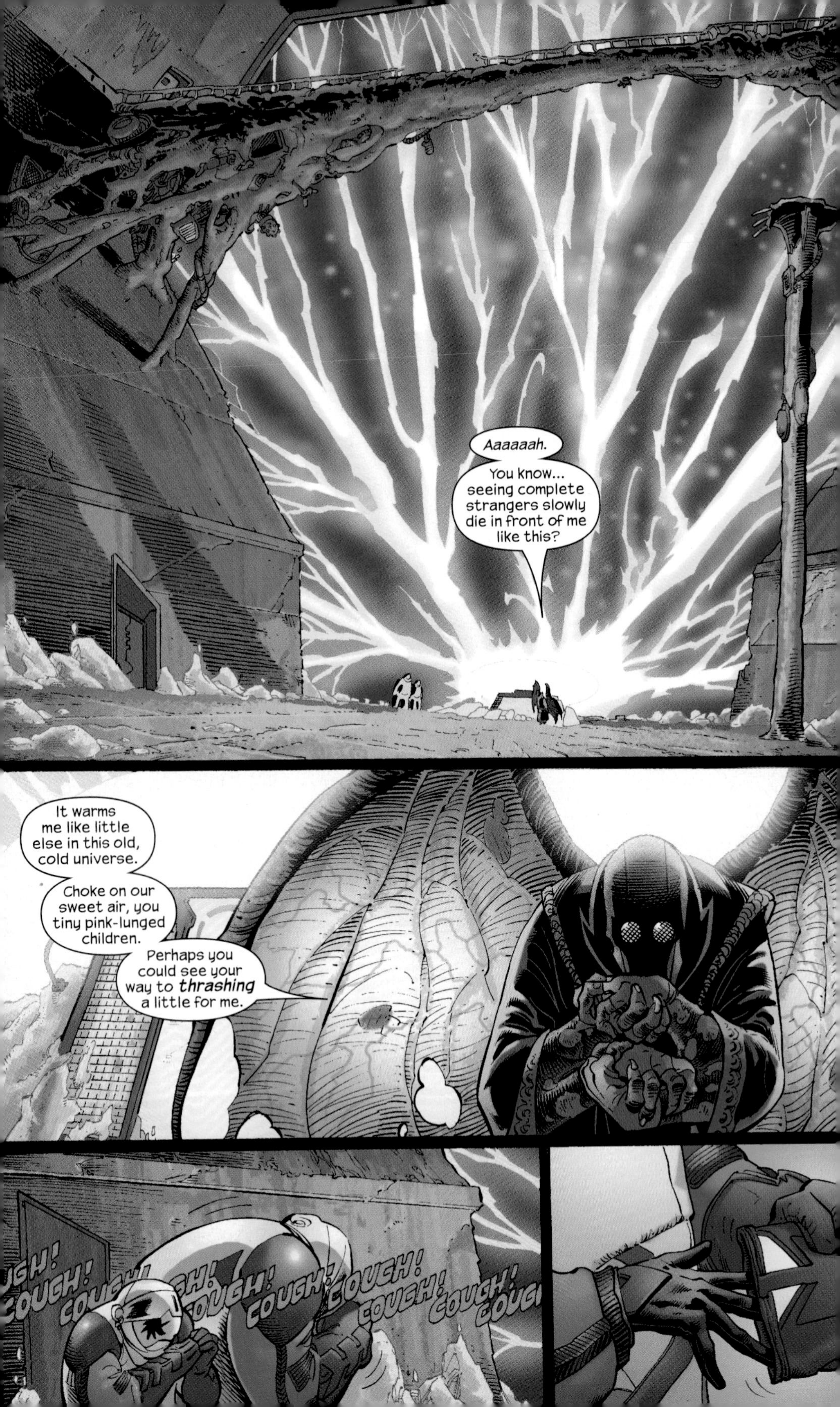
Aaaaaah.
You know... seeing complete strangers slowly die in front of me like this?
It warms me like little else in this old, cold universe.
Choke on our sweet air, you tiny pink-lunged children.
Perhaps you could see your way to *thrashing* a little for me.
COUGH! COUGH! COUGH! COUGH! COUGH! COUGH! COUGH!

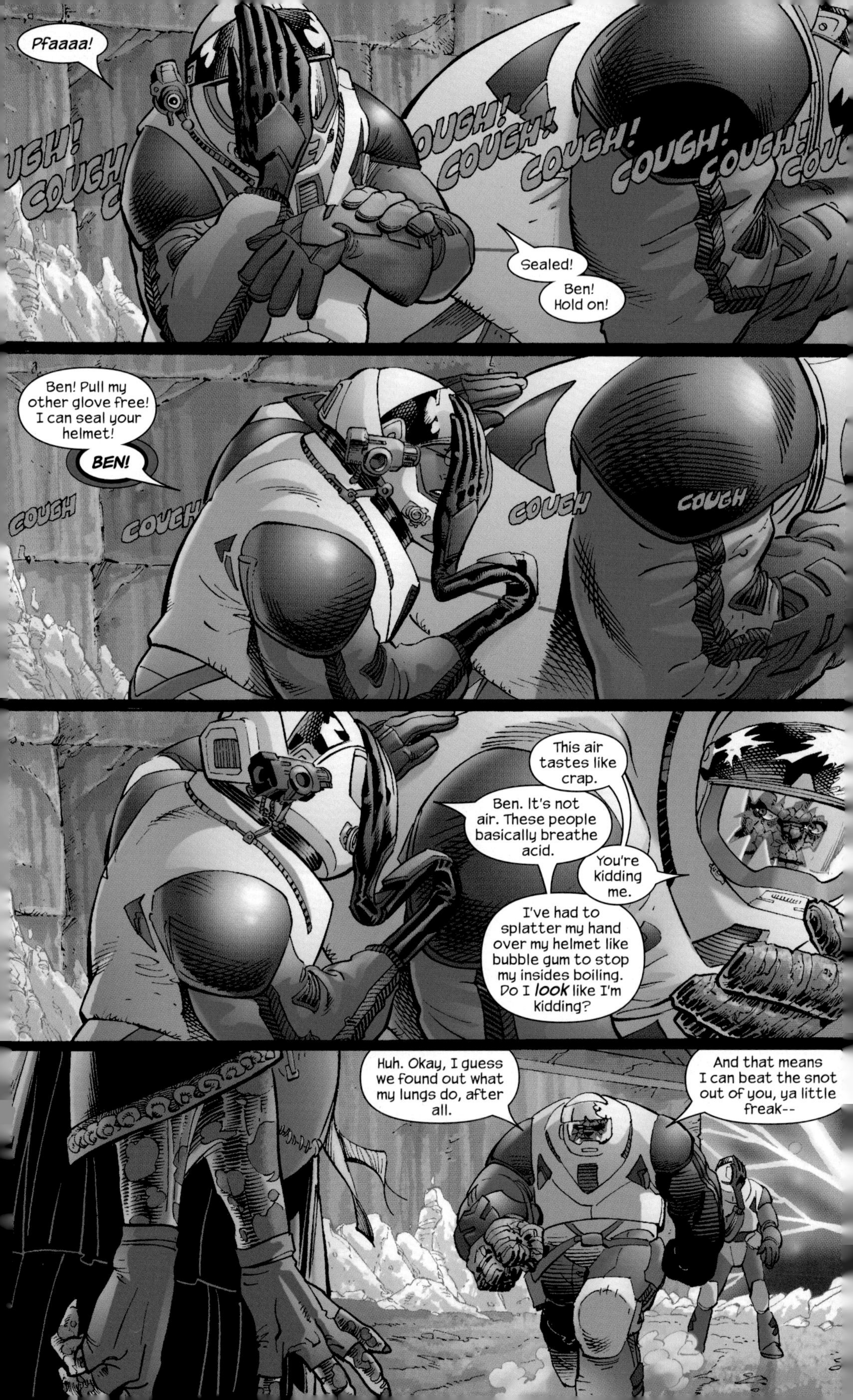
Pfaaaa!
COUGH! COUGH!
COUGH! COUGH!
COUGH! COUGH!
COUGH! COUGH!
Sealed!
Ben! Hold on!
Ben! Pull my other glove free! I can seal your helmet!
BEN!
COUGH
COUGH
COUGH
COUGH
This air tastes like crap.
Ben. It's not air. These people basically breathe acid.
You're kidding me.
I've had to splatter my hand over my helmet like bubble gum to stop my insides boiling. Do I *look* like I'm kidding?
Huh. Okay, I guess we found out what my lungs do, after all.
And that means I can beat the snot out of you, ya little freak--

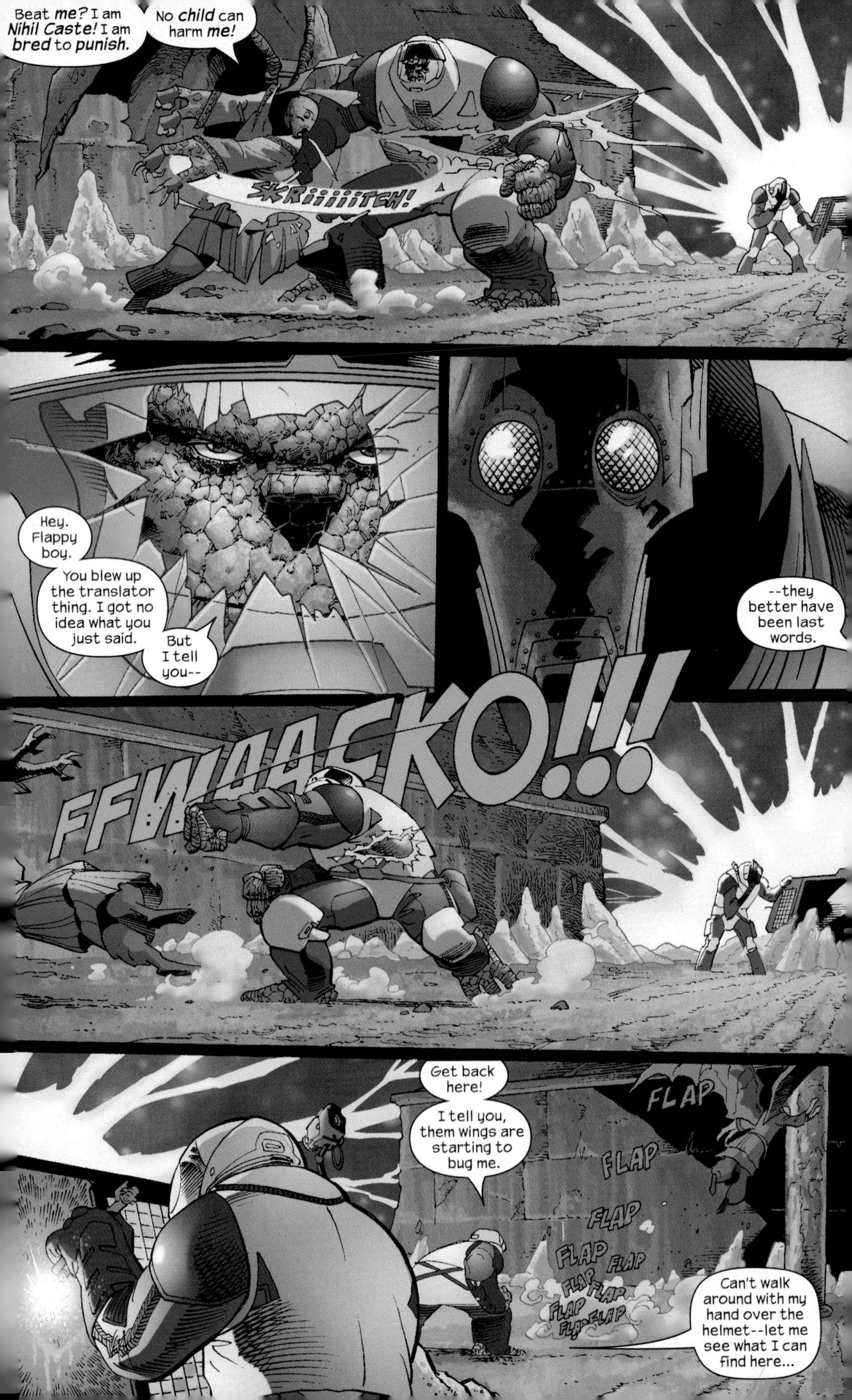
Beat me? I am Nihil Caste! I am bred to punish.
No child can harm me!
SKRIIIIITCH!
Hey. Flappy boy.
You blew up the translator thing. I got no idea what you just said.
But I tell you--
--they better have been last words.
FFWAACKO!!!
Get back here!
I tell you, them wings are starting to bug me.
FLAP
FLAP
FLAP
FLAP FLAP
FLAP FLAP
FLAP FLAP
Can't walk around with my hand over the helmet--let me see what I can find here...

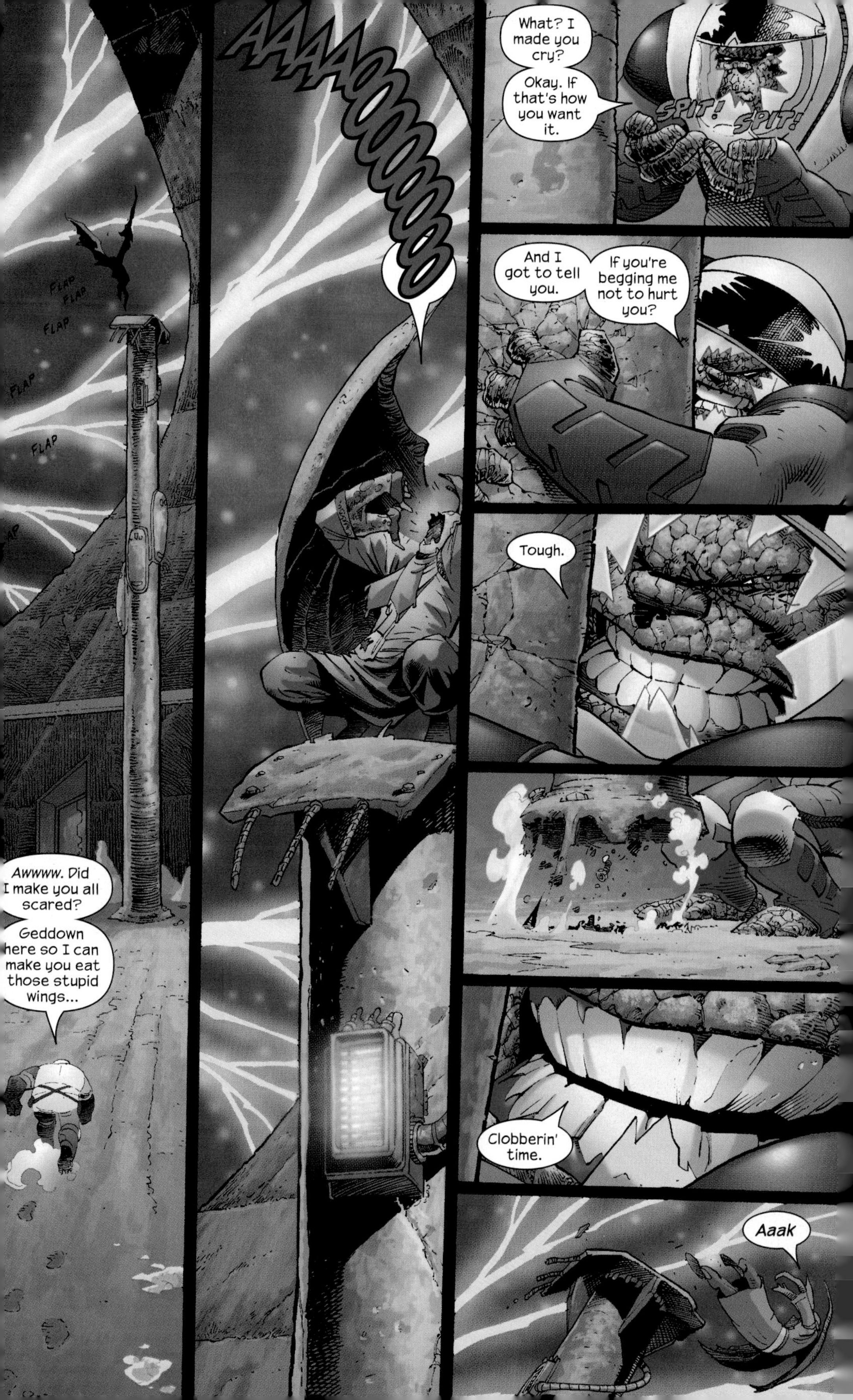

FLAP
FLAP
FLAP
FLAP
FLAP
Awwww. Did I make you all scared?
Geddown here so I can make you eat those stupid wings...
AAAAOOOOOOOOO
What? I made you cry?
Okay. If that's how you want it.
SPIT! SPIT!
And I got to tell you.
If you're begging me not to hurt you?
Tough.
Clobberin' time.
Aaak

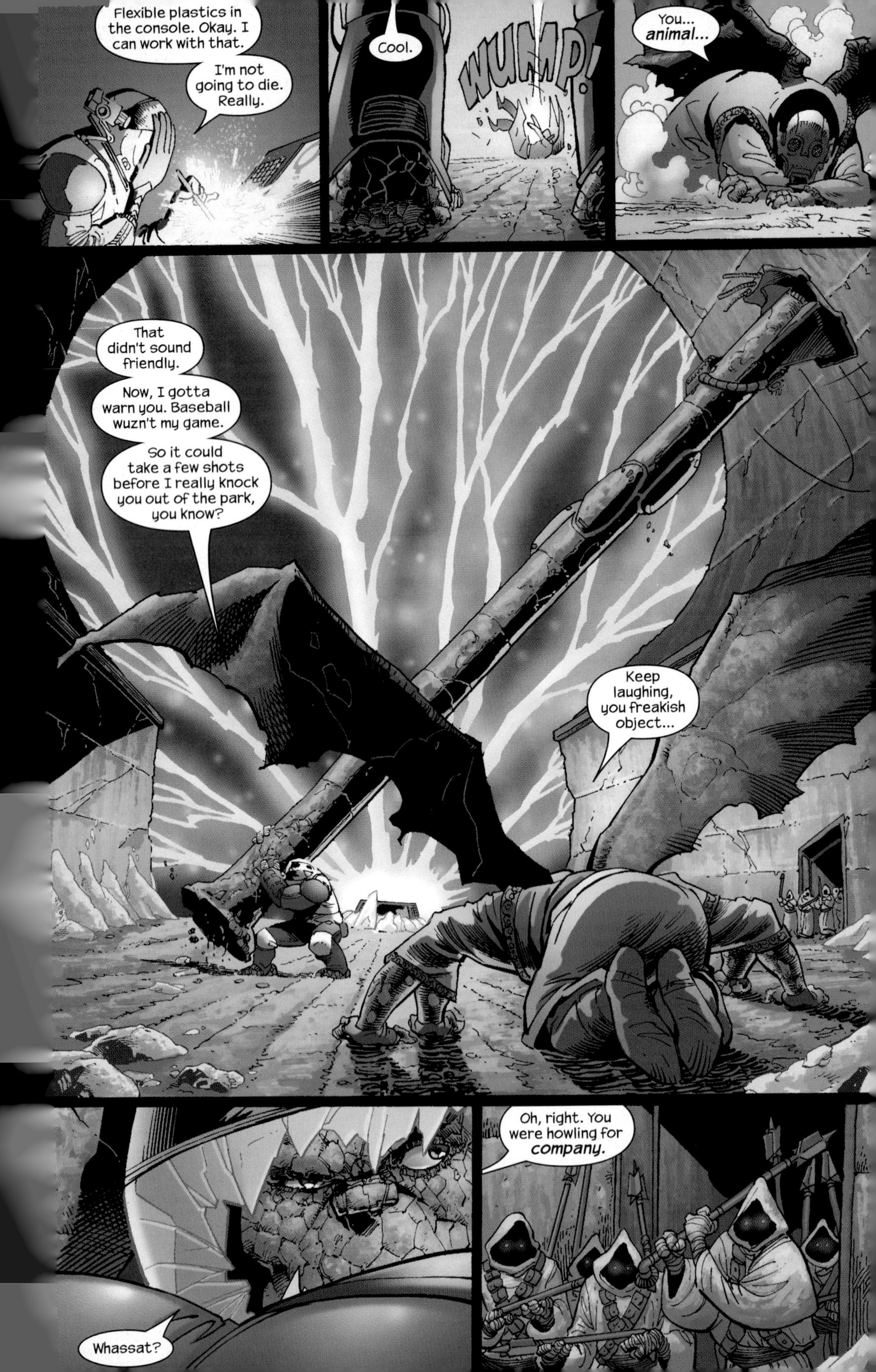
Flexible plastics in the console. Okay. I can work with that.
I'm not going to die. Really.
Cool.
WUMP!
You... animal...
That didn't sound friendly.
Now, I gotta warn you. Baseball wuzn't my game.
So it could take a few shots before I really knock you out of the park, you know?
Keep laughing, you freakish object...
Whassat?
Oh, right. You were howling for company.

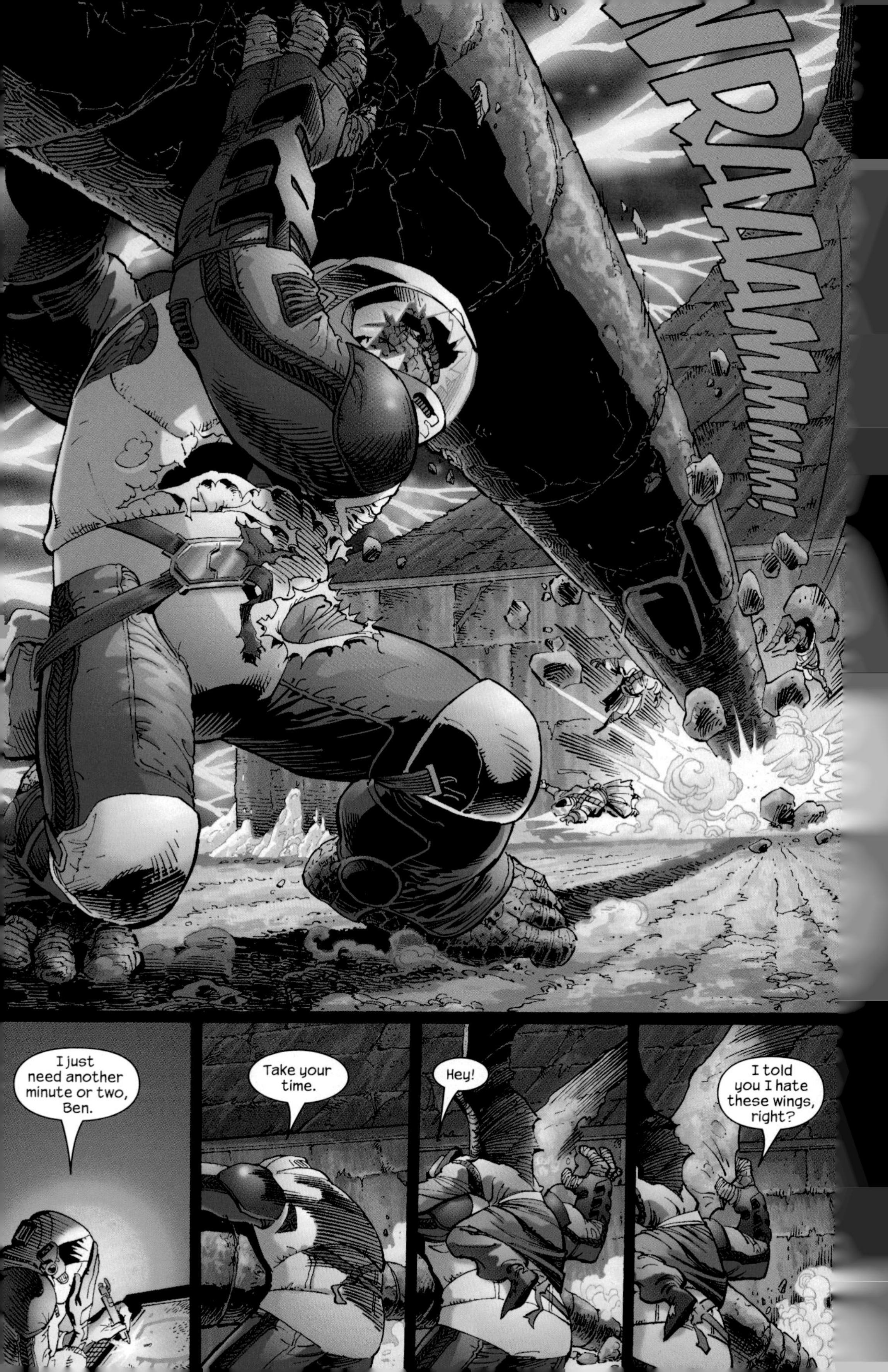
VRAAMMMM!
I just need another minute or two, Ben.
Take your time.
Hey!
I told you I hate these wings, right?

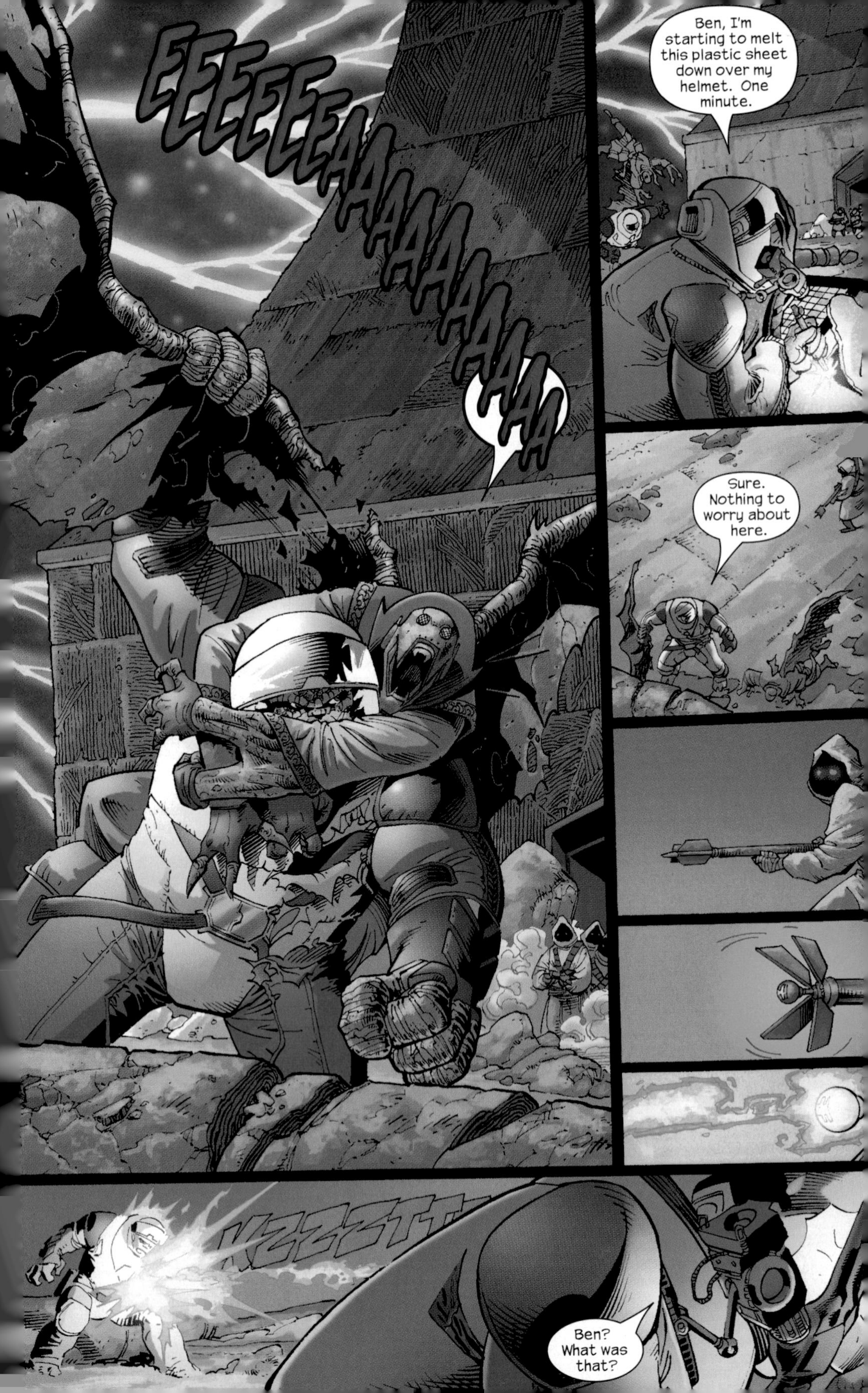
EEEEEEAAAAAAAAAAAAAAA
Ben, I'm starting to melt this plastic sheet down over my helmet. One minute.
Sure. Nothing to worry about here.
KZZZTT
Ben? What was that?

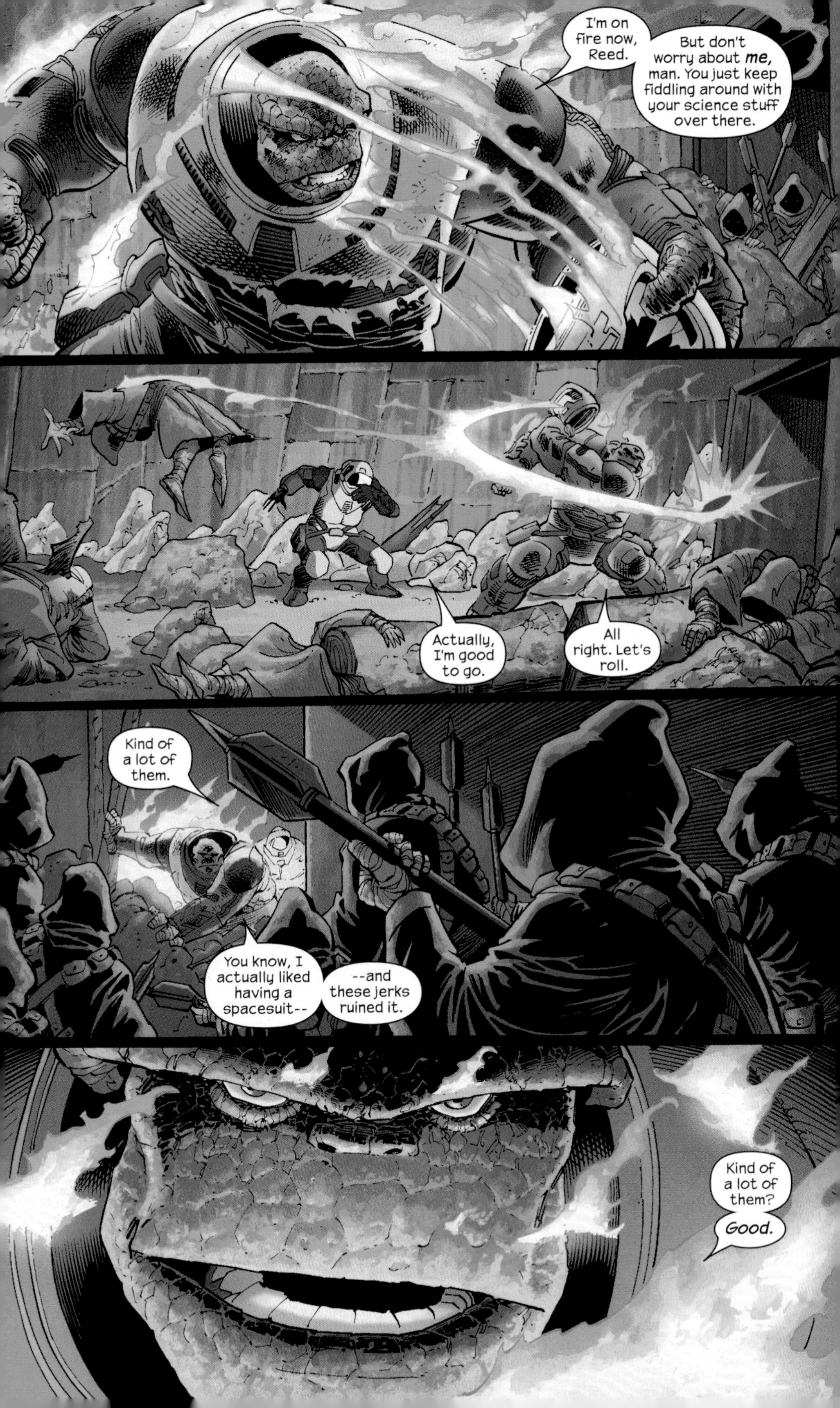
I'm on fire now, Reed.
But don't worry about *me,* man. You just keep fiddling around with your science stuff over there.
Actually, I'm good to go.
All right. Let's roll.
Kind of a lot of them.
You know, I actually liked having a spacesuit--
--and these jerks ruined it.
Kind of a lot of them? *Good.*

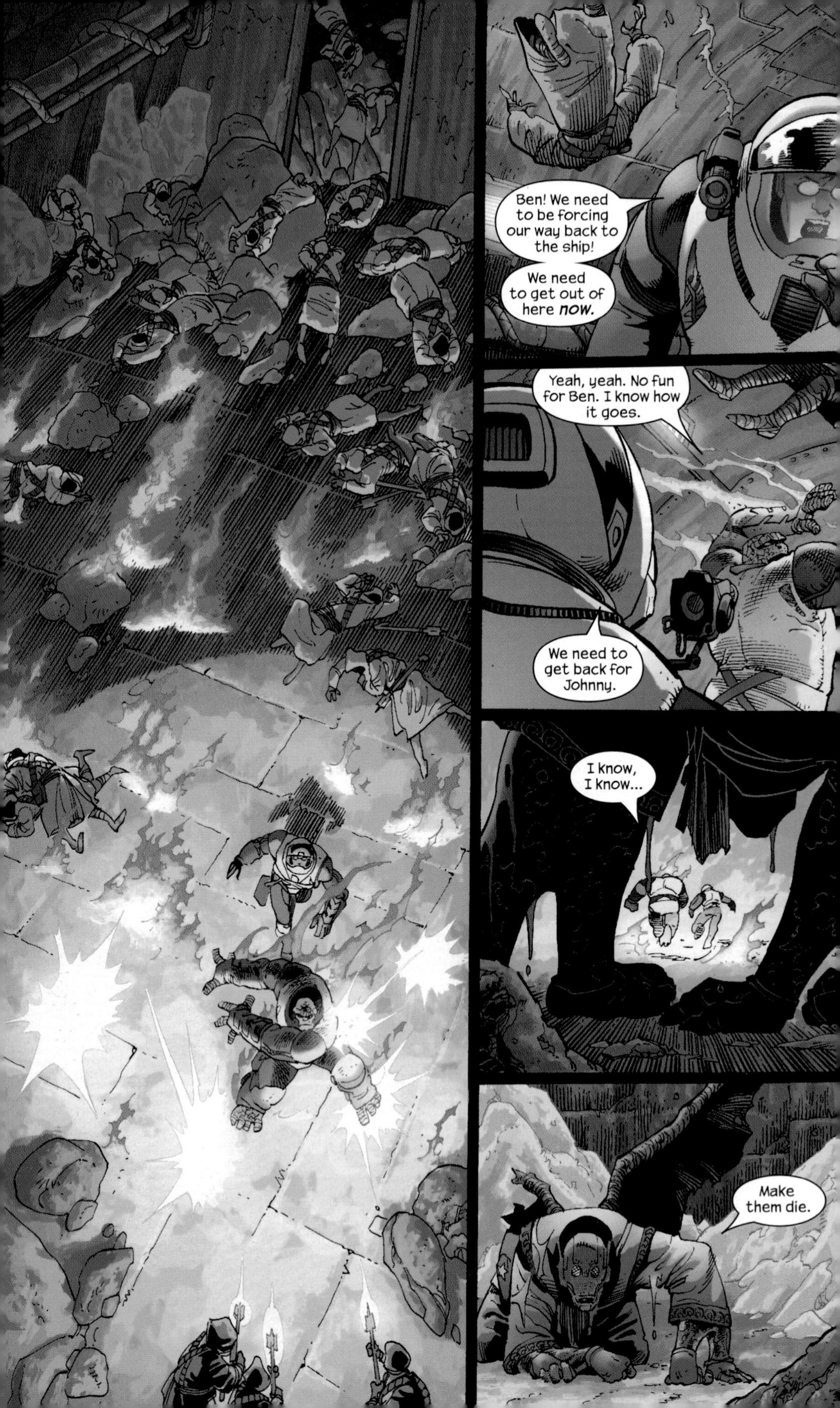
Ben! We need to be forcing our way back to the ship!
We need to get out of here *now.*
Yeah, yeah. No fun for Ben. I know how it goes.
We need to get back for Johnny.
I know, I know...
Make them die.

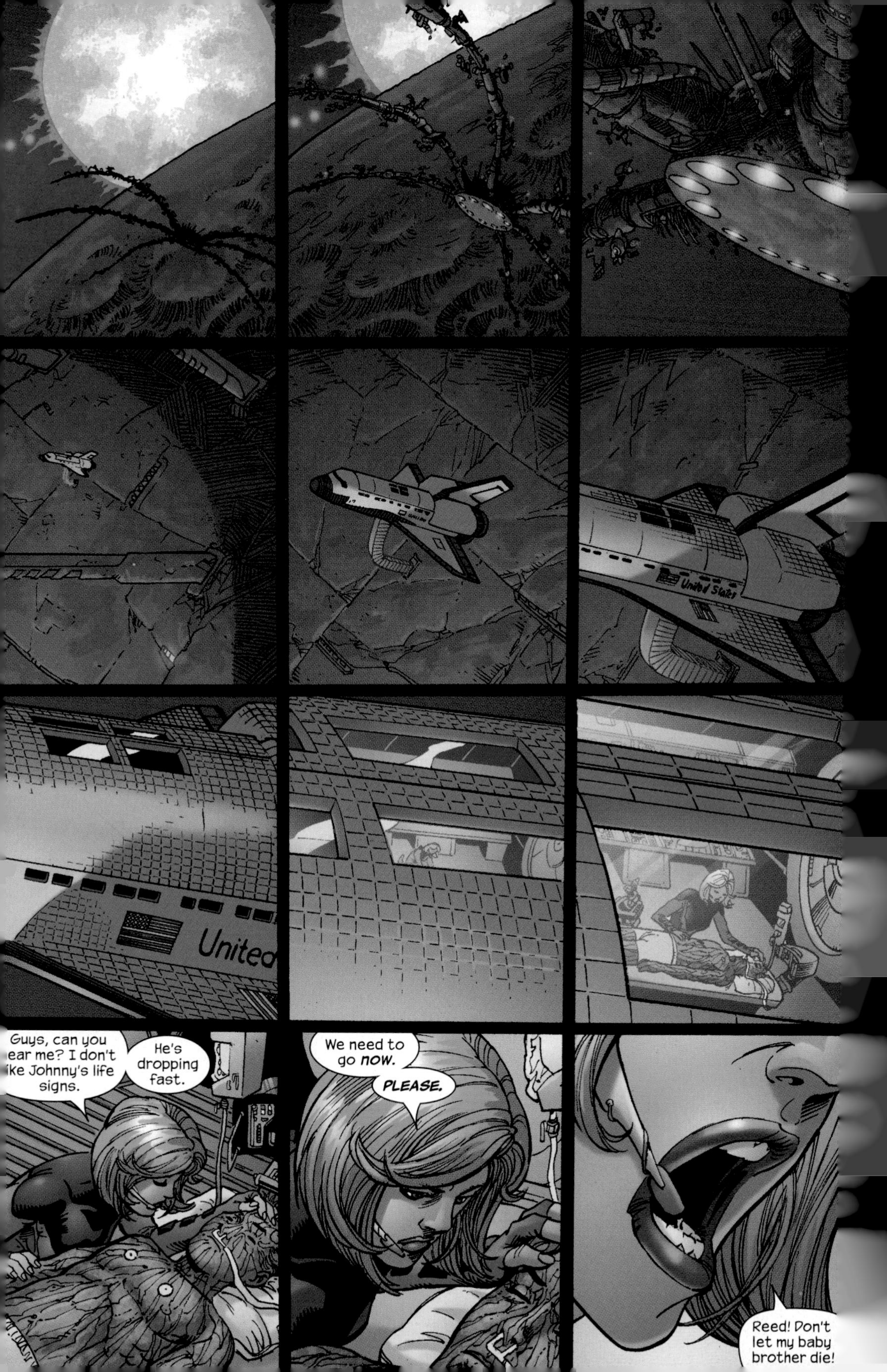
Guys, can you
ear me? I don't
ike Johnny's life
signs.
He's
dropping
fast.
We need to
go NOW.
PLEASE.
Reed! Don't
let my baby
brother die!

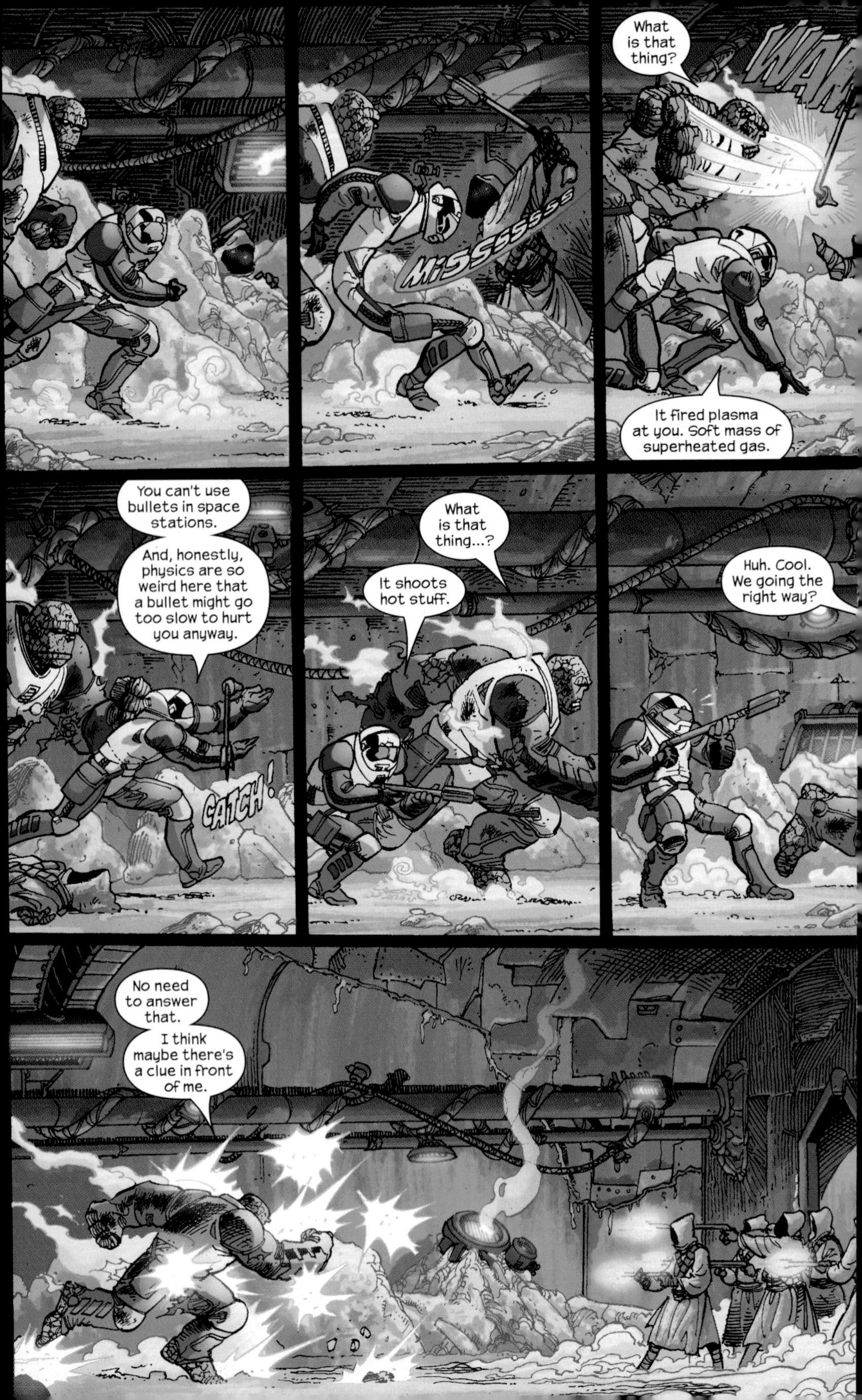
MISSSSSSSS
What is that thing?
WAM
It fired plasma at you. Soft mass of superheated gas.
You can't use bullets in space stations.
And, honestly, physics are so weird here that a bullet might go too slow to hurt you anyway.
CATCH!
What is that thing...?
It shoots hot stuff.
Huh. Cool. We going the right way?
No need to answer that.
I think maybe there's a clue in front of me.

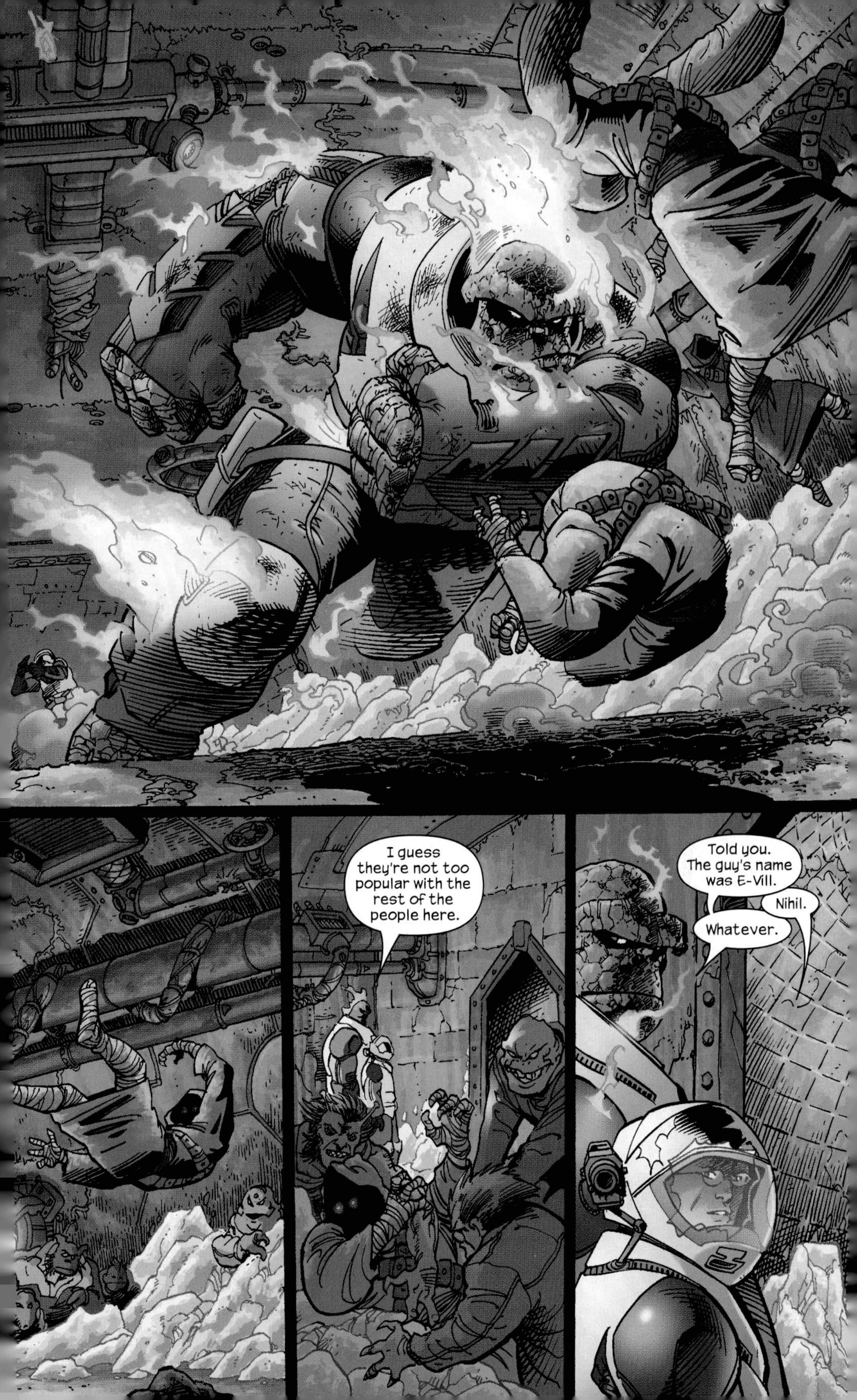
I guess they're not too popular with the rest of the people here.
Told you. The guy's name was E-Vill.
Nihil.
Whatever.

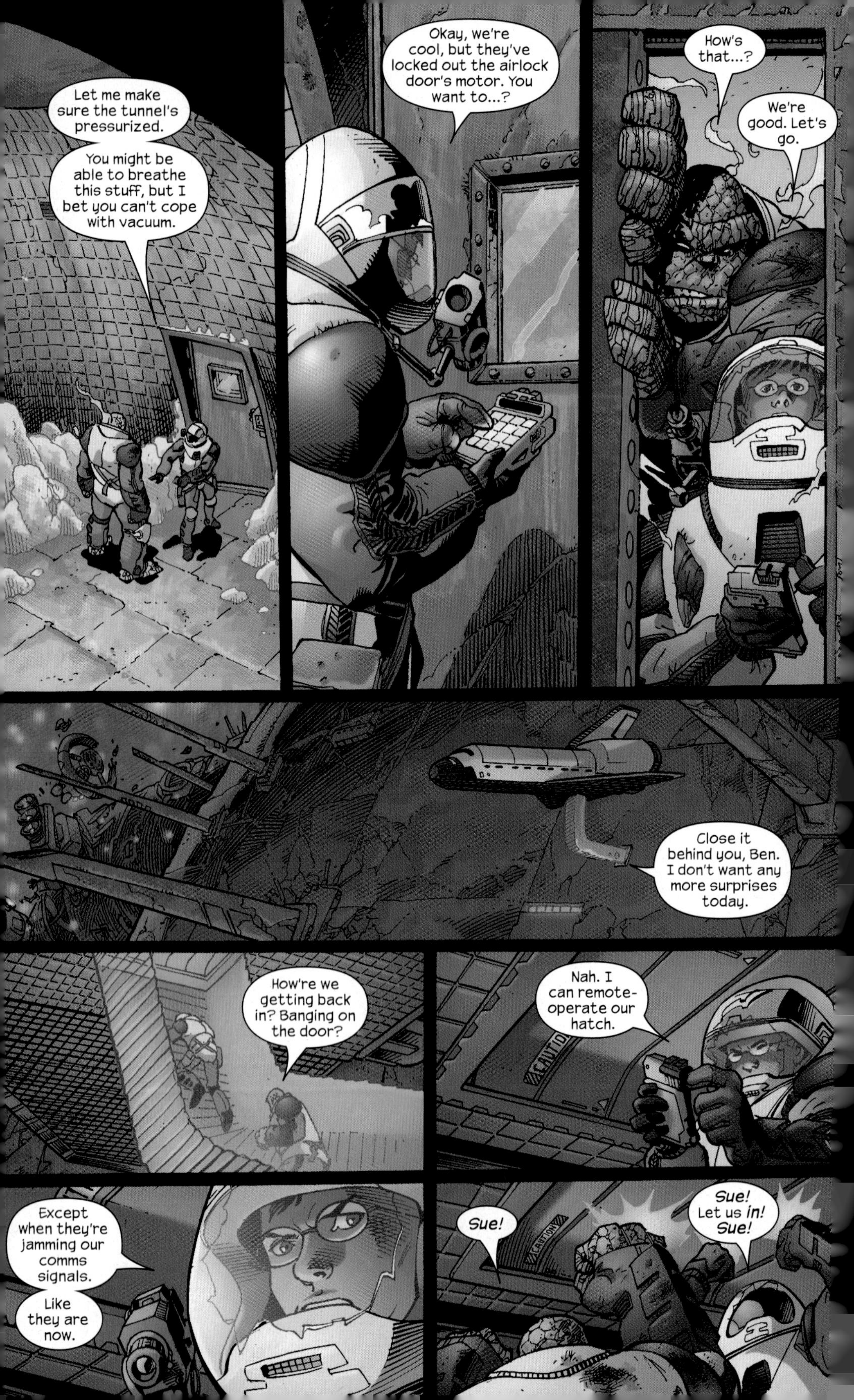
Let me make sure the tunnel's pressurized.
You might be able to breathe this stuff, but I bet you can't cope with vacuum.
Okay, we're cool, but they've locked out the airlock door's motor. You want to...?
How's that...?
We're good. Let's go.
Close it behind you, Ben. I don't want any more surprises today.
How're we getting back in? Banging on the door?
Nah. I can remote-operate our hatch.
Except when they're jamming our comms signals.
Like they are now.
Sue!
Sue! Let us in! Sue!

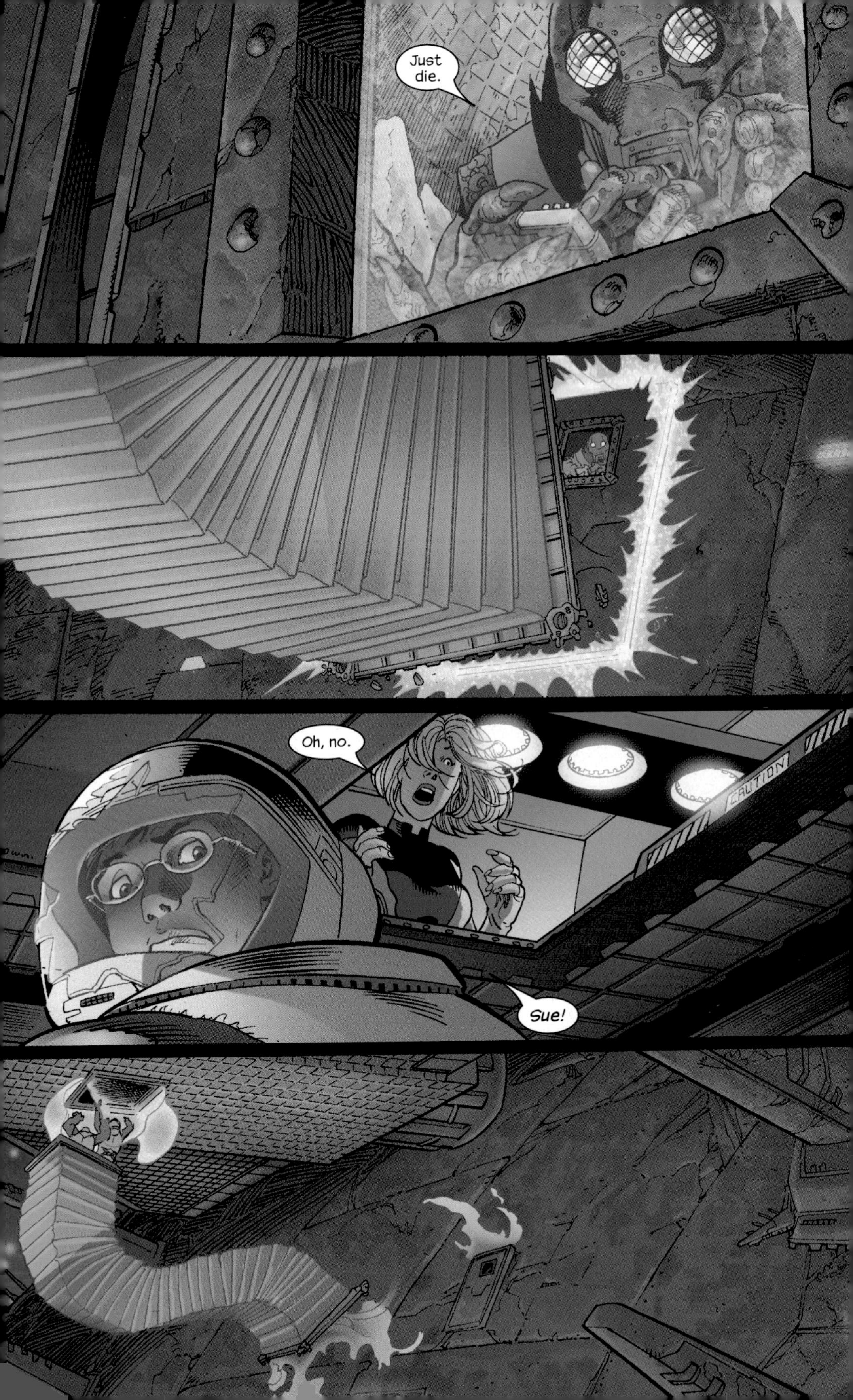
Just die.
Oh, no.
Sue!
CAUTION

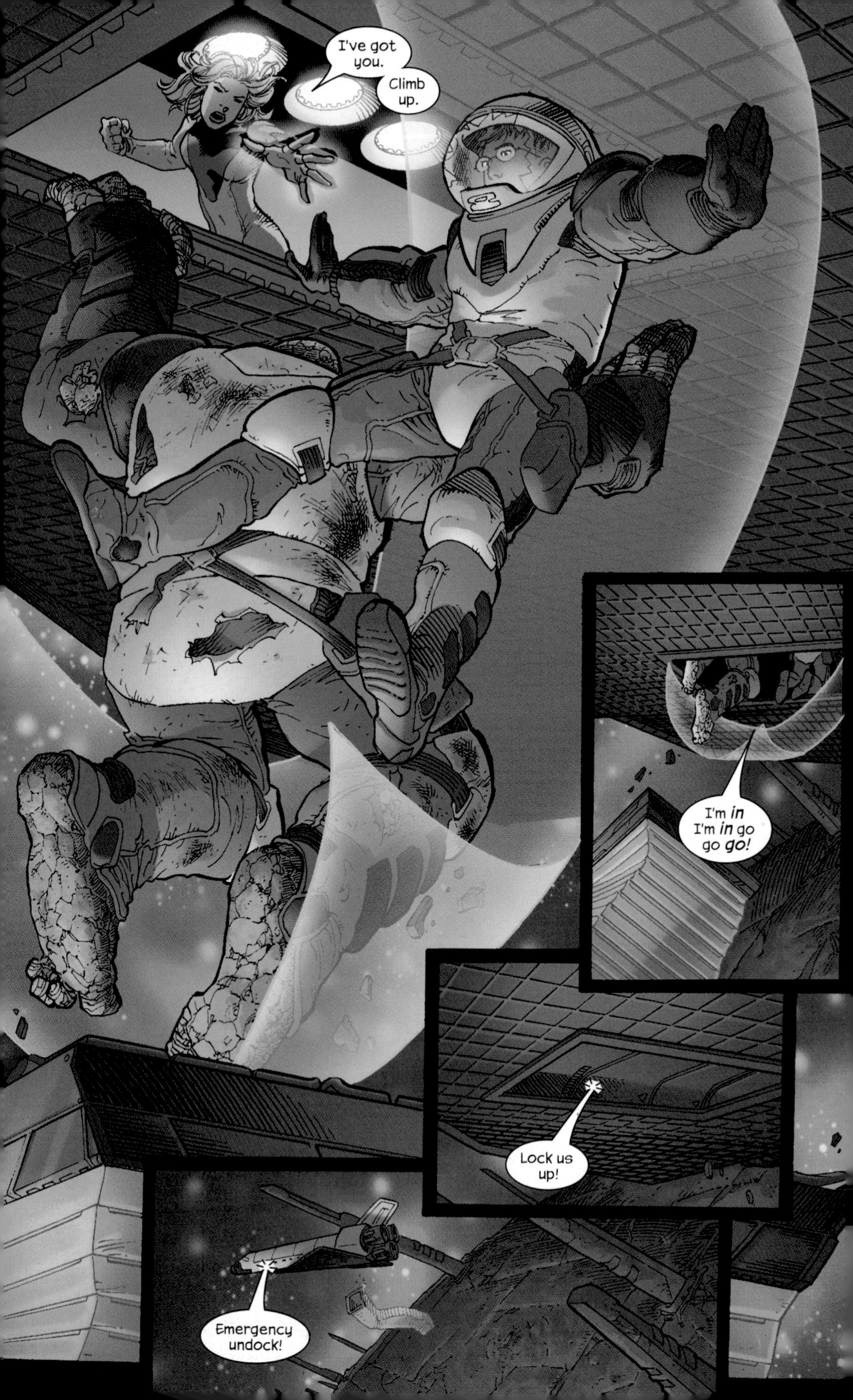
I've got you.
Climb up.
I'm *in* I'm *in* go go *go!*
Lock us up!
Emergency undock!

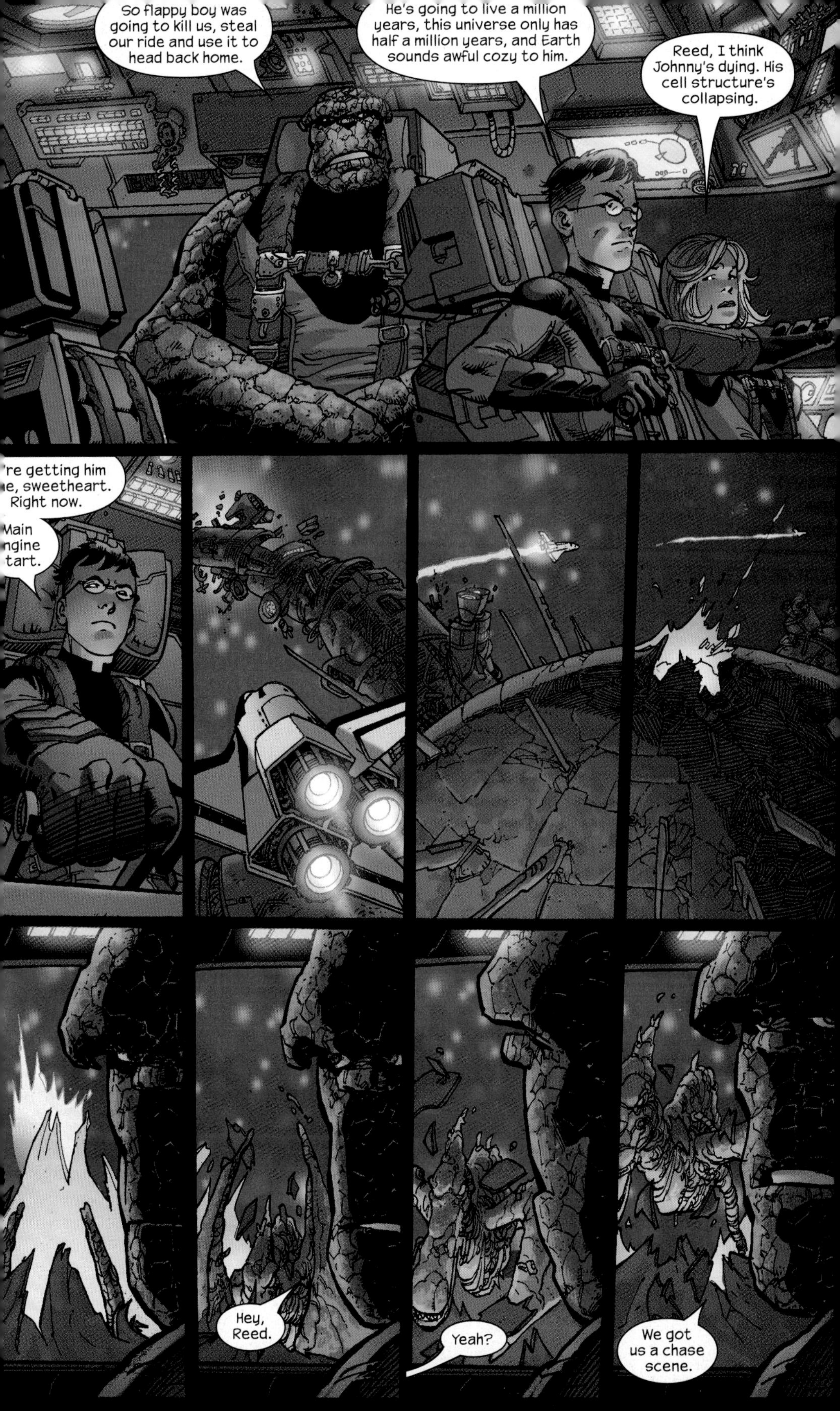
So flappy boy was going to kill us, steal our ride and use it to head back home.
He's going to live a million years, this universe only has half a million years, and Earth sounds awful cozy to him.
Reed, I think Johnny's dying. His cell structure's collapsing.
're getting him e, sweetheart. Right now.
Main ngine tart.
Hey, Reed.
Yeah?
We got us a chase scene.

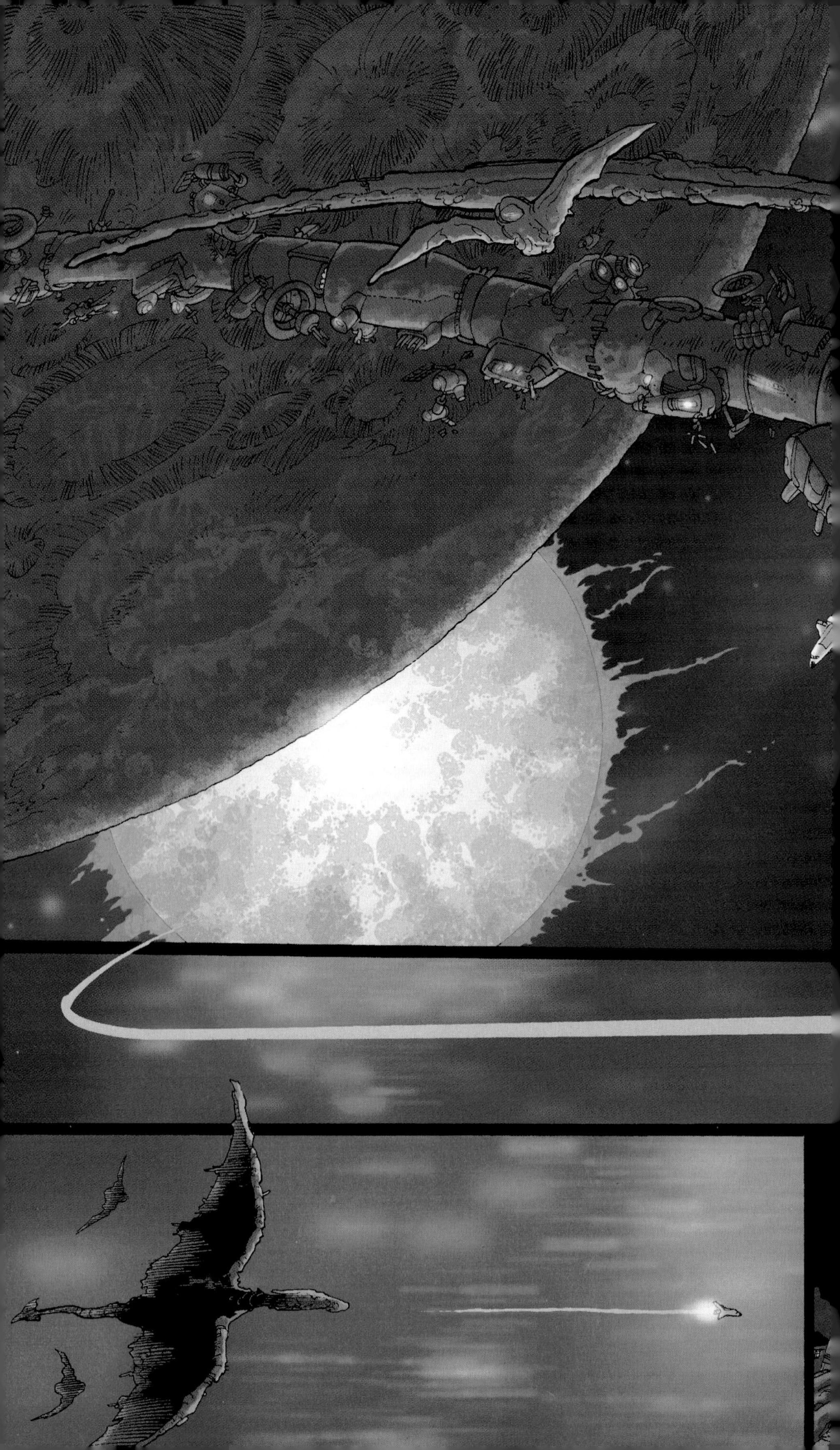

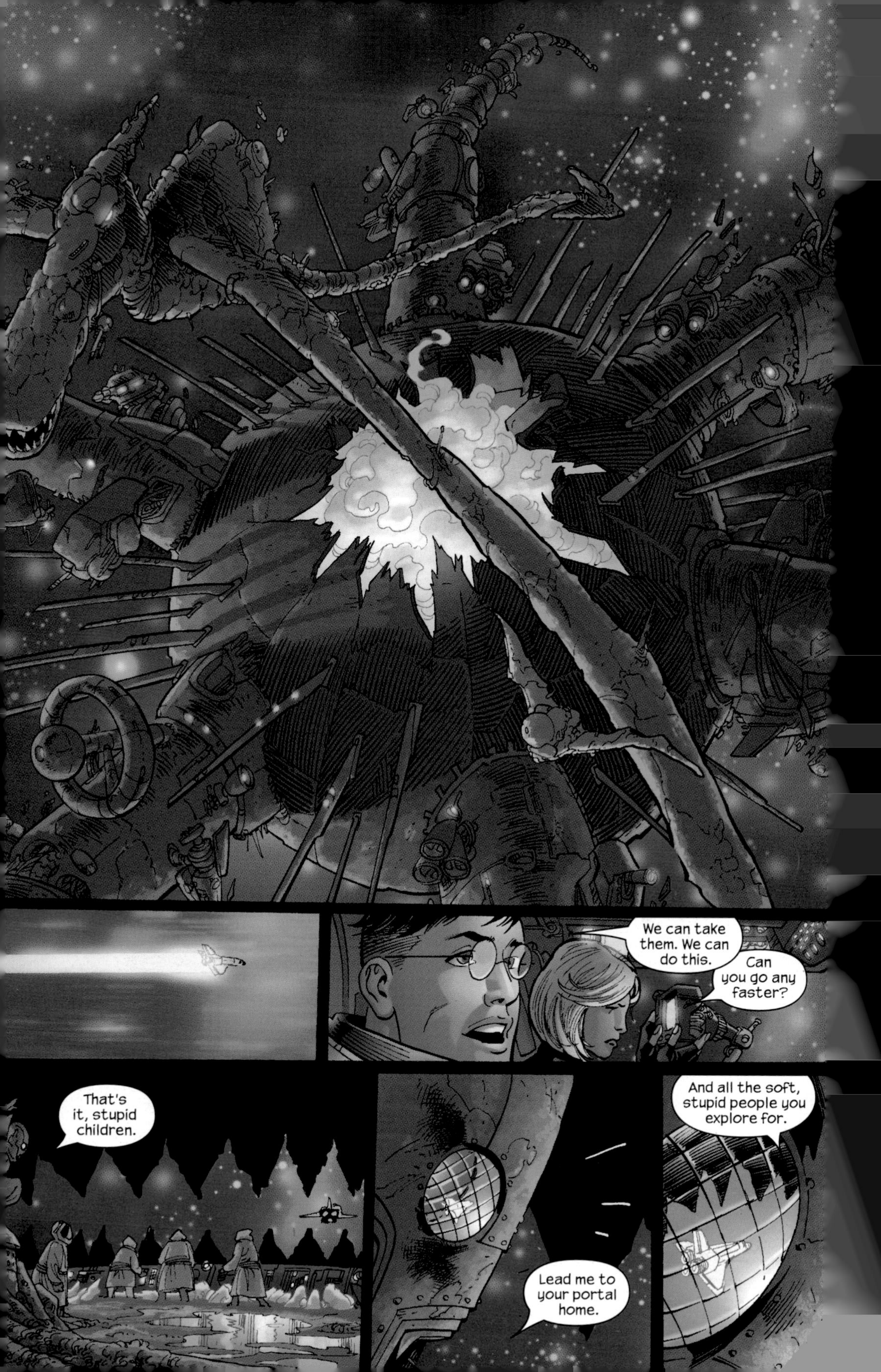
We can take them. We can do this.
Can you go any faster?
That's it, stupid children.
Lead me to your portal home.
And all the soft, stupid people you explore for.

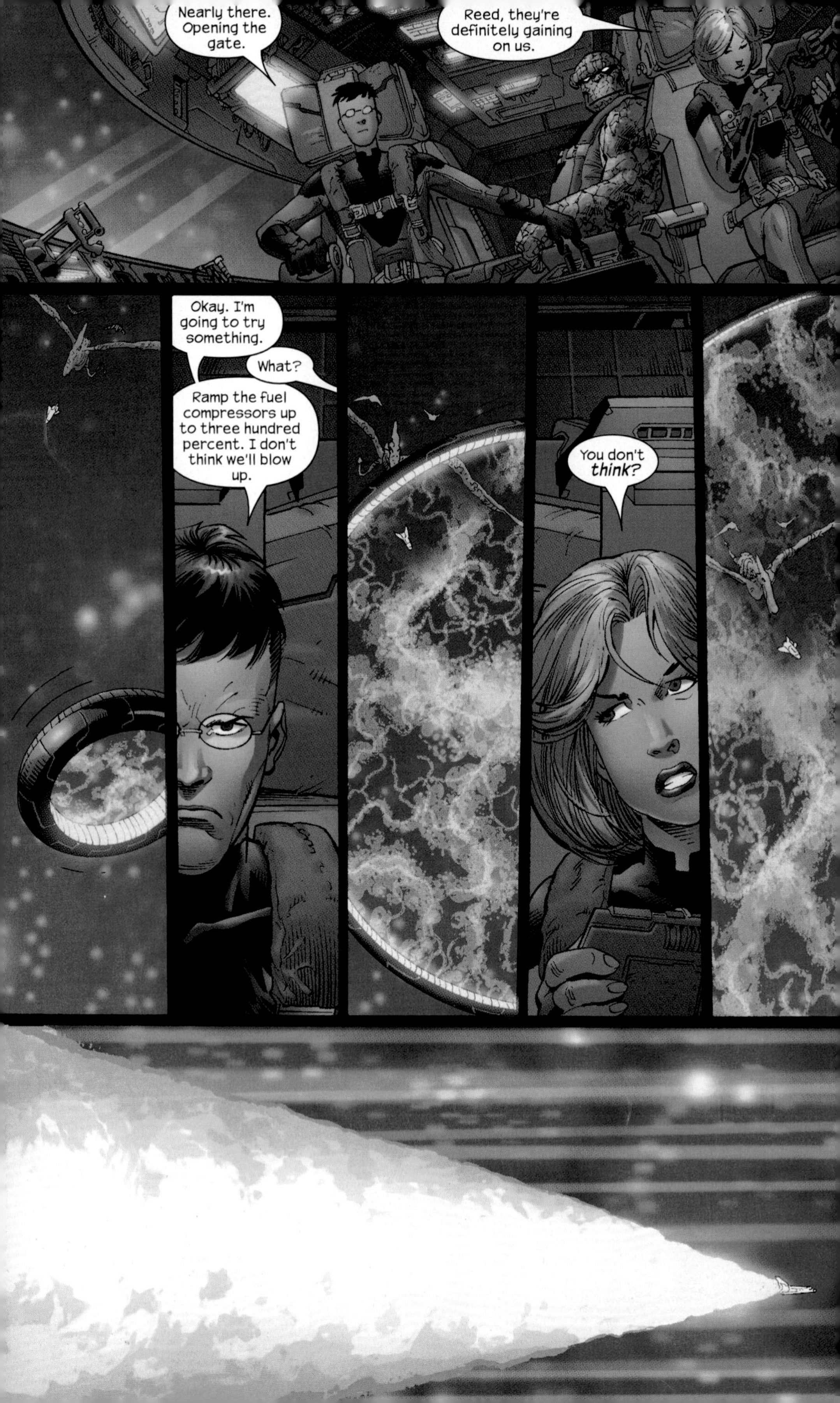
Nearly there. Opening the gate.
Reed, they're definitely gaining on us.
Okay. I'm going to try something.
What?
Ramp the fuel compressors up to three hundred percent. I don't think we'll blow up.
You don't *think*?

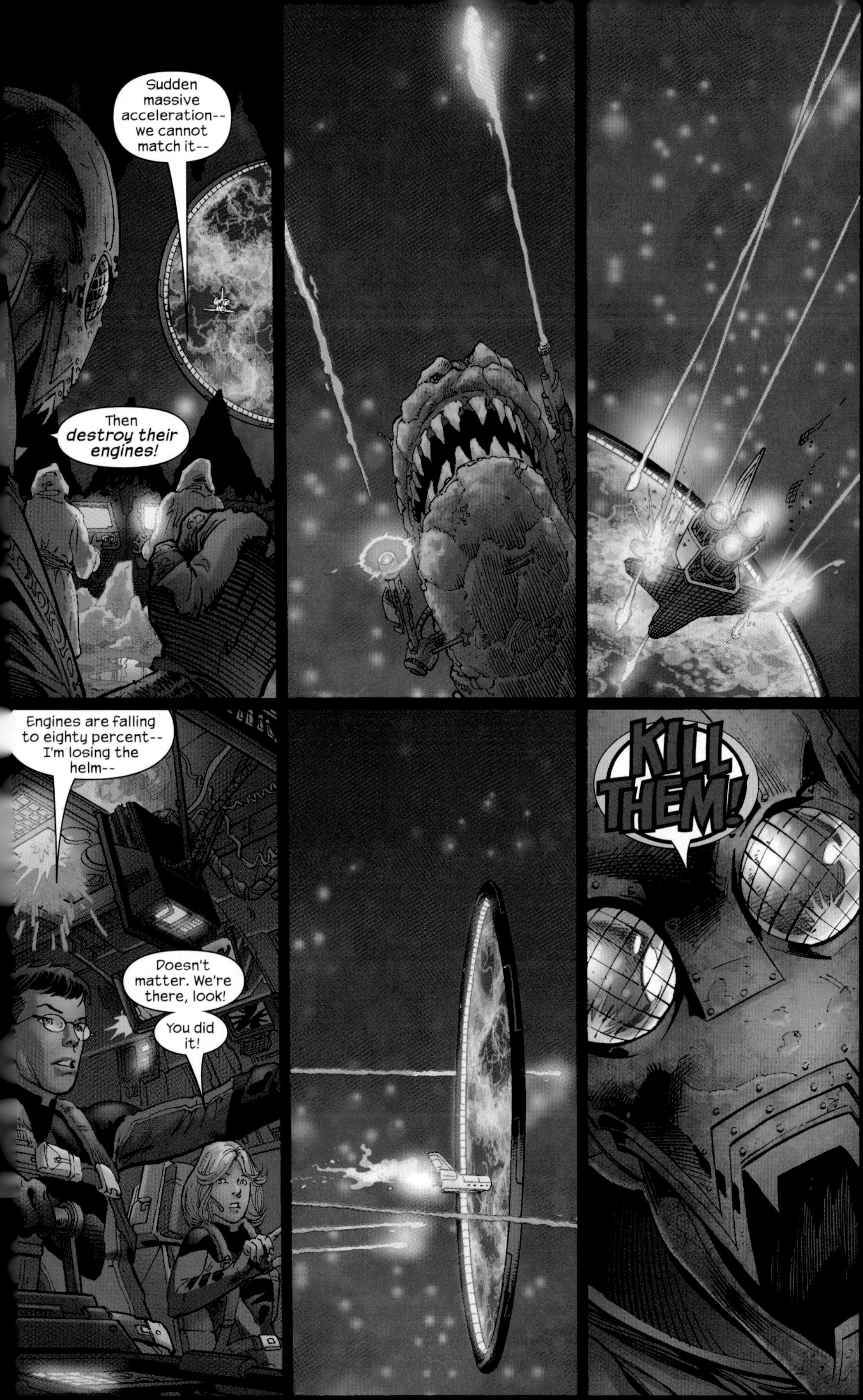
Sudden massive acceleration-- we cannot match it--
Then *destroy their engines!*
Engines are falling to eighty percent-- I'm losing the helm--
Doesn't matter. We're there, look!
You did it!
KILL THEM!

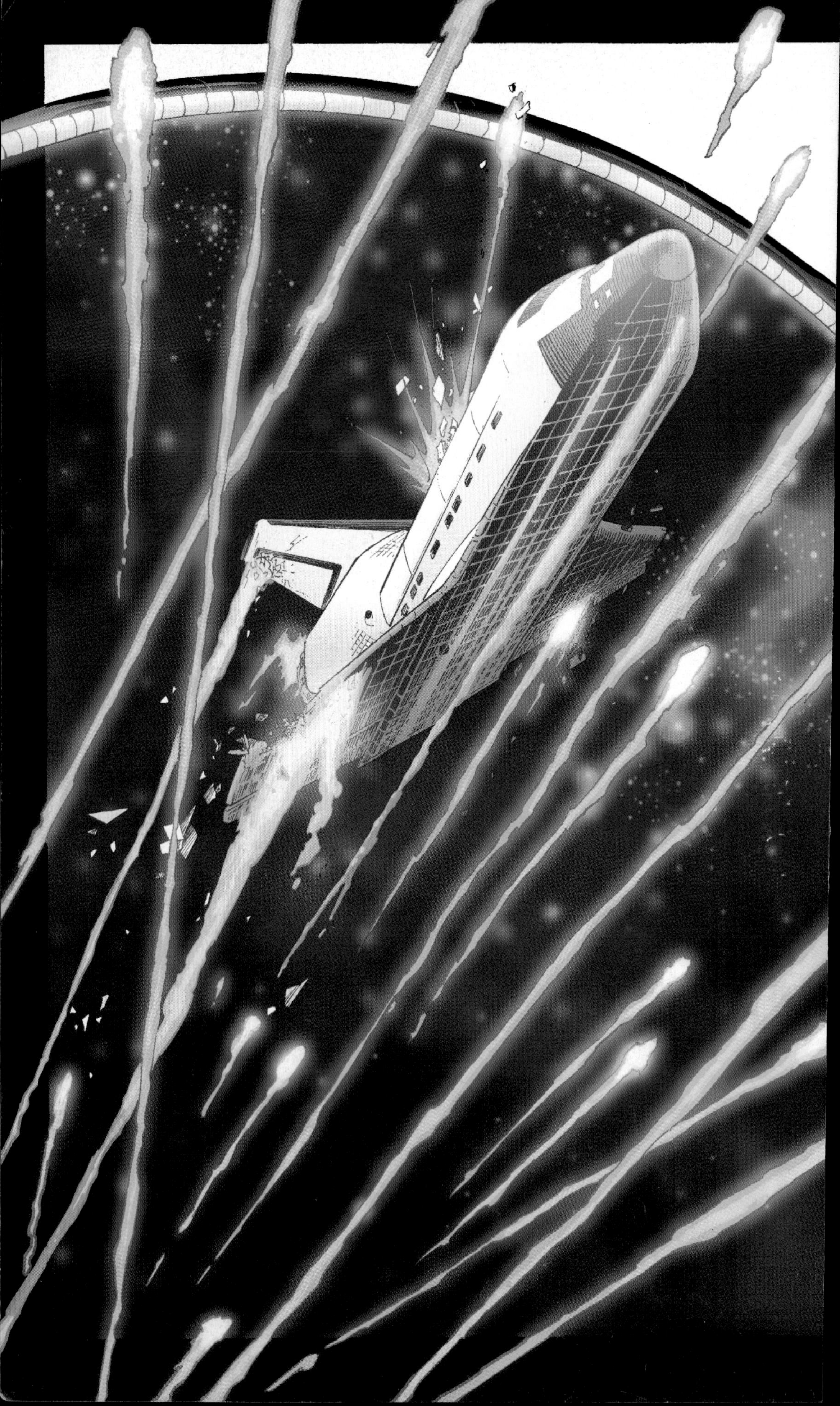

#18

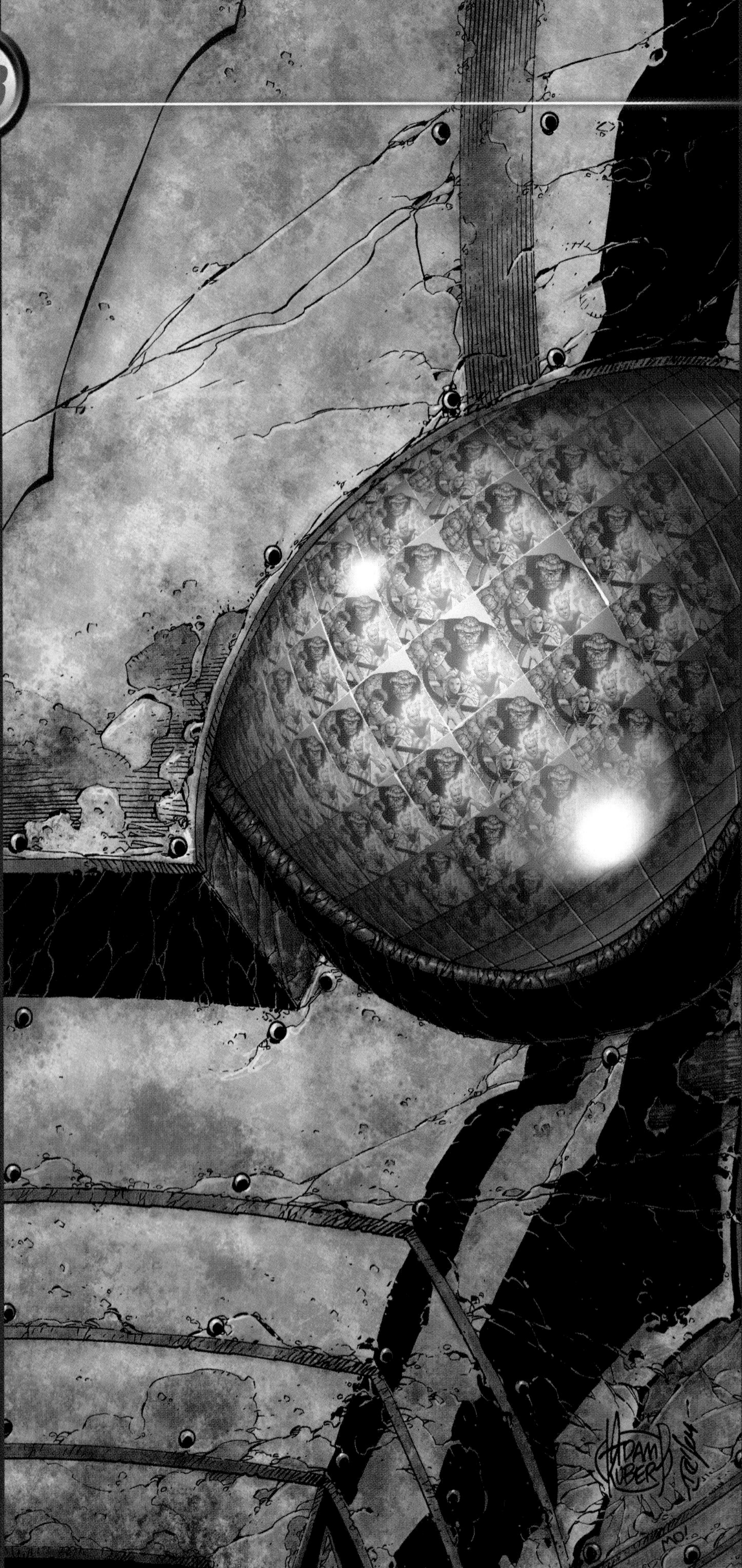

N-ZONE CONCLUSION

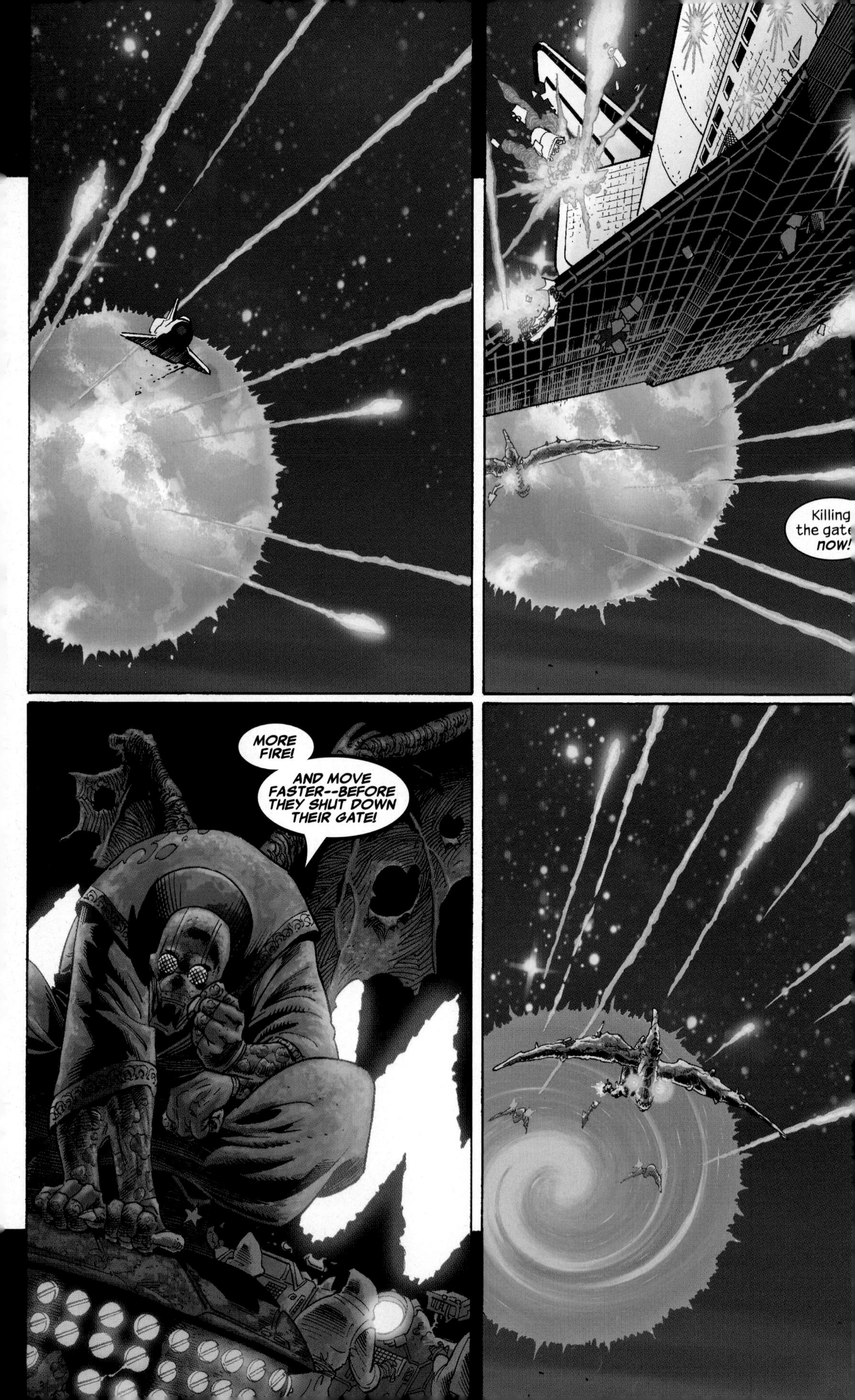
Killing the gate now!
MORE FIRE!
AND MOVE FASTER--BEFORE THEY SHUT DOWN THEIR GATE!

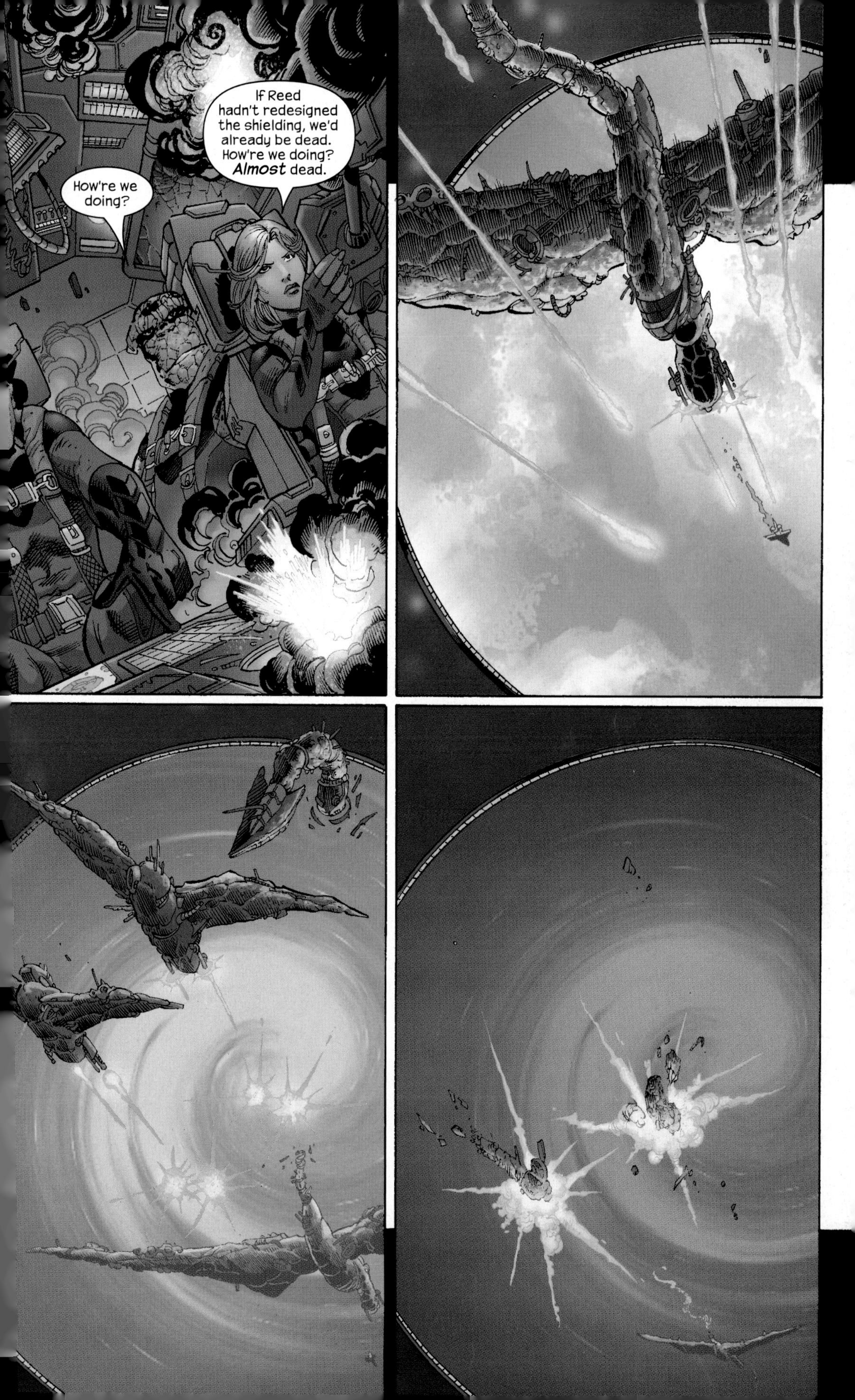
How're we doing?
If Reed hadn't redesigned the shielding, we'd already be dead. How're we doing? *Almost* dead.

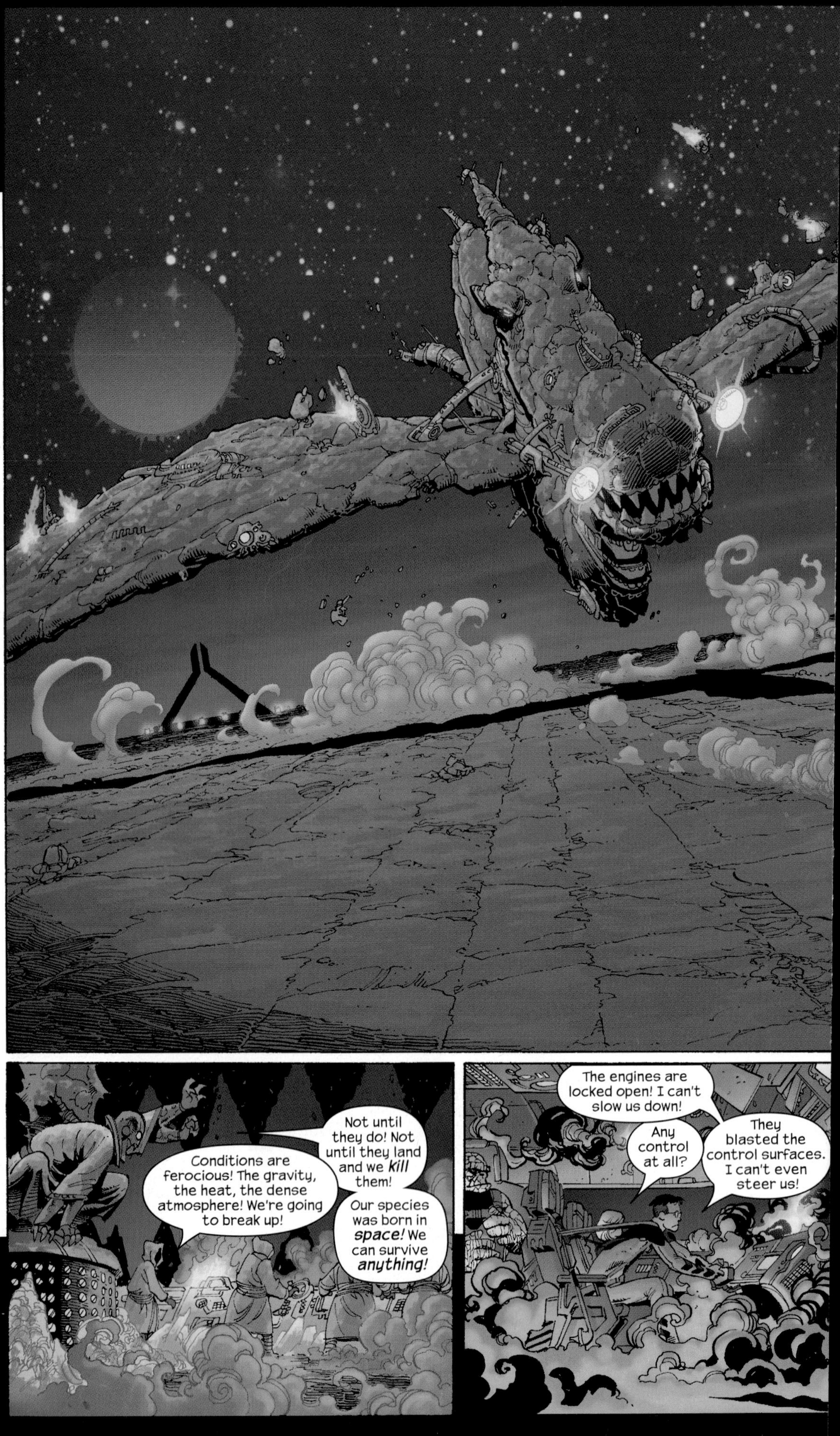
Conditions are ferocious! The gravity, the heat, the dense atmosphere! We're going to break up!
Not until they do! Not until they land and we *kill* them!
Our species was born in *space!* We can survive *anything!*
The engines are locked open! I can't slow us down!
Any control at all?
They blasted the control surfaces. I can't even steer us!

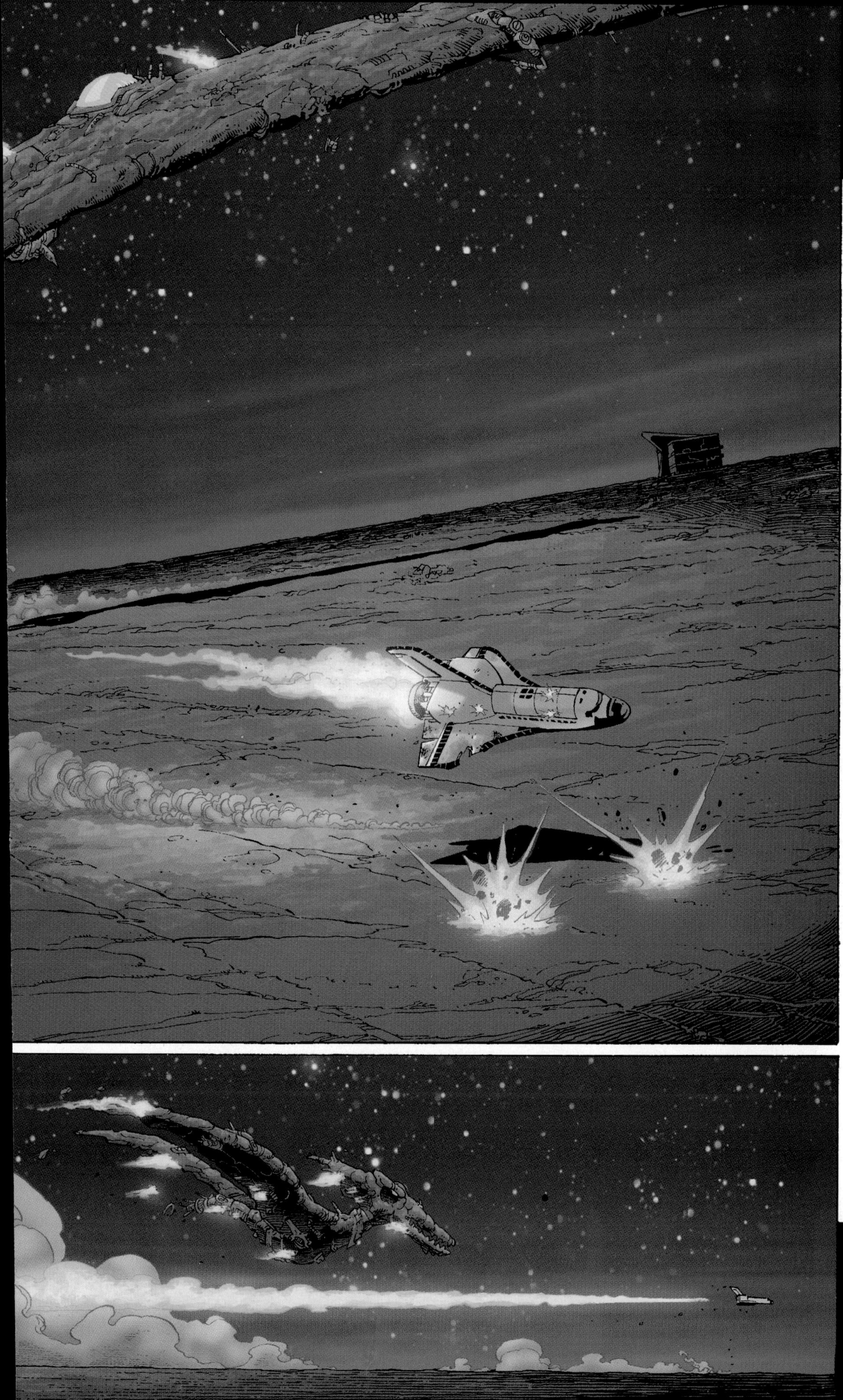

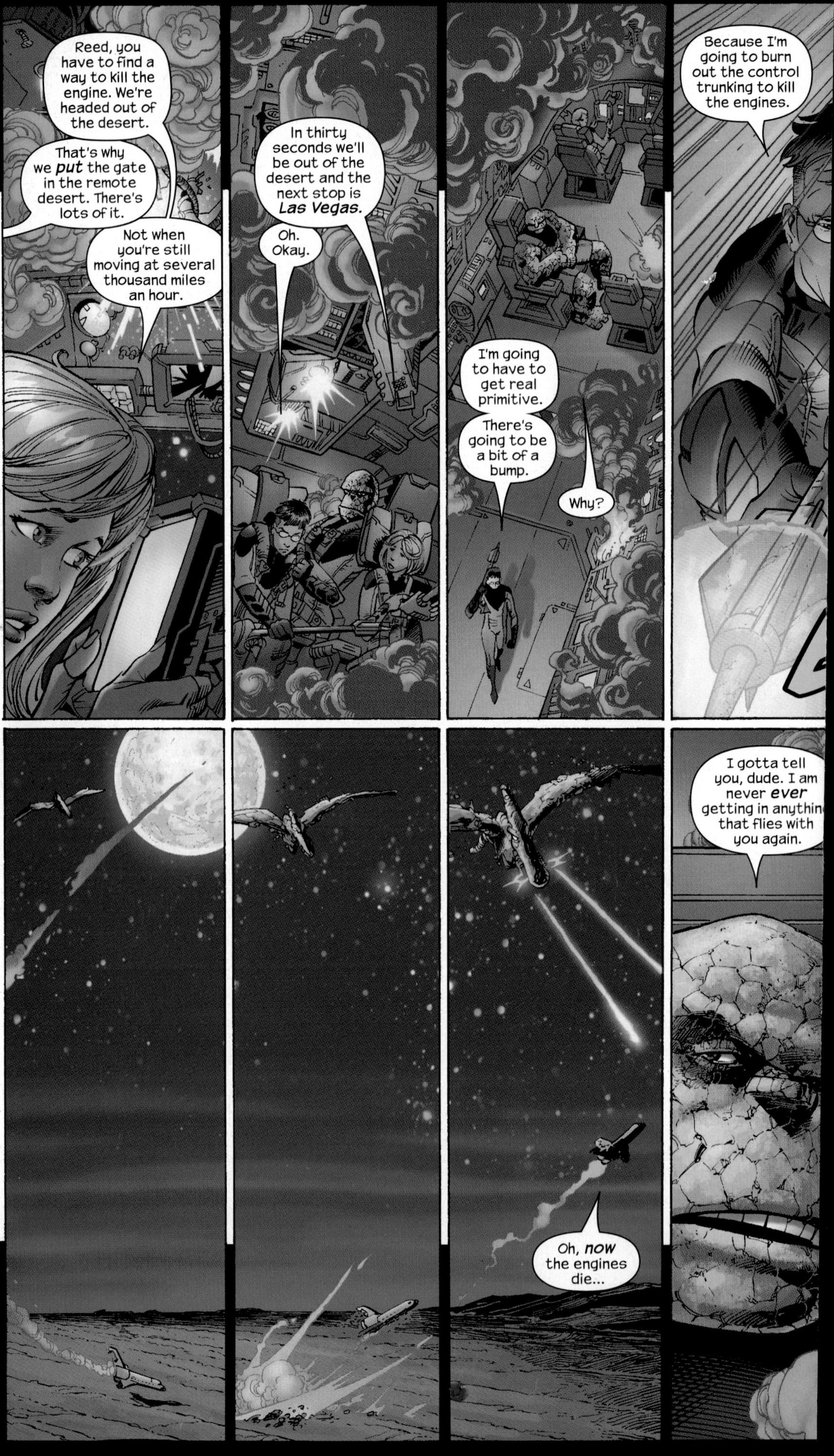
Reed, you have to find a way to kill the engine. We're headed out of the desert.
That's why we put the gate in the remote desert. There's lots of it.
Not when you're still moving at several thousand miles an hour.
In thirty seconds we'll be out of the desert and the next stop is Las Vegas.
Oh. Okay.
I'm going to have to get real primitive.
There's going to be a bit of a bump.
Why?
Because I'm going to burn out the control trunking to kill the engines.
Oh, now the engines die...
I gotta tell you, dude. I am never ever getting in anything that flies with you again.

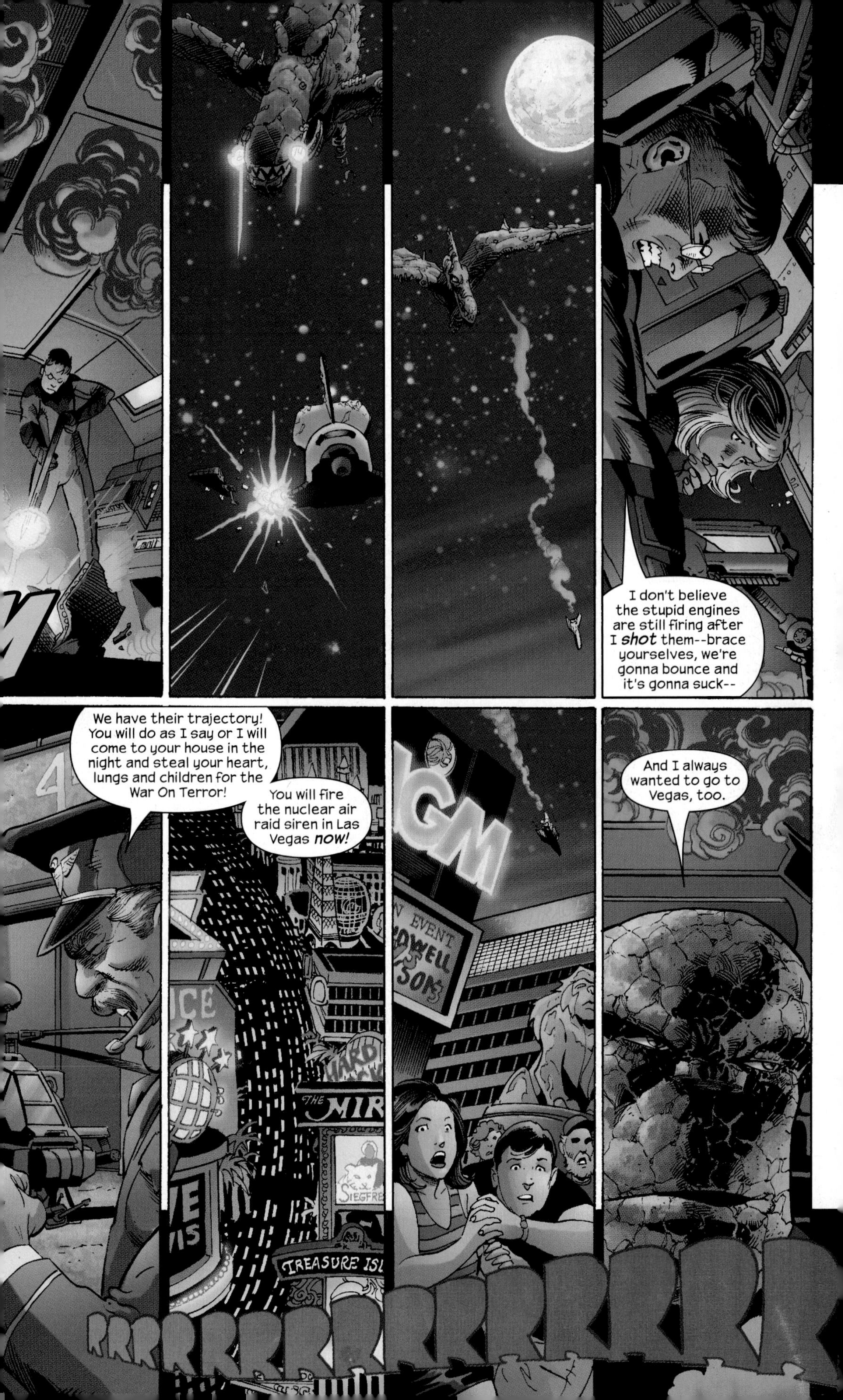

I don't believe the stupid engines are still firing after I *shot* them--brace yourselves, we're gonna bounce and it's gonna suck--
We have their trajectory! You will do as I say or I will come to your house in the night and steal your heart, lungs and children for the War On Terror!
You will fire the nuclear air raid siren in Las Vegas *now!*
And I always wanted to go to Vegas, too.
RRRRRRRRRRRRRRRRR

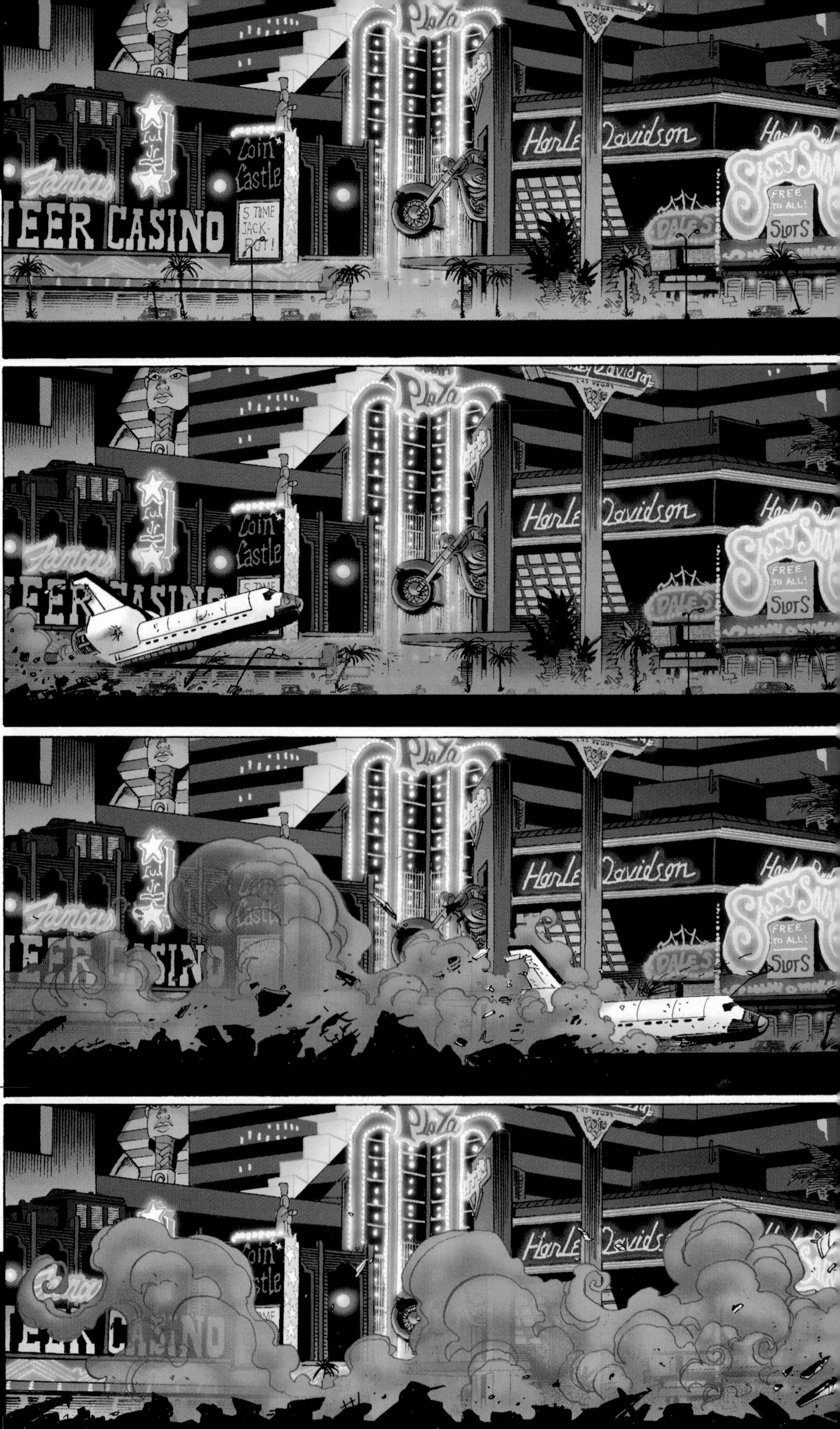

Famous
EER CASINO
Coin Castle
5 TIME JACK-POT!
Plaza
Harley Davidson
DALE'S
FREE TO ALL!
SLOTS

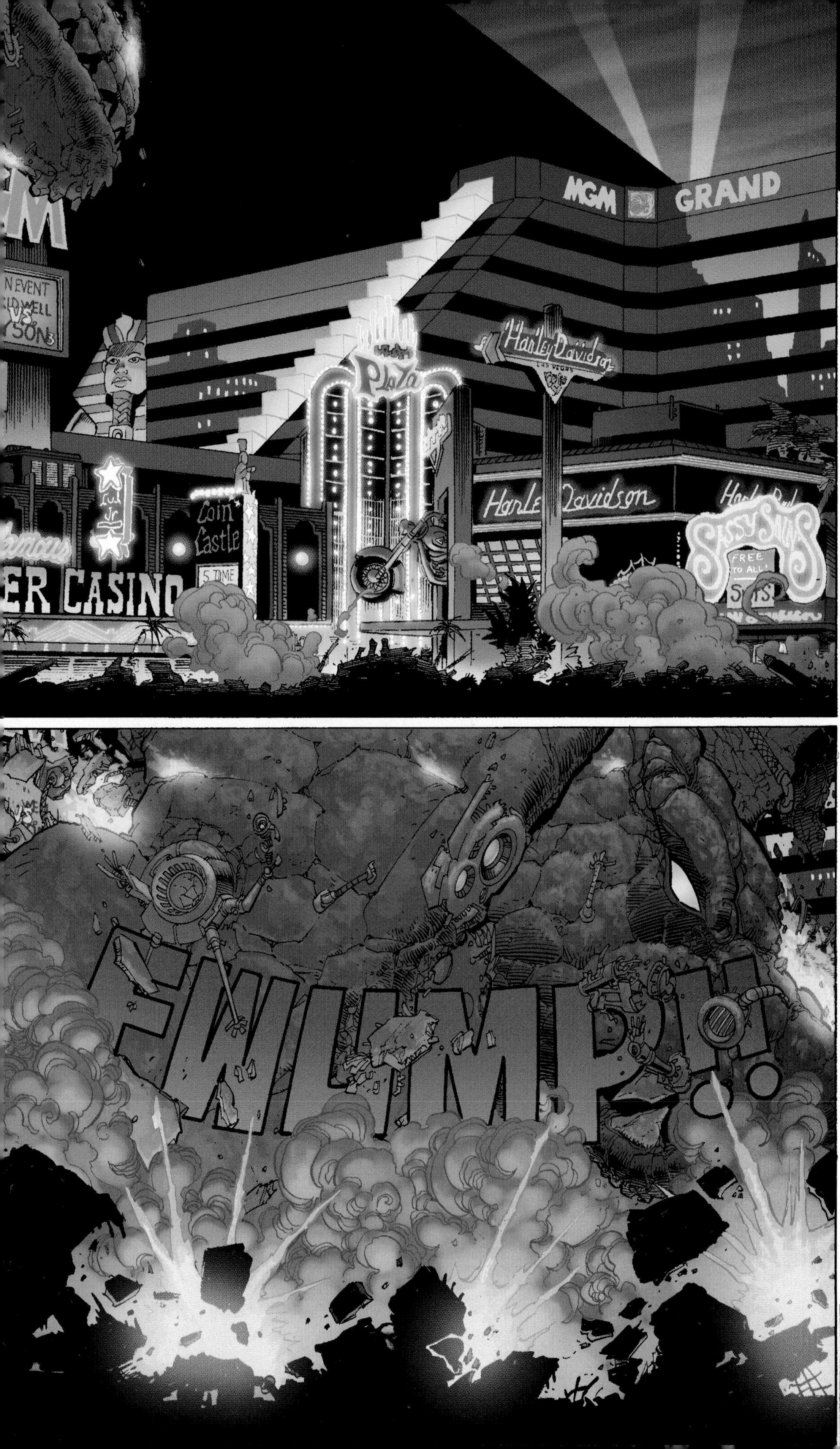

MGM GRAND
Harley Davidson
LAS VEGAS
Plaza
Coin Castle
5 TIME
ER CASINO
Harley Davidson
SASSY SALLY'S
FREE TO ALL!
FWUMP!!

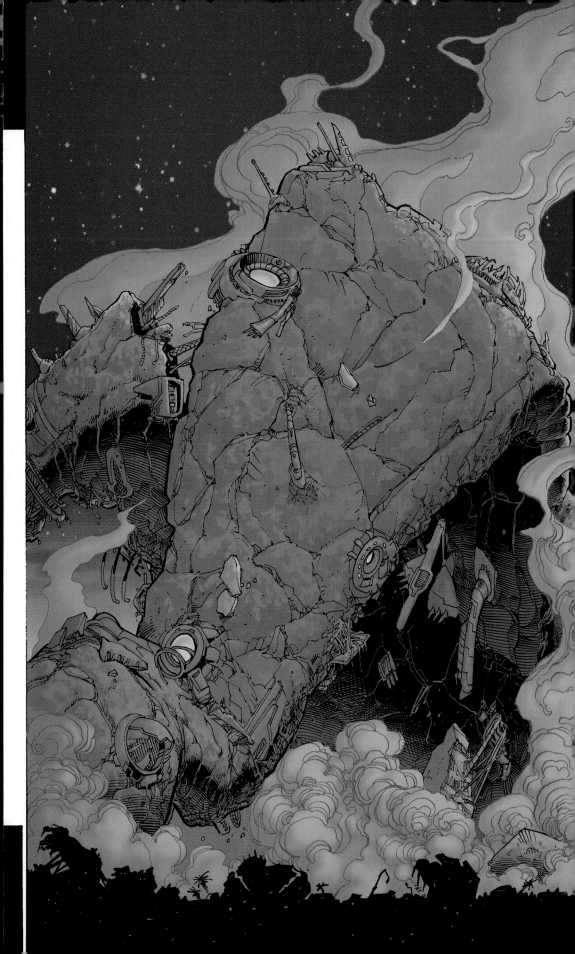

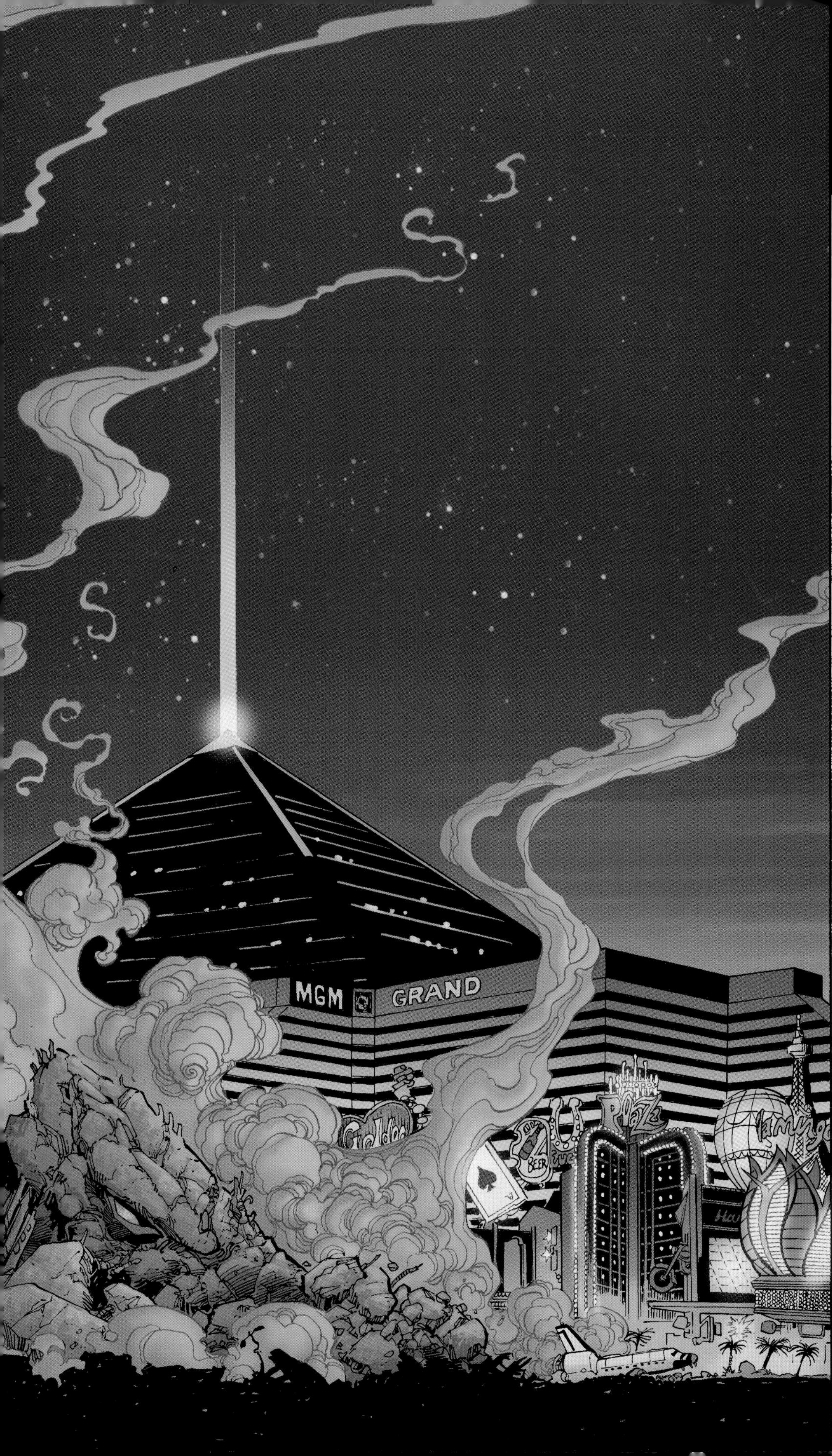
MGM
GRAND

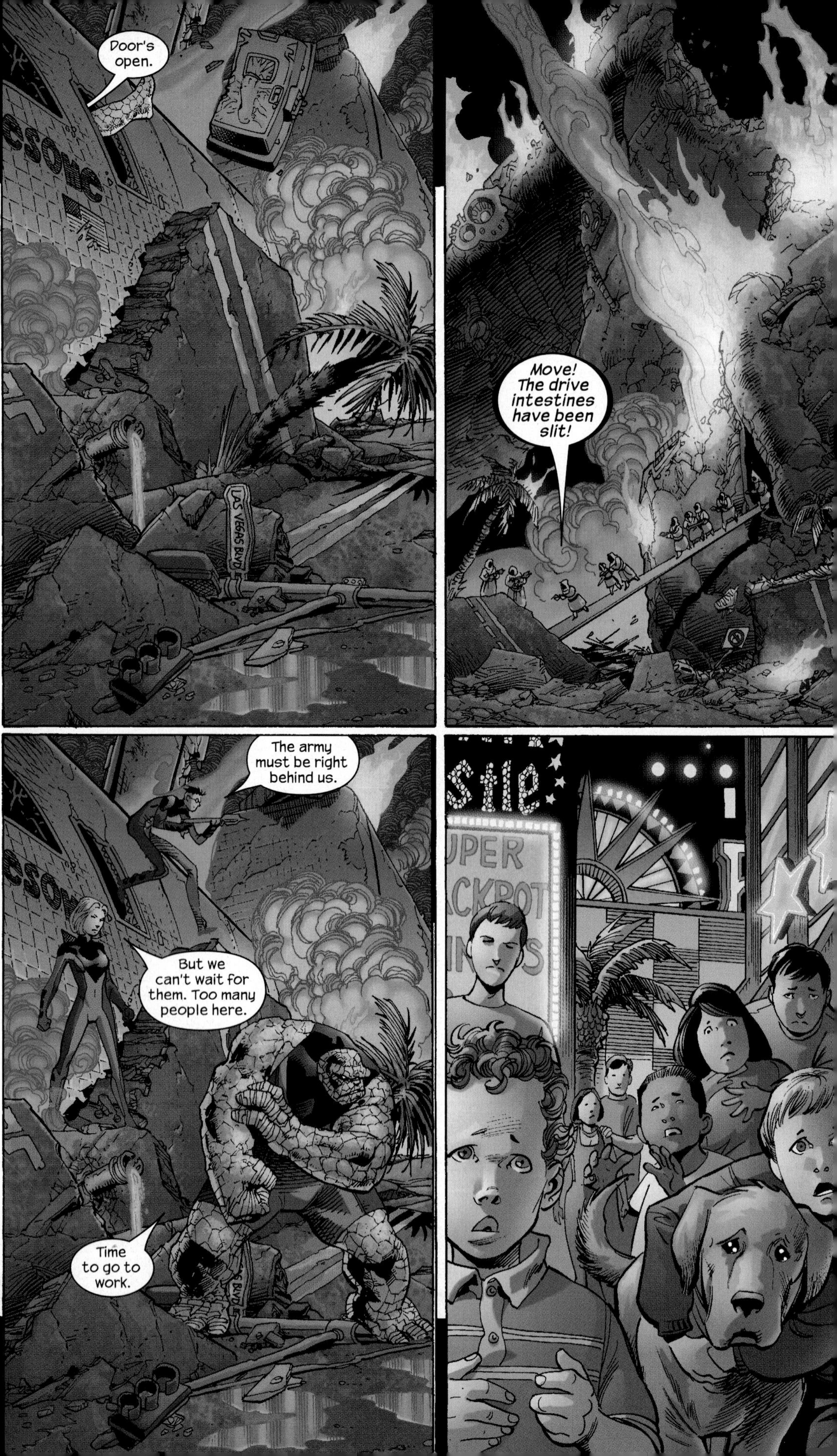
Door's open.
Move! The drive intestines have been slit!
LAS VEGAS BLVD
The army must be right behind us.
But we can't wait for them. Too many people here.
Time to go to work.

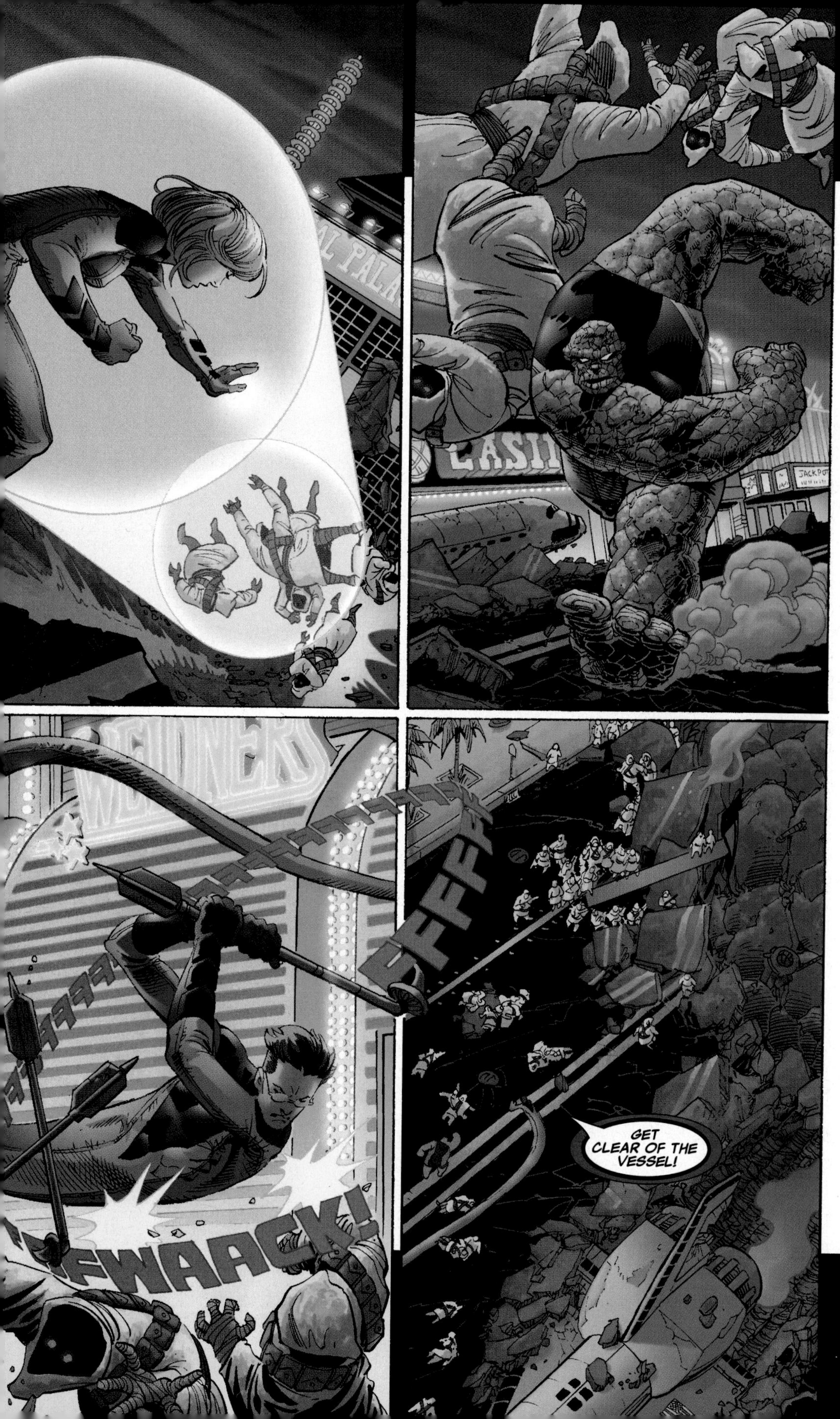
GET CLEAR OF THE VESSEL!
FWAACK!
JACKPOT

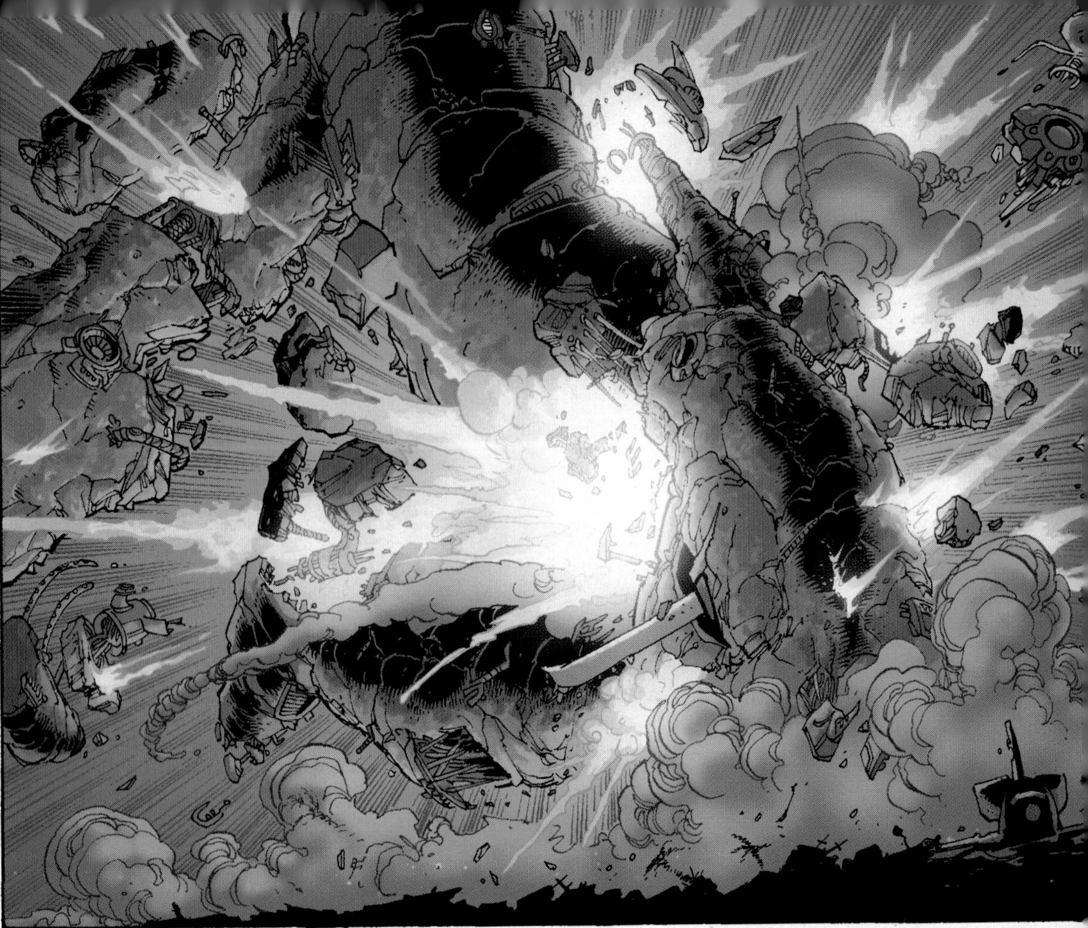

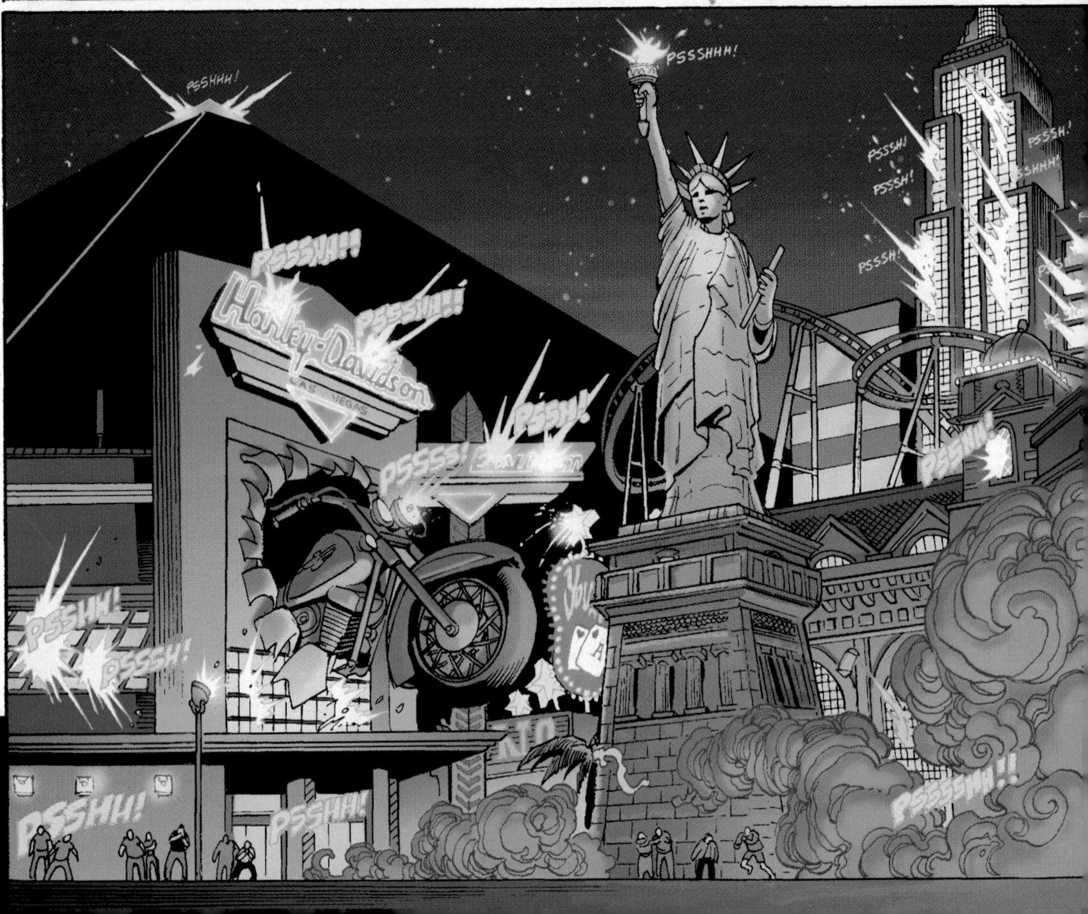
PSSHHH!
PSSSHHH!
PSSSHH!!
Harley-Davidson
LAS VEGAS
PSSSHH!!
PSSH!
PSSSS!
PSSSH!
PSSSH!
PSSSH!
PSSSH!
SSHHH!
PSSSHH!
PSSHH!
PSSSH!
PSSHH!
PSSHH!
PSSSHH!!

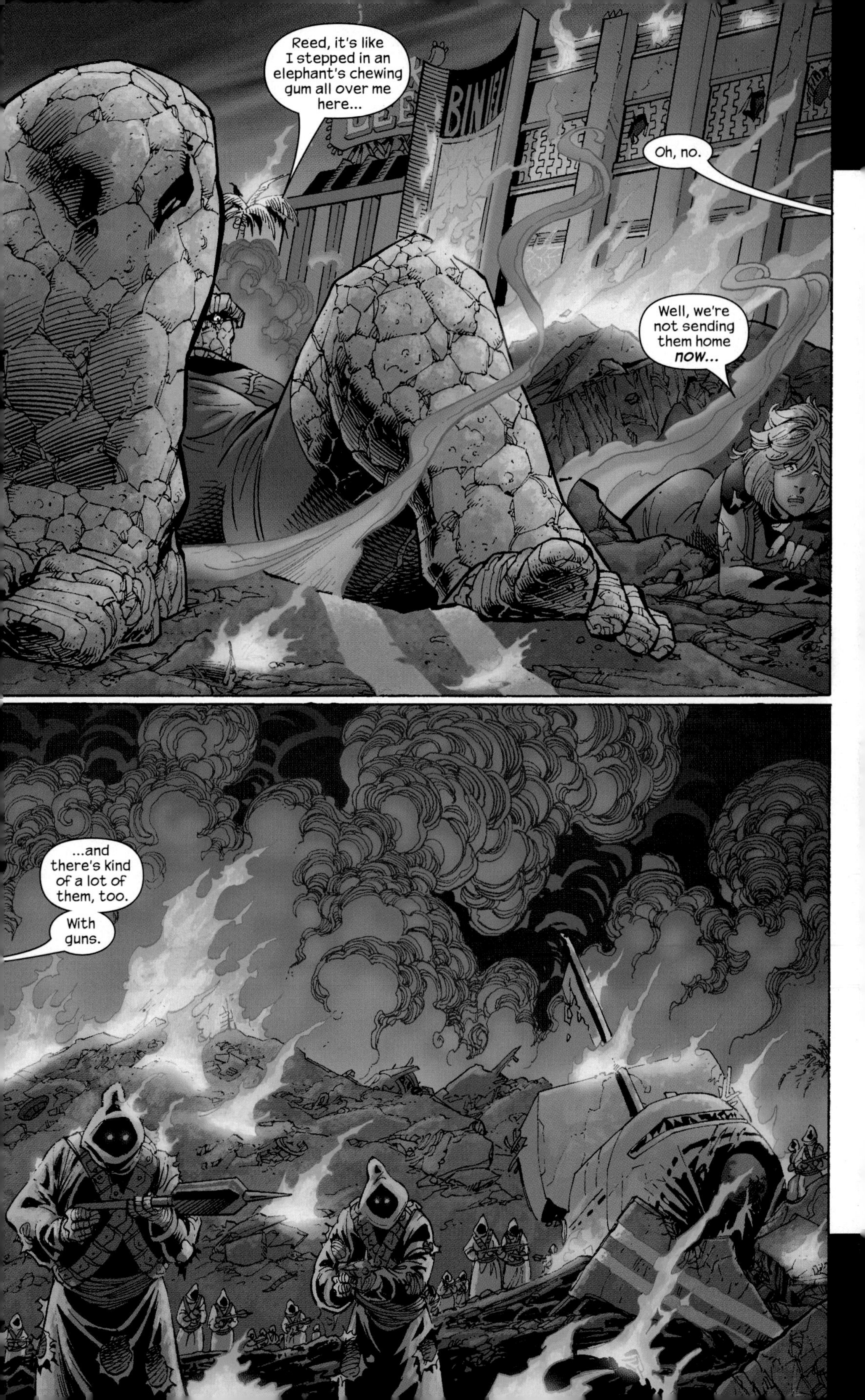
Reed, it's like I stepped in an elephant's chewing gum all over me here...
Oh, no.
Well, we're not sending them home *now*...
...and there's kind of a lot of them, too.
With guns.

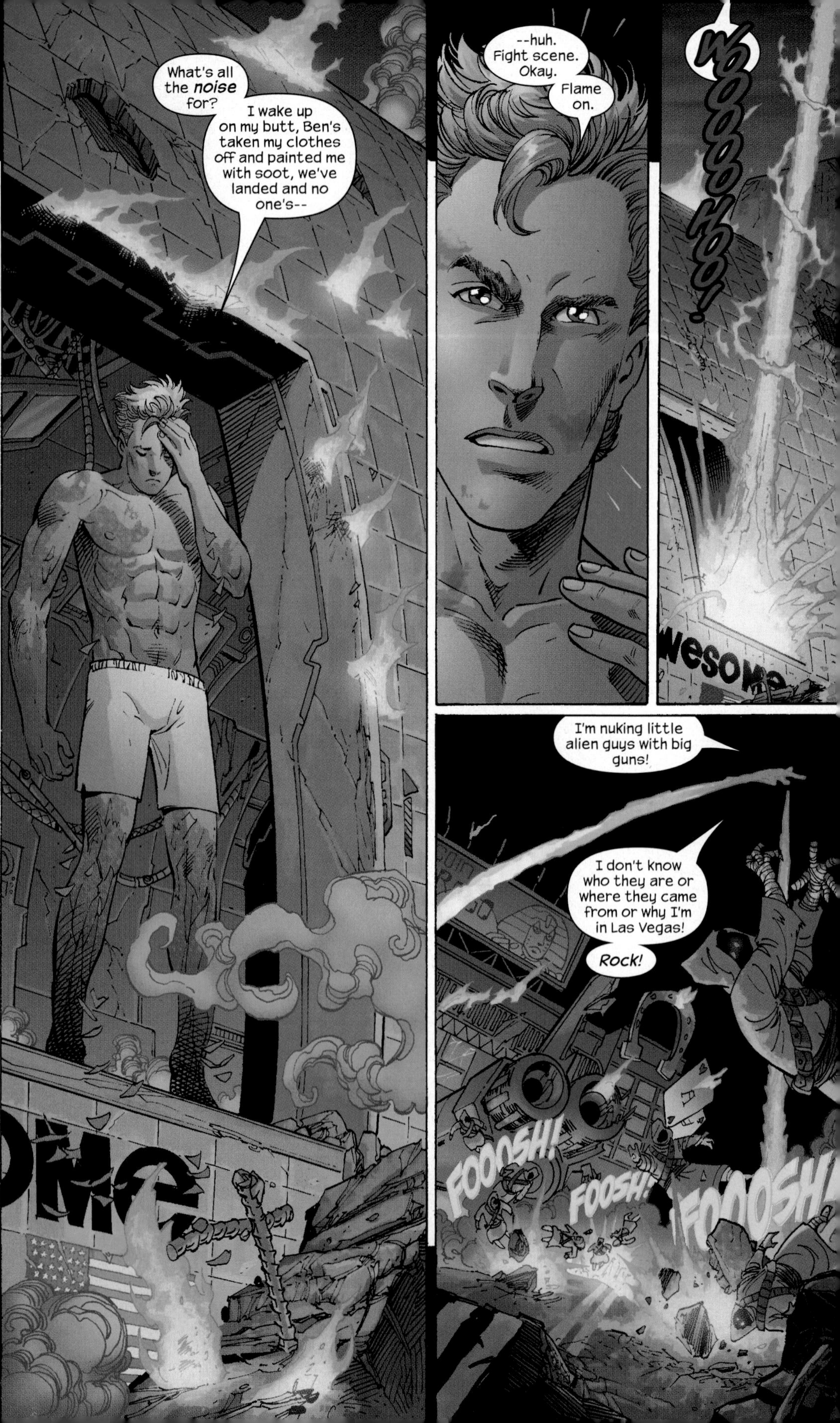

What's all the *noise* for?
I wake up on my butt, Ben's taken my clothes off and painted me with soot, we've landed and no one's--
--huh. Fight scene. Okay.
Flame on.
WOOOOOOHOO!
I'm nuking little alien guys with big guns!
I don't know who they are or where they came from or why I'm in Las Vegas!
Rock!
FOOOSH!
FOOSH!
FOOOSH!

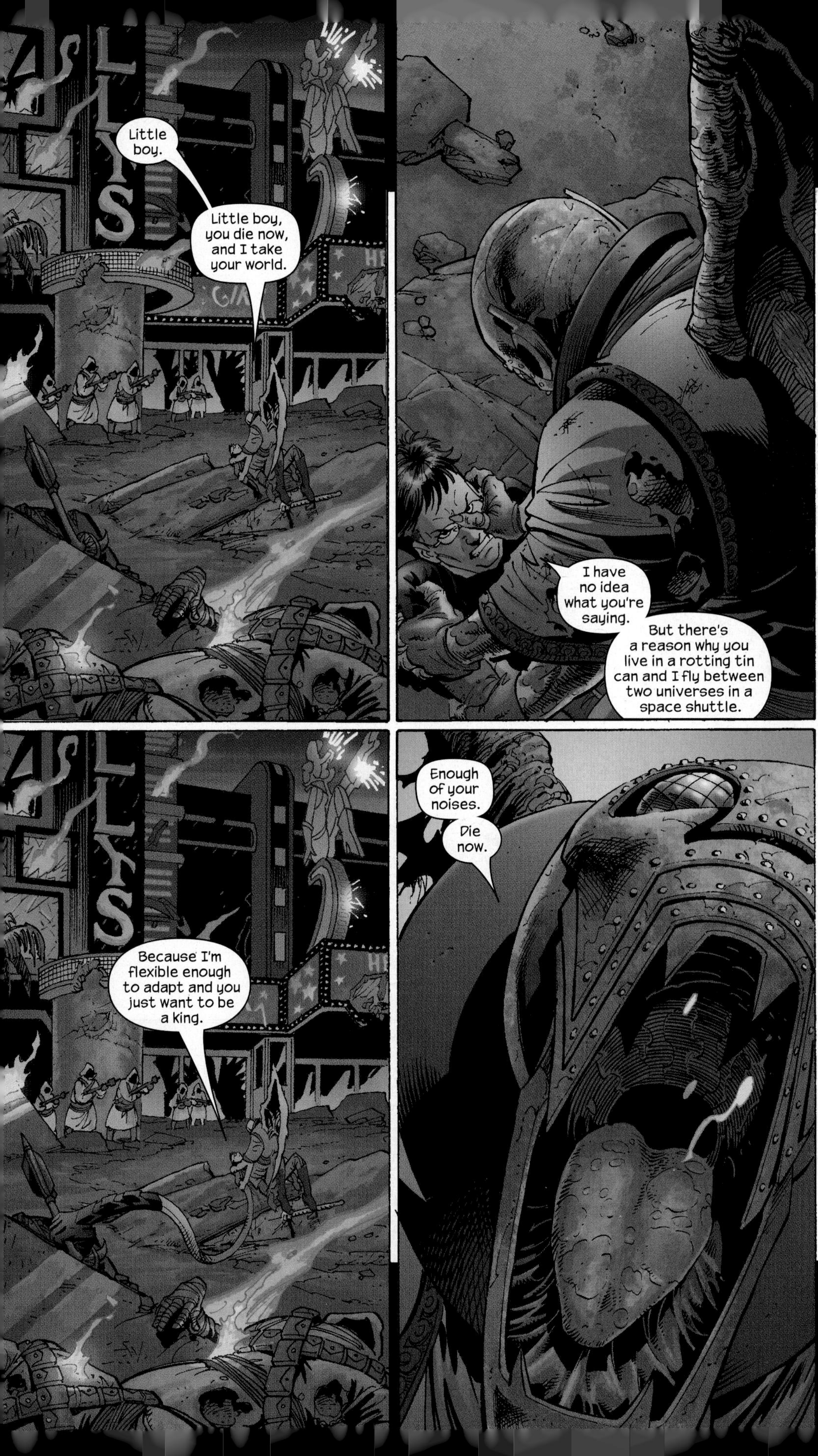

Little boy.
Little boy, you die now, and I take your world.
I have no idea what you're saying.
But there's a reason why you live in a rotting tin can and I fly between two universes in a space shuttle.
Because I'm flexible enough to adapt and you just want to be a king.
Enough of your noises.
Die now.

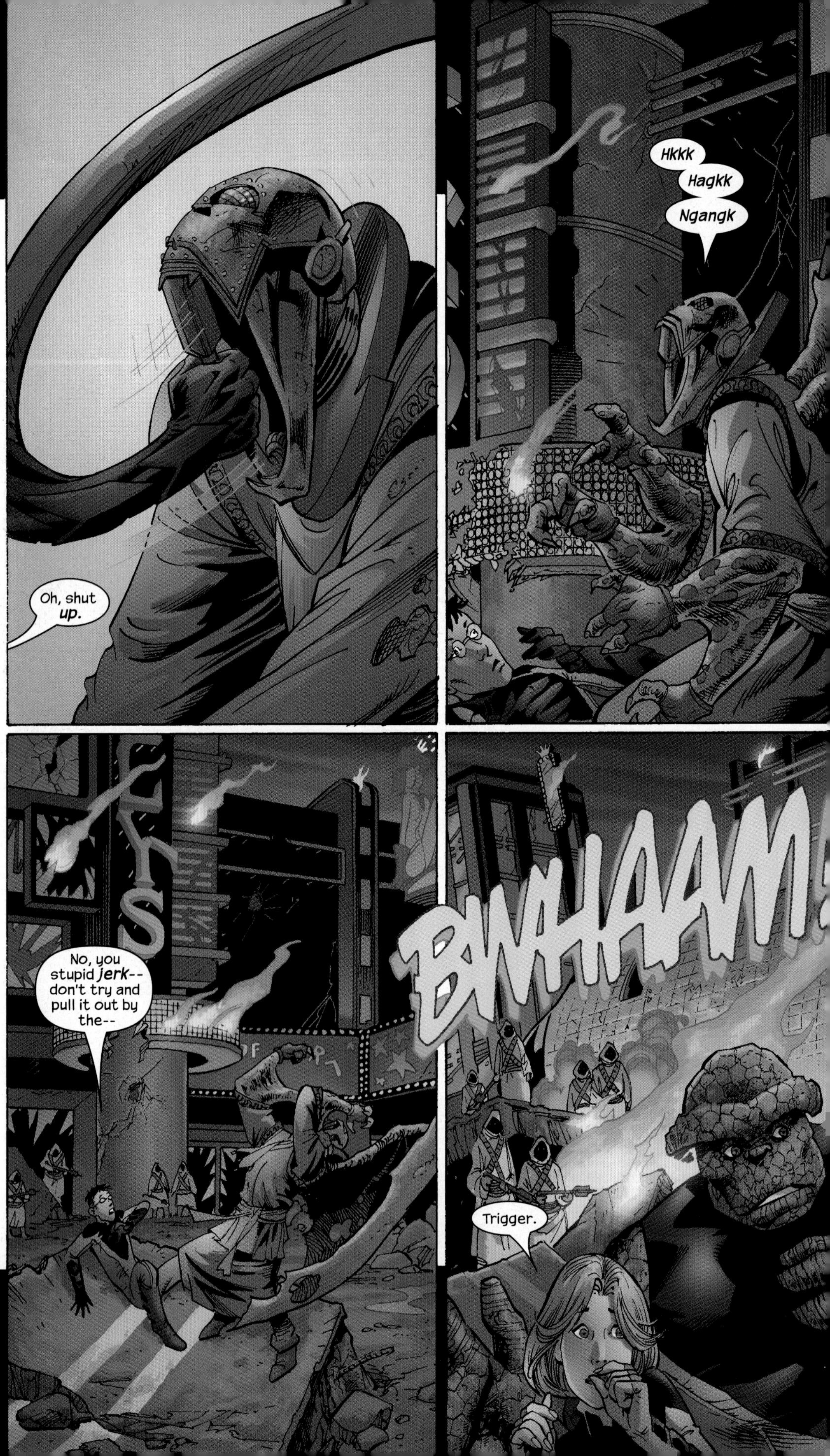
Hkkk
Hagkk
Ngangk
Oh, shut up.
No, you stupid jerk-- don't try and pull it out by the--
BWHAAM!
Trigger.

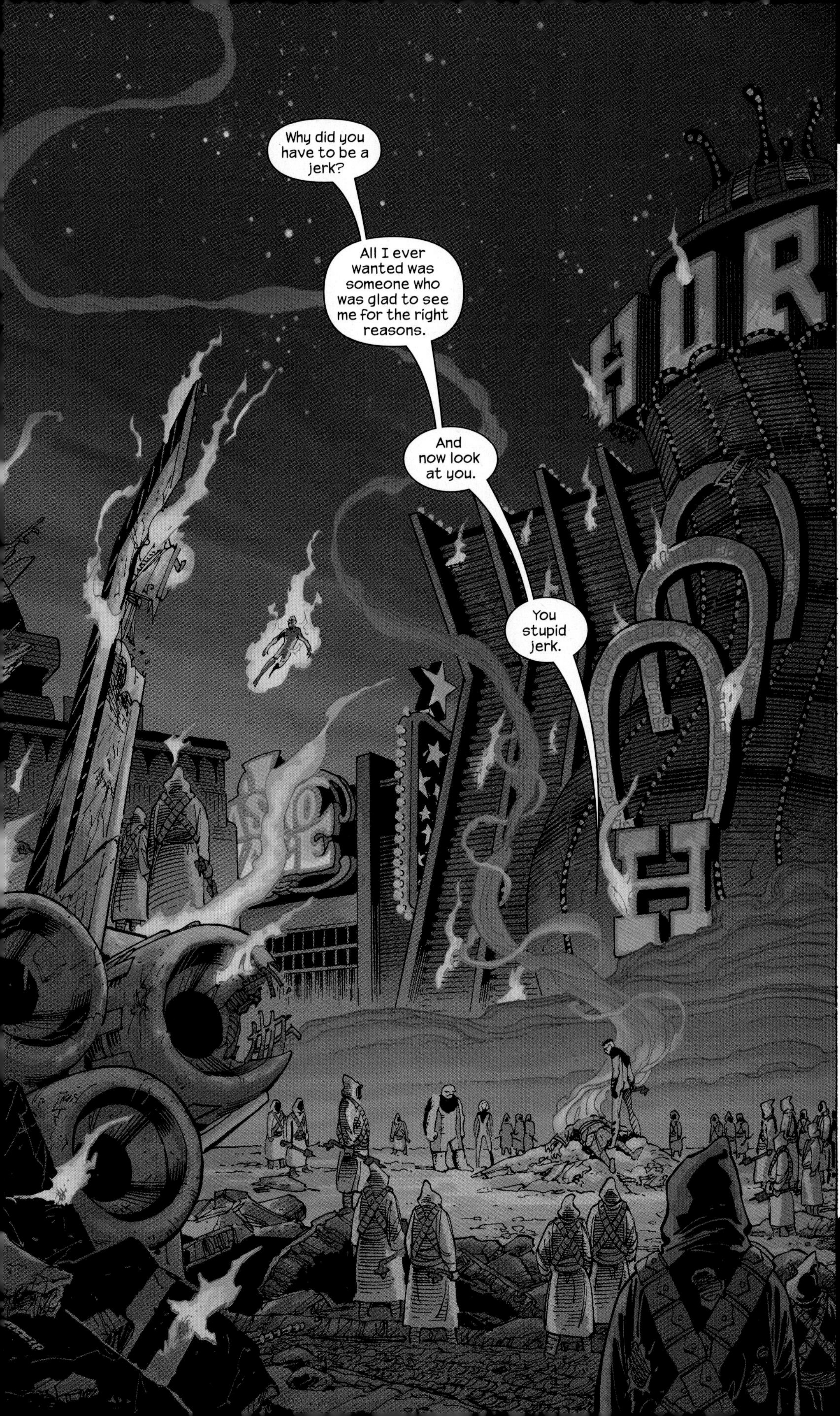
Why did you have to be a jerk?
All I ever wanted was someone who was glad to see me for the right reasons.
And now look at you.
You stupid jerk.

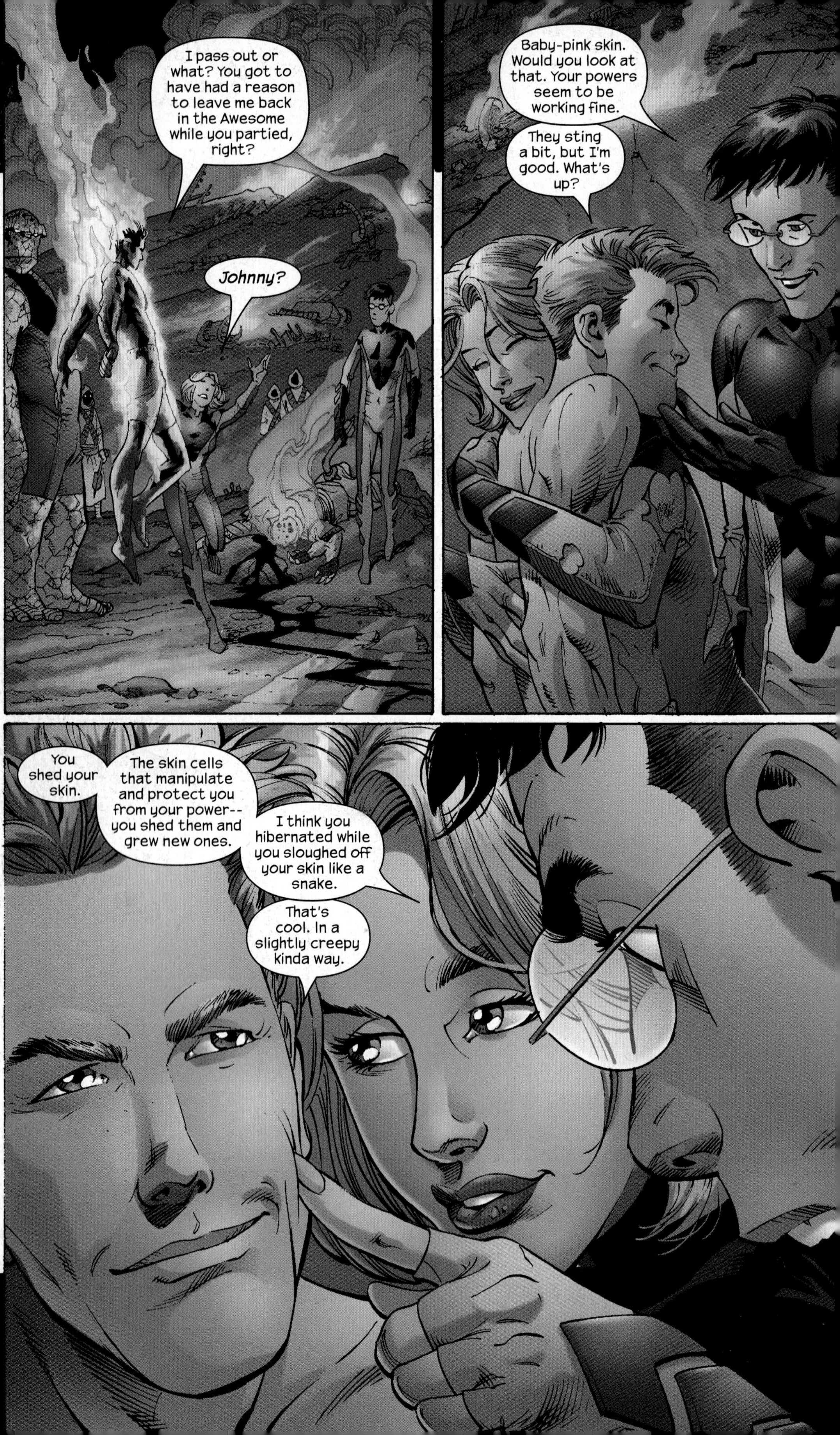
I pass out or what? You got to have had a reason to leave me back in the Awesome while you partied, right?
Johnny?
Baby-pink skin. Would you look at that. Your powers seem to be working fine.
They sting a bit, but I'm good. What's up?
You shed your skin.
The skin cells that manipulate and protect you from your power-- you shed them and grew new ones.
I think you hibernated while you sloughed off your skin like a snake.
That's cool. In a slightly creepy kinda way.

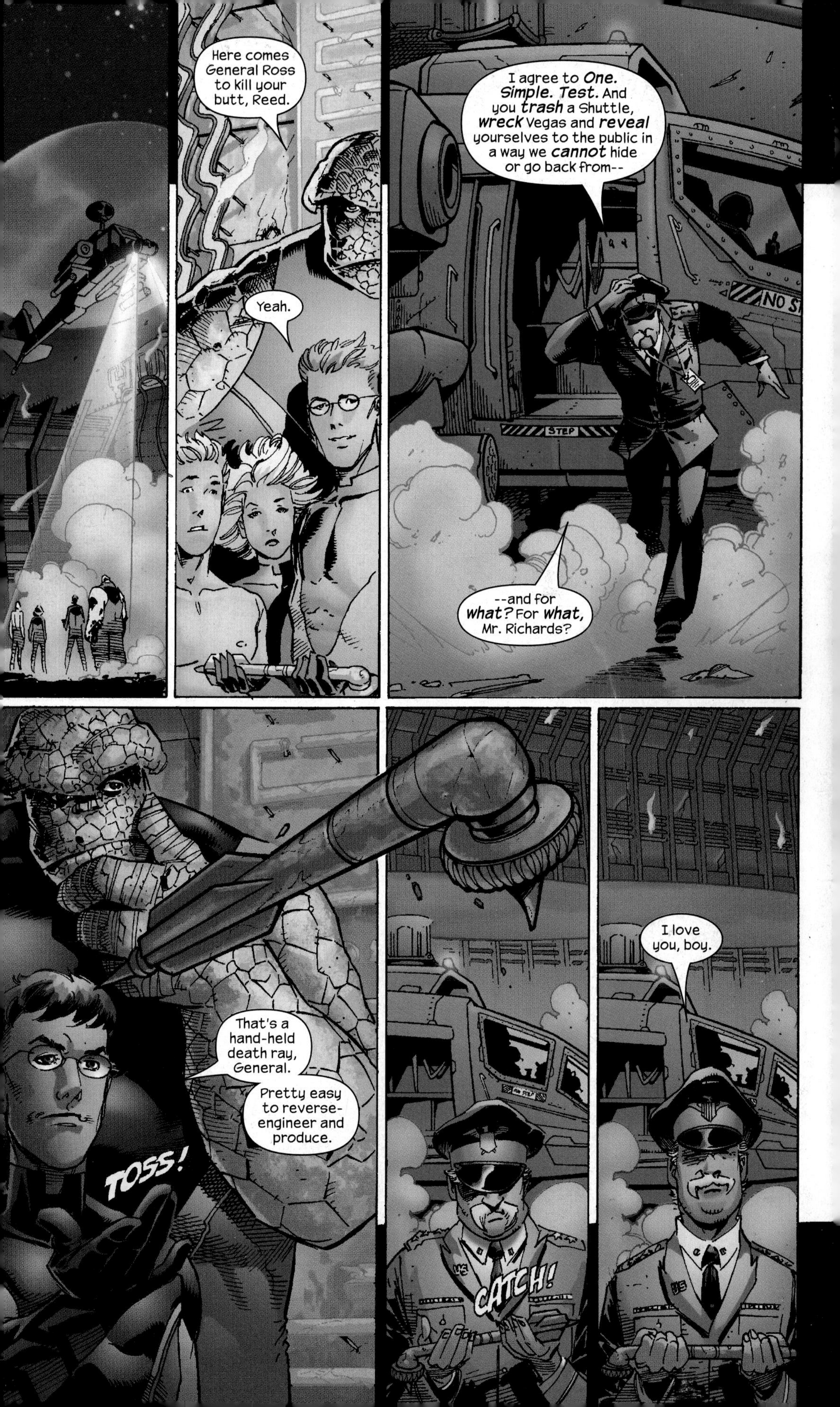
Here comes General Ross to kill your butt, Reed.
Yeah.
I agree to One. Simple. Test. And you trash a Shuttle, wreck Vegas and reveal yourselves to the public in a way we cannot hide or go back from--
--and for what? For what, Mr. Richards?
NO ST
STEP
That's a hand-held death ray, General.
Pretty easy to reverse-engineer and produce.
TOSS!
CATCH!
I love you, boy.

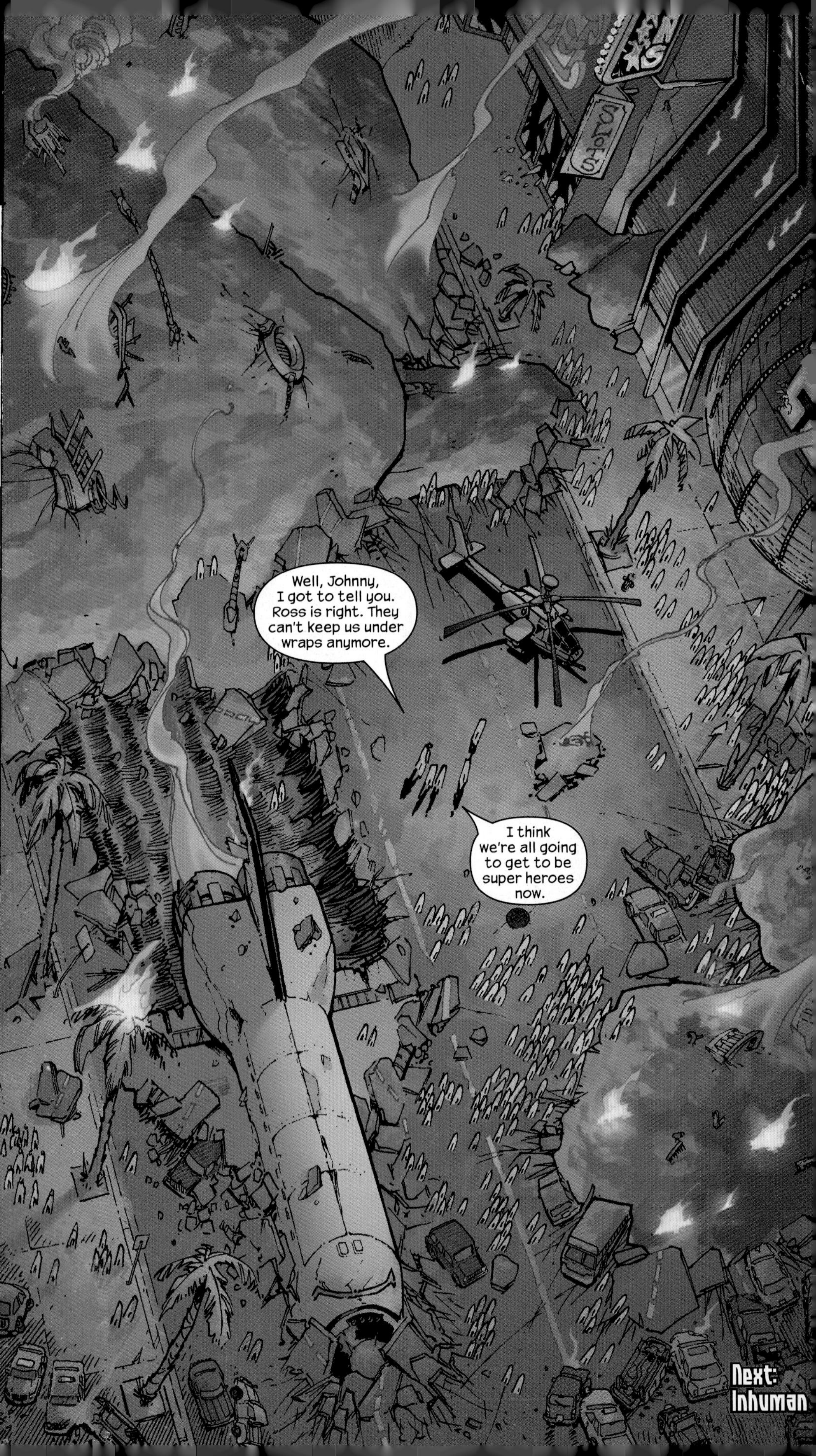
SLOTS
Well, Johnny, I got to tell you. Ross is right. They can't keep us under wraps anymore.
I think we're all going to get to be super heroes now.
Next: Inhuman